Deep Learning for Time Series Cookbook

Use PyTorch and Python recipes for forecasting, classification, and anomaly detection

Vitor Cerqueira

Luís Roque

Deep Learning for Time Series Cookbook

Group Product Manager: Ali Abidi

Publishing Product Manager: Sanjana Gupta

Book Project Manager: Aparna Ravikumar Nair

Senior Editor: Nazia Shaikh

Technical Editor: Rahul Limbachiya

Copy Editor: Safis Editing

Proofreader: Safis Editing

Indexer: Pratik Shirodkar

Production Designer: Prashant Ghare

Senior DevRel Marketing Coordinator: Vinishka Kalra

First published: March 2024

Production reference: 1210324

Published by Packt Publishing Ltd.

Grosvenor House

11 St Paul's Square

Birmingham

B3 1RB, UK

ISBN 978-1-80512-923-3

www.packtpub.com

Contributors

About the authors

Vitor Cerqueira is a machine learning researcher at the Faculty of Engineering at the University of Porto, working on a variety of projects concerning time-series data, including forecasting, anomaly detection, and meta-learning. Vitor earned his Ph.D. with honors, also from the University of Porto, and he also has a background in data analytics and mathematics. He has authored several peer-reviewed publications on related topics.

Luís Roque, is the Founder and Partner of ZAAI, a company focused on AI product development, consultancy, and investment in AI startups. He also serves as the Vice President of Data & AI at Marley Spoon, leading teams across data science, data analytics, data product, data engineering, machine learning operations, and platforms.

In addition, he holds the position of AI Advisor at CableLabs, where he contributes to integrating the broadband industry with AI technologies.

Luís is also a Ph.D. Researcher in AI at the University of Porto's AI&CS lab and oversees the Data Science Master's program at Nuclio Digital School in Barcelona. Previously, he co-founded HUUB, where he served as CEO until its acquisition by Maersk.

About the reviewer

Tuhin Sharma is a senior principal data scientist at Red Hat in the corporate development and strategy group. Prior to that, he worked at Hypersonix as an AI architect. He also co-founded and has been CEO of Binaize, a website conversion intelligence product for e-commerce SMBs. He received a master's degree from IIT in Roorkee and a bachelor's degree in computer science from IIEST in Shibpur. He loves to code and collaborate on open source and research projects. He has four research papers and five patents in the field of AI and NLP. He is a reviewer of the IEEE MASS conference in the AI track. He writes deep learning articles for O'Reilly in collaboration with the AWS MXNet team. He is a regular speaker at prominent AI conferences such as O'Reilly AI, ODSC, and GIDS.

Table of Contents

4

Forecasting with PyTorch Lightning   83

5

Global Forecasting Models   109

6

Advanced Deep Learning Architectures for Time Series Forecasting   133

8

Deep Learning for Time Series Classification   195

9

Deep Learning for Time Series Anomaly Detection   217

Preface

The writing of this book was motivated by the increasing demand for practical approaches to time series analysis and forecasting. Organizations across various sectors rely on time series analysis to gain insights into their operations. By leveraging time series, these organizations can make informed decisions and optimize their performance. Accurate forecasts are valuable assets across many application domains, such as retail or economics. These predictions help reduce uncertainty and enable better planning of operations. Overall, time series analysis is a valuable skill for data scientists to understand and extract meaningful insights from collections of observations that evolve over time.

Meanwhile, deep learning is driving recent important scientific and technological advances. It is a subset of machine learning and artificial intelligence where models are based on artificial neural networks. Deep learning is foundational to many technologies we use and hear about today, including ChatGPT, self-driving cars, and advanced image recognition tools. At the same time, deep learning methods require significant technical expertise to produce meaningful results.

This book guides machine learning practitioners and enthusiasts interested in applying deep learning to learn from time series data. We present clear and easy-to-follow code recipes for applying deep learning to time series data. While the content is tailored for beginners, more seasoned machine learning professionals can also find value in the nuances of more advanced techniques. The book presents a learn-by-doing approach to ensure that you not only understand the main concepts but also know how to apply them effectively.

The book covers several popular time series problems, such as forecasting, anomaly detection, and classification. These tasks are solved with different deep neural network architectures, including convolutional neural networks or transformers. We use the PyTorch ecosystem, a popular deep learning framework based on Python.

By the end of this book, you'll be able to solve different time series tasks using deep learning methods.

Who this book is for

This book is primarily designed for beginners to data science, and those who are eager to delve into the application of deep learning for time series analysis and forecasting. We assume that you have a basic understanding of Python, which will help you to navigate the coding recipes more easily. We also rely on popular data manipulation libraries such as pandas and NumPy. So, a familiarity with these will improve your reading experience.

We expect you to have basic knowledge concerning fundamental machine learning concepts and techniques. Understanding things such as supervised and unsupervised learning, as well as being familiar with classification, regression, cross-validation, and evaluation methodologies, is important to get the most out of this book.

What this book covers

Chapter 1, Getting Started with Time Series, introduces the main concepts behind time series. The chapter starts by defining a time series and describing how it can represent several real-world systems. Then, we explore the main features of time series data, including trend or seasonality. You'll also learn about several methods and techniques for time series analysis.

Chapter 2, Getting Started with PyTorch, provides an overview of how to use PyTorch to develop deep learning models in Python. We start by guiding you through the installation process of PyTorch, including how to set up the appropriate environment. This is followed by an introduction to defining a neural network structure in PyTorch, including the definition of layers and activation functions. Afterward, we walk through the process of training a neural network. By the end of the chapter, you will understand the fundamentals of using PyTorch for deep learning and be ready to tackle forecasting tasks with these new skills.

Chapter 3, Univariate Time Series Forecasting, focuses on using PyTorch to develop deep learning forecasting models for univariate time series. We begin by guiding you through preparing a time series for supervised learning. After that, we introduce different types of neural networks, including feed-forward, recurrent, and convolutional neural networks. We explain how they can be trained and how we can use them to tackle time series forecasting problems. We also cover common time series issues, such as trend and seasonality, and how to incorporate them into neural network models.

Chapter 4, Forecasting with PyTorch Lightning, explores the PyTorch Lightning ecosystem and how to use it to build neural networks using time series. You'll learn about data modules and data loaders, and how these can help you accelerate the process of building forecasting models. We also explore TensorBoard and callbacks, which are useful to drive the training process.

Chapter 5, Global Forecasting Models, describes how to handle forecasting problems involving collections of time series. You'll also learn about the intricacies of particular problems in forecasting, such as multi-step ahead predictions and predictions for multiple variables. Finally, we'll also explore how to optimize the parameters of a neural network using Ray Tune.

Chapter 6, Advanced Deep Learning Architectures for Time Series Forecasting, provides a comprehensive guide to using state-of-the-art architectures for time series forecasting. We cover how to train several models, such as DeepAR, N-BEATS, and TFT. Additionally, we explain each model's architecture and inner workings and how to apply them to specific forecasting problems.

Chapter 7, Probabilistic Time Series Forecasting, describes how to use deep learning for probabilistic time series forecasting. We introduce the concept of probabilistic forecasting and the key differences compared to traditional point forecasting. The chapter gives several examples of probabilistic forecasting problems that can be tackled using specific deep learning architectures.

Chapter 8, Deep Learning for Time Series Classification, focuses on using deep learning to tackle time series classification problems. The chapter introduces the concept of time series classification, which involves assigning a class label to a time series. We show how to tackle time series classification problems with different deep learning architectures, including residual and convolutional neural networks.

Chapter 9, Deep Learning for Time Series Anomaly Detection, gives an overview of how to use deep learning to detect abnormal patterns in a time series. For this use case, we introduce generative adversarial networks and auto-encoders, which are popular approaches to detecting anomalies in time series.

To get the most out of this book

We assume that you have basic knowledge of Python, data science, and machine learning. Coding and data manipulation using libraries such as NumPy or pandas should be familiar for a comfortable read. Readers should also know about basic concepts and techniques behind machine learning, including supervised and unsupervised learning, classification, regression, cross-validation, and evaluation.

Software/hardware covered in the book	OS requirements
Python (3.9)	Windows, Mac OS X, or Linux (any)
PyTorch Lightning (2.1.2)	
pandas (>=2.1)	
scikit-learn (1.3.2)	
NumPy (1.26.2)	
torch (2.1.1)	
PyTorch Forecasting (1.0.0)	
GluonTS (0.14.2)	

Further requirements will be detailed in the introduction of the chapters.

If you are using the digital version of this book, we advise you to type the code yourself or access the code via the GitHub repository (link available in the next section). Doing so will help you avoid any potential errors related to the copying and pasting of code.

Download the example code files

You can download the example code files for this book from GitHub at `https://github.com/PacktPublishing/Deep-Learning-for-Time-Series-Data-Cookbook`. If there's an update to the code, it will be updated on the existing GitHub repository.

We also have other code bundles from our rich catalog of books and videos available at `https://github.com/PacktPublishing/`. Check them out!

Conventions used

There are a number of text conventions used throughout this book.

`Code in text`: Indicates code words in text, database table names, folder names, filenames, file extensions, pathnames, dummy URLs, user input, and Twitter handles. Here is an example: "The main component of this module is the `setup()` method."

A block of code is set as follows:

```
from statsmodels.tsa.seasonal import seasonal_decompose
result = seasonal_decompose(x=series_daily, model='additive',
period=365)
```

Any command-line input or output is written as follows:

```
pip install pyod
```

Sections

In this book, you will find several headings that appear frequently (*Getting ready*, *How to do it...*, *How it works...*, *There's more...*, and *See also*).

To give clear instructions on how to complete a recipe, use these sections as follows:

Getting ready

This section tells you what to expect in the recipe and describes how to set up any software or any preliminary settings required for the recipe.

How to do it...

This section contains the steps required to follow the recipe.

How it works...

This section usually consists of a detailed explanation of what happened in the previous section.

There's more...

This section consists of additional information about the recipe in order to make you more knowledgeable about the recipe.

See also

This section provides helpful links to other useful information for the recipe.

Get in touch

Feedback from our readers is always welcome.

General feedback: If you have questions about any aspect of this book, mention the book title in the subject of your message and email us at customercare@packtpub.com.

Errata: Although we have taken every care to ensure the accuracy of our content, mistakes do happen. If you have found a mistake in this book, we would be grateful if you would report this to us. Please visit www.packtpub.com/support/errata, selecting your book, clicking on the Errata Submission Form link, and entering the details.

Piracy: If you come across any illegal copies of our works in any form on the Internet, we would be grateful if you would provide us with the location address or website name. Please contact us at copyright@packtpub.com with a link to the material.

If you are interested in becoming an author: If there is a topic that you have expertise in and you are interested in either writing or contributing to a book, please visit authors.packtpub.com.

Share Your Thoughts

Once you've read *Deep Learning for Time Series Cookbook*, we'd love to hear your thoughts! Scan the QR code below to go straight to the Amazon review page for this book and share your feedback.

https://packt.link/r/1-805-12923-6

Your review is important to us and the tech community and will help us make sure we're delivering excellent quality content.

Download a free PDF copy of this book

Thanks for purchasing this book!

Do you like to read on the go but are unable to carry your print books everywhere?

Is your eBook purchase not compatible with the device of your choice?

Don't worry, now with every Packt book you get a DRM-free PDF version of that book at no cost.

Read anywhere, any place, on any device. Search, copy, and paste code from your favorite technical books directly into your application.

The perks don't stop there, you can get exclusive access to discounts, newsletters, and great free content in your inbox daily

Follow these simple steps to get the benefits:

1. Scan the QR code or visit the link below

https://packt.link/free-ebook/978-1-80512-923-3

2. Submit your proof of purchase

3. That's it! We'll send your free PDF and other benefits to your email directly

1

Getting Started
with Time Series

In this chapter, we introduce the main concepts and techniques used in time series analysis. The chapter begins by defining time series and explaining why the analysis of these datasets is a relevant topic in data science. After that, we describe how to load time series data using the `pandas` library. The chapter dives into the basic components of a time series, such as trend and seasonality. One key concept of time series analysis covered in this chapter is that of stationarity. We will explore several methods to assess stationarity using statistical tests.

The following recipes will be covered in this chapter:

- Loading a time series using `pandas`
- Visualizing a time series
- Resampling a time series
- Dealing with missing values
- Decomposing a time series
- Computing autocorrelation
- Detecting stationarity
- Dealing with heteroskedasticity
- Loading and visualizing a multivariate time series
- Resampling a multivariate time series
- Analyzing the correlation among pairs of variables

By the end of this chapter, you will have a solid foundation in the main aspects of time series analysis. This includes loading and preprocessing time series data, identifying its basic components, decomposing time series, detecting stationarity, and expanding this understanding to a multivariate setting. This knowledge will serve as a building block for the subsequent chapters.

Technical requirements

To work through this chapter, you need to have Python 3.9 installed on your machine. We will work with the following libraries:

- pandas (2.1.4)
- numpy (1.26.3)
- statsmodels (0.14.1)
- pmdarima (2.0.4)
- seaborn (0.13.2)

You can install these libraries using pip:

```
pip install pandas numpy statsmodels pmdarima seaborn
```

In our setup, we used pip version 23.3.1. The code for this chapter can be found at the following GitHub URL: https://github.com/PacktPublishing/Deep-Learning-for-Time-Series-Data-Cookbook

Loading a time series using pandas

In this first recipe, we start by loading a dataset in a Python session using pandas. Throughout this book, we'll work with time series using pandas data structures. pandas is a useful Python package for data analysis and manipulation. Univariate time series can be structured as pandas Series objects, where the values of the series have an associated index or timestamp with a pandas.Index structure.

Getting ready

We will focus on a dataset related to solar radiation that was collected by the U.S. Department of Agriculture. The data, which contains information about solar radiation (in watts per square meter), spans from October 1, 2007, to October 1, 2013. It was collected at an hourly frequency totaling 52,608 observations.

You can download the dataset from the GitHub URL provided in the *Technical requirements* section of this chapter. You can also find the original source at the following URL: https://catalog. data.gov/dataset/data-from-weather-snow-and-streamflow-data-from-four-western-juniper-dominated-experimenta-b9e22.

How to do it...

The dataset is a .csv file. In pandas, we can load a .csv file using the pd.read_csv() function:

```
import pandas as pd
data = pd.read_csv('path/to/data.csv',
                   parse_dates=['Datetime'],
                   index_col='Datetime')
series = data['Incoming Solar']
```

In the preceding code, note the following:

- First, we import pandas using the import keyword. Importing this library is a necessary step to make its methods available in a Python session.

- The main argument to pd.read_csv is the file location. The parse_dates argument automatically converts the input variables (in this case, Datetime) into a datetime format. The index_col argument sets the index of the data to the Datetime column.

- Finally, we subset the data object using squared brackets to get the Incoming Solar column, which contains the information about solar radiation at each time step.

How it works...

The following table shows a sample of the data. Each row represents the level of the time series at a particular hour.

Datetime	Incoming Solar
2007-10-01 09:00:00	35.4
2007-10-01 10:00:00	63.8
2007-10-01 11:00:00	99.4
2007-10-01 12:00:00	174.5
2007-10-01 13:00:00	157.9
2007-10-01 14:00:00	345.8
2007-10-01 15:00:00	329.8
2007-10-01 16:00:00	114.6
2007-10-01 17:00:00	29.9
2007-10-01 18:00:00	10.9
2007-10-01 19:00:00	0.0

Table 1.1: Sample of an hourly univariate time series

The `series` object that contains the time series is a `pandas` Series data structure. This structure contains several methods for time series analysis. We could also create a Series object by calling `pd.Series` with a dataset and the respective time series. The following is an example of this: `pd.Series(data=values, index=timestamps)`, where `values` refers to the time series values and `timestamps` represents the respective timestamp of each observation.

Visualizing a time series

Now, we have a time series loaded in a Python session. This recipe walks you through the process of visualizing a time series in Python. Our goal is to create a line plot of the time series data, with the dates on the *x* axis and the value of the series on the *y* axis.

Getting ready

There are several data visualization libraries in Python. Visualizing a time series is useful to quickly identify patterns such as trends or seasonal effects. A graphic is an easy way to understand the dynamics of the data and to spot any anomalies within it.

In this recipe, we will create a time series plot using two different libraries: `pandas` and `seaborn`. `seaborn` is a popular data visualization Python library.

How to do it...

pandas Series objects contain a `plot()` method for visualizing time series. You can use it as follows:

```
series.plot(figsize=(12,6), title='Solar radiation time series')
```

The `plot()` method is called with two arguments. We use the `figsize` argument to change the size of the plot. In this case, we set the width and height of the figure to `12` and `6` inches, respectively. Another argument is `title`, which we set to `Solar radiation time series`. You can check the pandas documentation for a complete list of acceptable arguments.

You use it to plot a time series using `seaborn` as follows:

```
import matplotlib.pyplot as plt
import seaborn as sns

series_df = series.reset_index()

plt.rcParams['figure.figsize'] = [12, 6]

sns.set_theme(style='darkgrid')
sns.lineplot(data=series_df, x='Datetime', y='Incoming Solar')

plt.ylabel('Solar Radiation')
plt.xlabel('')
plt.title('Solar radiation time series')
plt.show()

plt.savefig('assets/time_series_plot.png')
```

The preceding code includes the following steps:

1. Import `seaborn` and `matplotlib`, two data visualization libraries.

2. Transform the time series into a `pandas` DataFrame object by calling the `reset_index()` method. This step is required because `seaborn` takes DataFrame objects as the main input.

3. Configure the figure size using `plt.rcParams` to a width of 12 inches and a height of 6 inches.

4. Set the plot theme to `darkgrid` using the `set_theme()` method.

5. Use the `lineplot()` method to build the plot. Besides the input data, it takes the name of the column for each of the axes: `Datetime` and `Incoming Solar` for the *x* axis and *y* axis, respectively.

6. Configure the plot parameters, namely the *y*-axis label (`ylabel`), *x*-axis label (`xlabel`), and `title`.

7. Finally, we use the `show` method to display the plot and `savefig` to store it as a `.png` file.

How it works...

The following figure shows the plot obtained from the `seaborn` library:

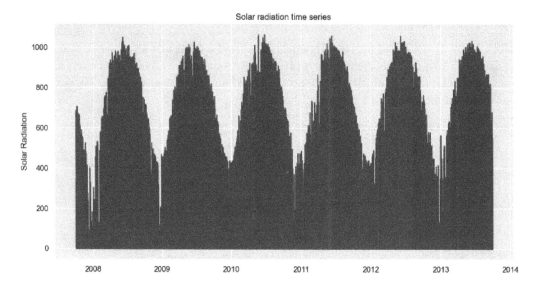

Figure 1.1: Time series plot using seaborn

The example time series shows a strong yearly seasonality, where the average level is lower at the start of the year. Apart from some fluctuations and seasonality, the long-term average level of the time series remains stable over time.

We learned about two ways of creating a time series plot. One uses the `plot()` method that is available in `pandas`, and another one uses `seaborn`, a Python library dedicated to data visualization. The first one provides a quick way of visualizing your data. But `seaborn` has a more powerful visualization toolkit that you can use to create beautiful plots.

There's more...

The type of plot created in this recipe is called a line plot. Both `pandas` and `seaborn` can be used to create other types of plots. We encourage you to go through the documentation to learn about these.

Resampling a time series

Time series resampling is the process of changing the frequency of a time series, for example, from hourly to daily. This task is a common preprocessing step in time series analysis and this recipe shows how to do it with `pandas`.

Getting ready

Changing the frequency of a time series is a common preprocessing step before analysis. For example, the time series used in the preceding recipes has an hourly granularity. Yet, our goal may be to study daily variations. In such cases, we can resample the data into a different period. Resampling is also an effective way of handling irregular time series – those that are collected in irregularly spaced periods.

How to do it...

We'll go over two different scenarios where resampling a time series may be useful: when changing the sampling frequency and when dealing with irregular time series.

The following code resamples the time series into a daily granularity:

```
series_daily = series.resample('D').sum()
```

The daily granularity is specified with the input D to the resample () method. The values of each corresponding day are summed together using the sum () method.

Most time series analysis methods work under the assumption that the time series is regular; in other words, it is collected in regularly spaced time intervals (for example, every day). But some time series are naturally irregular. For instance, the sales of a retail product occur at arbitrary timestamps as customers arrive at a store.

Let us simulate sale events with the following code:

```
import numpy as np
import pandas as pd

n_sales = 1000
start = pd.Timestamp('2023-01-01 09:00')
end = pd.Timestamp('2023-04-01')
n_days = (end - start).days + 1

irregular_series = pd.to_timedelta(np.random.rand(n_sales) * n_days,
                                   unit='D') + start
```

The preceding code creates `1000` sale events from `2023-01-01 09:00` to `2023-04-01`. A sample of this series is shown in the following table:

ID	Timestamp
1	2023-01-01 15:18:10
2	2023-01-01 15:28:15
3	2023-01-01 16:31:57
4	2023-01-01 16:52:29
5	2023-01-01 23:01:24
6	2023-01-01 23:44:39

Table 1.2: Sample of an irregular time series

Irregular time series can be transformed into a regular frequency by resampling. In the case of sales, we will count how many sales occurred each day:

```
ts_sales = pd.Series(0, index=irregular_series)
tot_sales = ts_sales.resample('D').count()
```

First, we create a time series of zeros based on the irregular timestamps (`ts_sales`). Then, we resample this dataset into a daily frequency (D) and use the `count()` method to count how many observations occur each day. The `tot_sales` reconstructed time series can be used for other tasks, such as forecasting daily sales.

How it works...

A sample of the reconstructed time series concerning solar radiation is shown in the following table:

Datetime	Incoming Solar
2007-10-01	1381.5
2007-10-02	3953.2
2007-10-03	3098.1
2007-10-04	2213.9

Table 1.3: Solar radiation time series after resampling

Resampling is a cornerstone preprocessing step in time series analysis. This technique can be used to change a time series into a different granularity or to convert an irregular time series into a regular one.

The summary statistic is an important input to consider. In the first case, we used `sum` to add the hourly solar radiation values observed each day. In the case of the irregular time series, we used the `count()` method to count how many events occurred in each period. Yet, you can use other summary statistics according to your needs. For example, using the mean would take the average value of each period to resample the time series.

There's more...

We resampled to daily granularity. A list of available options is available here: `https://pandas.pydata.org/docs/user_guide/timeseries.html#dateoffset-objects`.

Dealing with missing values

In this recipe, we'll cover how to impute time series missing values. We'll discuss different methods of imputing missing values and the factors to consider when choosing a method. We'll show an example of how to solve this problem using `pandas`.

Getting ready

Missing values are an issue that plagues all kinds of data, including time series. Observations are often unavailable for various reasons, such as sensor failure or annotation errors. In such cases, data imputation can be used to overcome this problem. Data imputation works by assigning a value based on some rule, such as the mean or some predefined value.

How to do it...

We start by simulating missing data. The following code removes 60% of observations from a sample of two years of the solar radiation time series:

```
import numpy as np

sample_with_nan = series_daily.head(365 * 2).copy()
size_na=int(0.6 * len(sample_with_nan))

idx = np.random.choice(a=range(len(sample_with_nan)),
                       size=size_na,
                       replace=False)

sample_with_nan[idx] = np.nan
```

We leverage the `np.random.choice()` method from numpy to select a random sample of the time series. The observations of this sample are changed to a missing value (`np.nan`).

In datasets without temporal order, it is common to impute missing values using central statistics such as the mean or median. This can be done as follows:

```
average_value = sample_with_nan.mean()
imp_mean = sample_with_nan.fillna(average_value)
```

Time series imputation must take into account the temporal nature of observations. This means that the assigned value should follow the dynamics of the series. A more common approach in time series is to impute missing data with the last known observation. This approach is implemented in the ffill() method:

```
imp_ffill = sample_with_nan.ffill()
```

Another, less common, approach that uses the order of observations is bfill():

```
imp_bfill = sample_with_nan.bfill()
```

The bfill() method imputes missing data with the next available observation in the dataset.

How it works...

The following figure shows the reconstructed time series after imputation with each method:

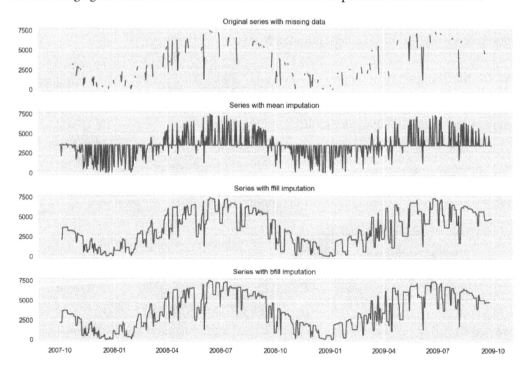

Figure 1.2: Imputing missing data with different strategies

The mean imputation approach misses the time series dynamics, while both ffill and bfill lead to a reconstructed time series with similar dynamics as the original time series. Usually, ffill is preferable because it does not break the temporal order of observations, that is, using future information to alter (impute) the past.

There's more…

The imputation process can also be carried out using some conditions, such as limiting the number of imputed observations. You can learn more about this in the documentation pages of these functions, for example, `https://pandas.pydata.org/docs/reference/api/pandas.DataFrame.ffill.html`.

Decomposing a time series

Time series decomposition is the process of splitting a time series into its basic components, such as trend or seasonality. This recipe explores different techniques to solve this task and how to choose among them.

Getting ready

A time series is composed of three parts – trend, seasonality, and the remainder:

- The trend characterizes the long-term change in the level of a time series. Trends can be upward (increase in level) or downward (decrease in level), and they can also change over time.

- Seasonality refers to regular variations in fixed periods, such as every day. The solar radiation time series plotted in the preceding recipe shows a clear yearly seasonality. Solar radiation is higher during summer and lower during winter.

- The remainder (also called irregular) of the time series is what is left after removing the trend and seasonal components.

Breaking a time series into its components is useful to understand the underlying structure of the data.

We'll describe the process of time series decomposition with two methods: the classical decomposition approach and a method based on local regression. You'll also learn how to extend the latter method to time series with multiple seasonal patterns.

How to do it...

There are several approaches for decomposing a time series into its basic parts. The simplest method is known as classical decomposition. This approach is implemented in the statsmodels library and can be used as follows:

```
from statsmodels.tsa.seasonal import seasonal_decompose

result = seasonal_decompose(x=series_daily,
                            model='additive',
                            period=365)
```

Besides the dataset, you need to specify the period and the type of model. For a daily time series with a yearly seasonality, the period should be set to 365, which is the number of days in a year. The model parameter can be either additive or multiplicative. We'll go into more detail about this in the next section.

Each component is stored as an attribute of the results in an object:

```
result.trend
result.seasonal
result.resid
```

Each of these attributes returns a time series with the respective component.

Arguably, one of the most popular methods for time series decomposition is **STL** (which stands for **Seasonal and Trend decomposition using LOESS**). This method is also available on statsmodels:

```
from statsmodels.tsa.seasonal import STL

result = STL(endog=series_daily, period=365).fit()
```

In the case of STL, you don't need to specify a model as we did with the classical method.

Usually, time series decomposition approaches work under the assumption that the dataset contains a single seasonal pattern. Yet, time series collected in high sampling frequencies (such as hourly or daily) can contain multiple seasonal patterns. For example, an hourly time series can show both regular daily and weekly variations.

The MSTL() method (short for **Multiple STL**) extends MSTL for time series with multiple seasonal patterns. You can specify the period for each seasonal pattern in a tuple as the input for the period argument. An example is shown in the following code:

```
from statsmodels.tsa.seasonal import MSTL

result = MSTL(endog=series_daily, periods=(7, 365)).fit()
```

In the preceding code, we passed two periods as input: 7 and 365. These periods attempt to capture weekly and yearly seasonality in a daily time series.

How it works...

In a given time step i, the value of the time series (Y_i) can be decomposed using an additive model, as follows:

$$Y_i = Trend_i + Seasonality_i + Remainder_i$$

This decomposition can also be multiplicative:

$$Y_i = Trend_i \times Seasonality_i \times Remainder_i$$

The most appropriate approach, additive or multiplicative, depends on the input data. But you can turn a multiplicative decomposition into an additive one by transforming the data with the logarithm function. The logarithm stabilizes the variance, thus making the series additive regarding its components.

The results of the classical decomposition are shown in the following figure:

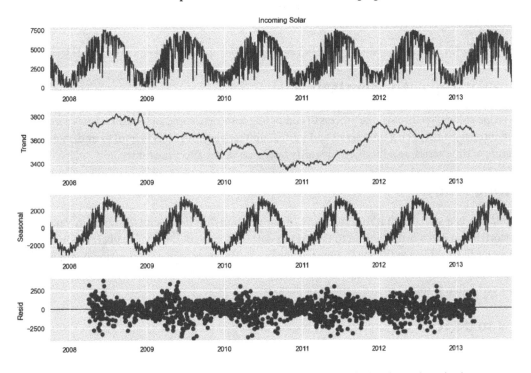

Figure 1.3: Time series components after decomposition with the classical method

In the classical decomposition, the trend is estimated using a moving average, for example, the average of the last 24 hours (for hourly series). Seasonality is estimated by averaging the values of each period. STL is a more flexible method for decomposing a time series. It can handle complex patterns, such as irregular trends or outliers. STL leverages **LOESS**, which stands for **locally weighted scatterplot smoothing**, to extract each component.

There's more...

Decomposition is usually done for data exploration purposes. But it can also be used as a preprocessing step for forecasting. For example, some studies show that removing seasonality before training a neural network improves forecasting performance.

See also

You can learn more about this in the following references:

- Hewamalage, Hansika, Christoph Bergmeir, and Kasun Bandara. "Recurrent neural networks for time series forecasting: Current status and future directions." *International Journal of Forecasting* 37.1 (2021): 388-427.

- Hyndman, Rob J., and George Athanasopoulos. *Forecasting: Principles and Practice.* OTexts, 2018.

Computing autocorrelation

This recipe guides you through the process of computing autocorrelation. Autocorrelation is a measure of the correlation between a time series and itself at different lags, and it is helpful to understand the structure of time series, specifically, to quantify how past values affect the future.

Getting ready

Correlation is a statistic that measures the linear relationship between two random variables. Autocorrelation extends this notion to time series data. In time series, the value observed in a given time step will be similar to the values observed before it. The autocorrelation function quantifies the linear relationship between a time series and a lagged version of itself. A lagged time series refers to a time series that is shifted over a number of periods.

How to do it...

We can compute the autocorrelation function using statsmodels:

```
from statsmodels.tsa.stattools import acf

acf_scores = acf(x=series_daily, nlags=365)
```

The inputs to the function are a time series and the number of lags to analyze. In this case, we compute autocorrelation up to 365 lags, a full year of data.

We can also use statsmodels to compute the partial autocorrelation function. This measure extends the autocorrelation by controlling for the correlation of the time series at shorter lags:

```
from statsmodels.tsa.stattools import pacf

pacf_scores = pacf(x=series_daily, nlags=365)
```

The statsmodels library also provides functions to plot the results of autocorrelation analysis:

```
from statsmodels.graphics.tsaplots import plot_acf, plot_pacf

plot_acf(series_daily, lags=365)
plot_pacf(series_daily, lags=365)
```

How it works...

The following figure shows the autocorrelation of the daily solar radiation time series up to 365 lags.

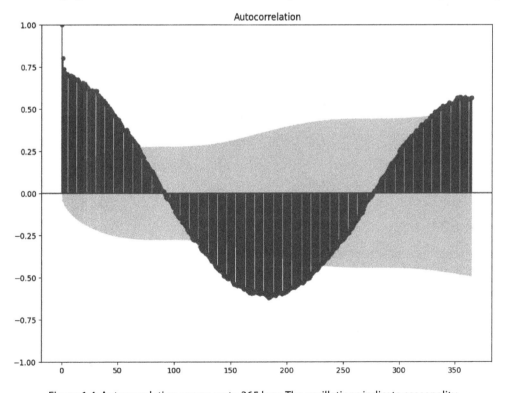

Figure 1.4: Autocorrelation scores up to 365 lags. The oscillations indicate seasonality

The oscillations in this plot are due to the yearly seasonal pattern. The analysis of autocorrelation is a useful approach to detecting seasonality.

There's more...

The autocorrelation at each seasonal lag is usually large and positive. Besides, sometimes autocorrelation decays slowly along the lags, which indicates the presence of a trend. You can learn more about this from the following URL: https://otexts.com/fpp3/components.html.

The partial autocorrelation function is an important tool for identifying the order of autoregressive models. The idea is to select the number of lags whose partial autocorrelation is significant.

Detecting stationarity

Stationarity is a central concept in time series analysis and an important assumption made by many time series models. This recipe walks you through the process of testing a time series for stationarity.

Getting ready

A time series is stationary if its statistical properties do not change. It does not mean that the series does not change over time, just that the way it changes does not itself change over time. This includes the level of the time series, which is constant under stationary conditions. Time series patterns such as trend or seasonality break stationarity. Therefore, it may help to deal with these issues before modeling. As we described in the *Decomposing a time series* recipe, there is evidence that removing seasonality improves the forecasts of deep learning models.

We can stabilize the mean level of the time series by differencing. Differencing is the process of taking the difference between consecutive observations. This process works in two steps:

1. Estimate the number of differencing steps required for stationarity.

2. Apply the required number of differencing operations.

How to do it...

We can estimate the required differencing steps with statistical tests, such as the augmented Dickey-Fuller test, or the KPSS test. These are implemented in the ndiffs() function, which is available in the pmdarima library:

```
from pmdarima.arima import ndiffs

ndiffs(x=series_daily, test='adf')
```

Besides the time series, we pass `test='adf'` as an input to set the method to the augmented Dickey-Fuller test. The output of this function is the number of differencing steps, which in this case is 1. Then, we can differentiate the time series using the `diff()` method:

```
series_changes = series_daily.diff()
```

Differencing can also be applied over seasonal periods. In such cases, seasonal differencing involves computing the difference between consecutive observations of the same seasonal period:

```
from pmdarima.arima import nsdiffs

nsdiffs(x=series_changes, test='ch', m=365)
```

Besides the data and the test (`ch` for Canova-Hansen), we also specify the number of periods. In this case, this parameter is set to `365` (number of days in a year).

How it works...

The differenced time series is shown in the following figure.

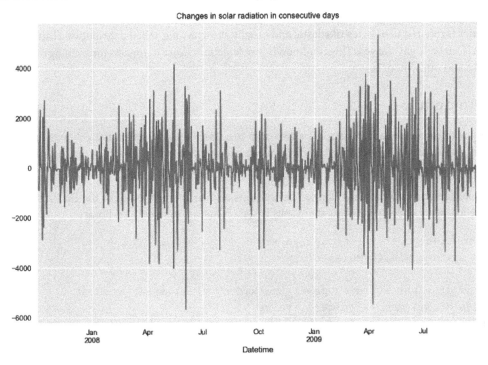

Figure 1.5: Sample of the series of changes between consecutive periods after differencing

Differencing works as a preprocessing step. First, the time series is differenced until it becomes stationary. Then, a forecasting model is created based on the differenced time series. The forecasts provided by the model can be transformed to the original scale by reverting the differencing operations.

There's more...

In this recipe, we focused on two particular methods for testing stationarity. You can check other options in the function documentation: https://alkaline-ml.com/pmdarima/modules/generated/pmdarima.arima.ndiffs.html.

Dealing with heteroskedasticity

In this recipe, we delve into the variance of time series. The variance of a time series is a measure of how spread out the data is and how this dispersion evolves over time. You'll learn how to handle data with a changing variance.

Getting ready

The variance of time series can change over time, which also violates stationarity. In such cases, the time series is referred to as heteroskedastic and usually shows a long-tailed distribution. This means the data is left- or right-skewed. This condition is problematic because it impacts the training of neural networks and other models.

How to do it...

Dealing with non-constant variance is a two-step process. First, we use statistical tests to check whether a time series is heteroskedastic. Then, we use transformations such as the logarithm to stabilize the variance.

We can detect heteroskedasticity using statistical tests such as the White test or the Breusch-Pagan test. The following code implements these tests based on the statsmodels library:

```
import statsmodels.stats.api as sms
from statsmodels.formula.api import ols

series_df = series_daily.reset_index(drop=True).reset_index()
series_df.columns = ['time', 'value']
series_df['time'] += 1

olsr = ols('value ~ time', series_df).fit()

_, pval_white, _, _ = sms.het_white(olsr.resid, olsr.model.exog)
_, pval_bp, _, _ = sms.het_breuschpagan(olsr.resid, olsr.model.exog)
```

The preceding code follows these steps:

1. Import the `statsmodels` modules `ols` and `stats`.

2. Create a DataFrame based on the values of the time series and the row they were collected at (`1` for the first observation).

3. Create a linear model that relates the values of the time series with the `time` column.

4. Run `het_white` (White) and `het_breuschpagan` (Breusch-Pagan) to apply the variance tests.

The output of the tests is a p-value, where the null hypothesis posits that the time series has constant variance. So, if the p-value is below the significance value, we reject the null hypothesis and assume heteroskedasticity.

The simplest way to deal with non-constant variance is by transforming the data using the logarithm. This operation can be implemented as follows:

```
import numpy as np

class LogTransformation:
    @staticmethod
    def transform(x):
        xt = np.sign(x) * np.log(np.abs(x) + 1)
        return xt

    @staticmethod
    def inverse_transform(xt):
        x = np.sign(xt) * (np.exp(np.abs(xt)) - 1)
        return x
```

The preceding code is a Python class called `LogTransformation`. It contains two methods: `transform()` and `inverse_transform()`. The first transforms the data using the logarithm and the second reverts that operation.

We apply the `transform()` method to the time series as follows:

```
series_log = LogTransformation.transform(series_daily)
```

The log is a particular case of Box-Cox transformation that is available in the `scipy` library. You can implement this method as follows:

```
series_transformed, lmbda = stats.boxcox(series_daily)
```

The `stats.boxcox()` method estimates a transformation parameter, `lmbda`, which can be used to revert the operation.

How it works...

The transformations outlined in this recipe stabilize the variance of a time series. They also bring the data distribution closer to the Normal distribution. These transformations are especially useful for neural networks as they help avoid saturation areas. In neural networks, saturation occurs when the model becomes insensitive to different inputs, thus compromising the training process.

There's more...

The Yeo-Johnson power transformation is similar to the Box-Cox transformation but allows for negative values in the time series. You can learn more about this method with the following link: `https://docs.scipy.org/doc/scipy/reference/generated/scipy.stats.yeojohnson.html`.

See also

You can learn more about the importance of the logarithm transformation in the following reference:

Bandara, Kasun, Christoph Bergmeir, and Slawek Smyl. "Forecasting across time series databases using recurrent neural networks on groups of similar series: A clustering approach." *Expert Systems with Applications* 140 (2020): 112896.

Loading and visualizing a multivariate time series

So far, we've learned how to analyze univariate time series. Yet, multivariate time series are also relevant in real-world problems. This recipe explores how to load a multivariate time series. Before, we used the `pandas` Series structure to handle univariate time series. Multivariate time series are better structured as `pandas` DataFrame objects.

Getting ready

A multivariate time series contains multiple variables. The concepts underlying time series analysis are extended to cases where multiple variables evolve over time and are interrelated with each other. The relationship between the different variables can be difficult to model, especially when the number of these variables is large.

In many real-world applications, multiple variables can influence each other and exhibit a temporal dependency. For example, in weather modeling, the incoming solar radiation is correlated with other meteorological variables, such as air temperature or humidity. Considering these variables with a single multivariate model can be fundamental for modeling the dynamics of the data and getting better predictions.

We'll continue to study the solar radiation dataset. This time series is extended by including extra meteorological information.

How to do it...

We'll start by reading a multivariate time series. Like in the *Loading a time series using pandas* recipe, we resort to pandas and read a .csv file into a DataFrame data structure:

```
import pandas as pd

data = pd.read_csv('path/to/multivariate_ts.csv',
                   parse_dates=['datetime'],
                   index_col='datetime')
```

The parse_dates and index_col arguments ensure that the index of the DataFrame is a DatetimeIndex object. This is important so that pandas treats this object as a time series. After loading the time series, we can transform and visualize it using the plot() method:

```
data_log = LogTransformation.transform(data)

sample = data_log.tail(1000)

mv_plot = sample.plot(figsize=(15, 8),
                      title='Multivariate time series',
                      xlabel='',
                      ylabel='Value')

mv_plot.legend(fancybox=True, framealpha=1)
```

The preceding code follows these steps:

1. First, we transform the data using the logarithm.

2. We take the last 1,000 observations to make the visualization less cluttered.

3. Finally, we use the plot() method to create a visualization. We also call legend to configure the legend of the plot.

How it works...

A sample of the multivariate time series is displayed in the following figure:

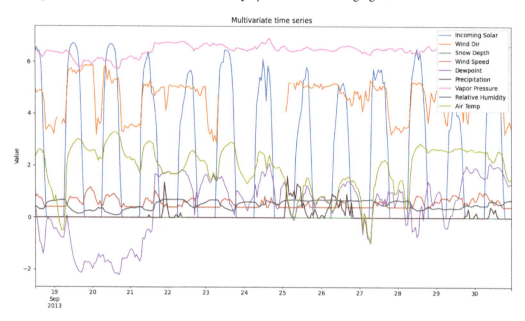

Figure 1.6: Multivariate time series plot

The process of loading a multivariate time series works like the univariate case. The main difference is that a multivariate time series is stored in Python as a DataFrame object rather than a Series one.

From the preceding plot, we can notice that different variables follow different distributions and have distinct average and dispersion levels.

Resampling a multivariate time series

This recipe revisits the topic of resampling but focuses on multivariate time series. We'll explain why resampling can be a bit tricky for multivariate time series due to the eventual need to use distinct summary statistics for different variables.

Getting ready

When resampling a multivariate time, you may need to apply different summary statistics depending on the variable. For example, you may want to sum up the solar radiation observed at each hour to get a sense of how much power you could generate. Yet, taking the average, instead of the sum, is more sensible when summarizing wind speed because this variable is not cumulative.

How to do it...

We can pass a Python dictionary that details which statistic should be applied to each variable. Then, we can pass this dictionary to the agg () method, as follows:

```
stat_by_variable = {
    'Incoming Solar': 'sum',
    'Wind Dir': 'mean',
    'Snow Depth': 'sum',
    'Wind Speed': 'mean',
    'Dewpoint': 'mean',
    'Precipitation': 'sum',
    'Vapor Pressure': 'mean',
    'Relative Humidity': 'mean',
    'Air Temp': 'max',
}

data_daily = data.resample('D').agg(stat_by_variable)
```

We aggregate the time series into a daily periodicity using different summary statistics. For example, we want to sum up the solar radiation observed each day. For the air temperature variable (Air Temp), we take the maximum value observed each day.

How it works...

By using a dictionary to pass different summary statistics, we can adjust the frequency of the time series in a more flexible way. Note that if you wanted to apply the mean for all variables, you would not need a dictionary. A simpler way would be to run data.resample('D').mean().

Analyzing correlation among pairs of variables

This recipe walks you through the process of using correlation to analyze a multivariate time series. This task is useful to understand the relationship among the different variables in the series and thereby understand its dynamics.

Getting ready

A common way to analyze the dynamics of multiple variables is by computing the correlation of each pair. You can use this information to perform feature selection. For example, when pairs of variables are highly correlated, you may want to keep only one of them.

How to do it...

First, we compute the correlation among each pair of variables:

```
corr_matrix = data_daily.corr(method='pearson')
```

We can visualize the results using a heatmap from the seaborn library:

```
import seaborn as sns
import matplotlib.pyplot as plt

sns.heatmap(data=corr_matrix,
            cmap=sns.diverging_palette(230, 20, as_cmap=True),
            xticklabels=data_daily.columns,
            yticklabels=data_daily.columns,
            center=0,
            square=True,
            linewidths=.5,
            cbar_kws={"shrink": .5})

plt.xticks(rotation=30)
```

Heatmaps are a common way of visualizing matrices. We pick a diverging color set from sns. diverging_palette to distinguish between negative correlation (blue) and positive correlation (red).

How it works...

The following figure shows the heatmap with the correlation results:

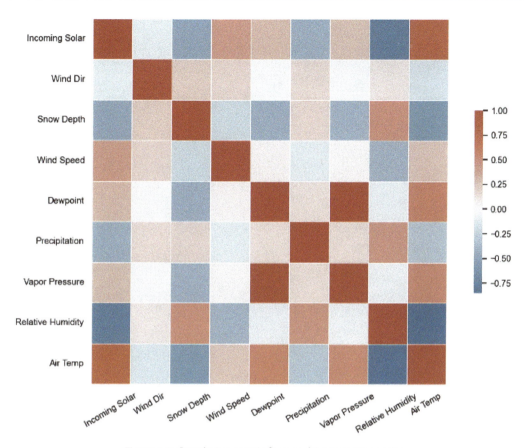

Figure 1.7: Correlation matrix for a multivariate time series

The corr() method computes the correlation among each pair of variables in the data_daily object. In this case, we use the Pearson correlation with the method='pearson' argument. Kendall and Spearman are two common alternatives to the Pearson correlation.

2

Getting Started with PyTorch

In this chapter, we'll explore **PyTorch**, a leading deep learning library in Python.

We go over several operations that are useful for understanding how neural networks are built using PyTorch. Besides tensor operations, we will also explore how to train different types of neural networks. Specifically, we will focus on feedforward, recurrent, **long short-term memory** (**LSTM**), and 1D convolutional networks.

In later chapters, we will also cover other types of neural networks, such as transformers. Here, we will use synthetic data for demonstrative purposes, which will help us showcase both the implementation and theory behind each model.

Upon completing this chapter, you will have gained a robust understanding of PyTorch, equipping you with the tools for more advanced deep learning projects.

In this chapter, we will cover the following recipes:

- Installing PyTorch
- Basic operations in PyTorch
- Advanced operations in PyTorch
- Building a simple neural network with PyTorch
- Training a feedforward neural network
- Training a recurrent neural network
- Training an LSTM neural network
- Training a convolutional neural network

Technical requirements

Before starting, you will need to ensure that your system meets the following technical requirements:

- **Python 3.9**: You can download Python from `https://www.python.org/downloads/`.
- pip (23.3.1) or Anaconda: These are popular package managers for Python. pip comes with Python by default. Anaconda can be downloaded from `https://www.anaconda.com/products/distribution`.
- torch (2.2.0): The main library we will be using for deep learning in this chapter.
- **CUDA (optional)**: If you have a CUDA-capable GPU on your machine, you can install a version of PyTorch that supports CUDA. This will enable computations on your GPU and can significantly speed up your deep learning experiments.

It's worth noting that the code presented in this chapter is platform-independent and should run on any system with the preceding requirements satisfied.

The code for this chapter can be found at the following GitHub URL: `https://github.com/PacktPublishing/Deep-Learning-for-Time-Series-Data-Cookbook`.

Installing PyTorch

To start with PyTorch, we need to install it first. As of the time of writing, PyTorch supports Linux, macOS, and Windows platforms. Here, we will guide you through the installation process on these operating systems.

Getting ready

PyTorch is usually installed via `pip` or Anaconda. We recommend creating a new Python environment before installing the library, especially if you will be working on multiple Python projects on your system. This is to prevent any conflicts between different versions of Python libraries that different projects may require.

How to do it...

Let's see how to install `PyTorch`. We'll describe how to do this using either `pip` or `Anaconda`. We'll also provide some information about how to use a CUDA environment.

If you're using `pip`, Python's package manager, you can install PyTorch by running the following command in your terminal:

```
pip install torch
```

With the Anaconda Python distribution, you can install PyTorch using the following command:

```
conda install pytorch torchvision -c pytorch
```

If you have a CUDA-capable GPU on your machine, you can install a version of PyTorch that supports CUDA to enable computations on your GPU. This can significantly speed up your deep learning experiments. The PyTorch website provides a tool that generates the appropriate installation command based on your needs. Visit the PyTorch website, select your preferences (such as OS, package manager, Python version, and CUDA version) in the **Quick Start Locally** section, and then copy the generated command into your terminal.

How it works...

After you've installed PyTorch, you can verify that everything is working correctly by opening a Python interpreter and running the following code:

```
import torch
print(torch.__version__)
```

This should output the version of PyTorch that you installed. Now, you're ready to start using PyTorch for deep learning!

In the next sections, we will familiarize ourselves with the basics of PyTorch and build our first neural network.

Basic operations in PyTorch

Before we start building neural networks with PyTorch, it is essential to understand the basics of how to manipulate data using this library. In PyTorch, the fundamental unit of data is the tensor, a generalization of matrices to an arbitrary number of dimensions (also known as a multidimensional array).

Getting ready

A tensor can be a number (a 0D tensor), a vector (a 1D tensor), a matrix (a 2D tensor), or any multi-dimensional data (a 3D tensor, a 4D tensor, and so on). PyTorch provides various functions to create and manipulate tensors.

How to do it...

Let's start by importing PyTorch:

```
import torch
```

We can create a tensor in `PyTorch` using various techniques. Let's start by creating tensors from lists:

```
t1 = torch.tensor([1, 2, 3])
print(t1)
t2 = torch.tensor([[1, 2], [3, 4]])
print(t2)
```

PyTorch can seamlessly integrate with NumPy, allowing for easy tensor creation from NumPy arrays:

```
import numpy as np
np_array = np.array([5, 6, 7])
t3 = torch.from_numpy(np_array)
print(t3)
```

PyTorch also provides functions to generate tensors with specific values, such as zeros or ones:

```
t4 = torch.zeros((3, 3))
print(t4)
t5 = torch.ones((3, 3))
print(t5)
t6 = torch.eye(3)
print(t6)
```

These are commonly used methods in NumPy that are also available in `PyTorch`.

How it works...

Now that we know how to create tensors, let's look at some basic operations. We can perform all standard arithmetic operations on tensors:

```
result = t1 + t3
print(result)
result = t3 - t1
print(result)
result = t1 * t3
print(result)
result = t3 / t1
print(result)
```

You can reshape tensors using the `.reshape()` method:

```
t7 = torch.arange(9) # Creates a 1D tensor [0, 1, 2, ..., 8]
t8 = t7.reshape((3, 3)) # Reshapes the tensor to a 3x3 matrix
print(t8)
```

This is a brief introduction to tensor operations in `PyTorch`. As you dive deeper, you'll find that `PyTorch` offers various operations to manipulate tensors, giving you the flexibility and control needed to implement complex deep learning models and algorithms.

Advanced operations in PyTorch

After exploring basic tensor operations, let's now dive into more advanced operations in `PyTorch`, specifically the linear algebra operations that form the backbone of most numerical computations in deep learning.

Getting ready

Linear algebra is a subset of mathematics. It deals with vectors, vector spaces, and linear transformations between these spaces, such as rotations, scaling, and shearing. In the context of deep learning, we deal with high-dimensional vectors (tensors), and operations on these vectors play a crucial role in the internal workings of models.

How to do it...

Let's start by revisiting the tensors we created in the previous section:

```
print(t1)
print(t2)
```

The dot product of two vectors is a scalar that measures the vectors' direction and magnitude. In `PyTorch`, we can calculate the dot product of two 1D tensors using the `torch.dot()` function:

```
dot_product = torch.dot(t1, t3)
print(dot_product)
```

Unlike element-wise multiplication, matrix multiplication, also known as the dot product, is the operation of multiplying two matrices to produce a new matrix. `PyTorch` provides the `torch.mm()` function to perform matrix multiplication:

```
matrix_product = torch.mm(t2, t5)
print(matrix_product)
```

The transpose of a matrix is a new matrix whose rows are the columns of the original matrix and whose columns are the rows. You can compute the transpose of a tensor using the `.T` attribute:

```
t_transposed = t2.T
print(t_transposed)
```

There are other operations you can perform, such as calculating the determinant of a matrix and finding the inverse of a matrix. Let's look at a couple of these operations:

```
det = torch.det(t2)
print(det)
inverse = torch.inverse(t2)
print(inverse)
```

Note that these two operations are only defined for 2D tensors (matrices).

How it works...

PyTorch is a highly optimized library for performing basic and advanced operations, particularly linear algebra operations that are crucial in deep learning.

These operations make PyTorch a powerful tool for building and training neural networks and performing high-level computations in a more general context. In the next section, we will use these building blocks to start constructing deep learning models.

Building a simple neural network with PyTorch

This section will build a simple two-layer neural network from scratch using only basic tensor operations to solve a time series prediction problem. We aim to demonstrate how one might manually implement a feedforward pass, backpropagation, and optimization steps without leveraging PyTorch's predefined layers and optimization routines.

Getting ready

We use synthetic data for this demonstration. Suppose we have a simple time series data of 100 samples, each with 10 time steps. Our task is to predict the next time step based on the previous ones:

```
X = torch.randn(100, 10)
y = torch.randn(100, 1)
```

Now, let's create a neural network.

How to do it...

Let's start by defining our model parameters and their initial values. Here, we are creating a simple two-layer network, so we have two sets of weights and biases:

We use the requires_grad_() function to tell PyTorch that we want to compute gradients with respect to these tensors during the backward pass.

Next, we define our model. For this simple network, we'll use a sigmoid activation function for the hidden layer:

```
input_size = 10
hidden_size = 5
output_size = 1
W1 = torch.randn(hidden_size, input_size).requires_grad_()
b1 = torch.zeros(hidden_size, requires_grad=True)
W2 = torch.randn(output_size, hidden_size).requires_grad_()
b2 = torch.zeros(output_size, requires_grad=True)

def simple_neural_net(x, W1, b1, W2, b2):
    z1 = torch.mm(x, W1.t()) + b1
    a1 = torch.sigmoid(z1)
    z2 = torch.mm(a1, W2.t()) + b2
    return z2
```

Now, we're ready to train our model. Let's define the learning rate and the number of epochs:

```
lr = 0.01
epochs = 100
loss_fn = torch.nn.MSELoss()

for epoch in range(epochs):
    y_pred = simple_neural_net(X, W1, b1, W2, b2)
    loss = loss_fn(y_pred.squeeze(), y)
    loss.backward()

    with torch.no_grad():
        W1 -= lr * W1.grad
        b1 -= lr * b1.grad
        W2 -= lr * W2.grad
        b2 -= lr * b2.grad

    W1.grad.zero_()
    b1.grad.zero_()
    W2.grad.zero_()
    b2.grad.zero_()
    if epoch % 10 == 0:
        print(f'Epoch: {epoch} \t Loss: {loss.item()}')
```

This basic code demonstrates the essential parts of a neural network: the forward pass, where we compute predictions; the backward pass, where gradients are computed; and the update step, where we adjust our weights to minimize the loss.

There's more...

This chapter is focused on exploring the intricacies of the training process of a neural network. In future chapters, we'll show how to train deep neural networks without worrying about most of these details.

Training a feedforward neural network

This recipe walks you through the process of building a feedforward neural network using PyTorch.

Getting ready

Feedforward neural networks, also known as **multilayer perceptrons** (**MLPs**), are one of the simplest types of artificial neural networks. The data flows from the input layer to the output layer, passing through hidden layers without any loop. In this type of neural network, all hidden units in one layer are connected to the units of the following layer.

How to do it...

Let's create a simple feedforward neural network using PyTorch. First, we need to import the necessary PyTorch modules:

```
import torch
import torch.nn as nn
```

Now, we can define a simple feedforward neural network with one hidden layer:

```
class Net(nn.Module):
    def __init__(self):
        super(Net, self).__init__()
        self.fc1 = nn.Linear(10, 5)
        self.fc2 = nn.Linear(5, 1)

    def forward(self, x):
        x = torch.relu(self.fc1(x))
        x = self.fc2(x)
        return x

net = Net()
print(net)
```

In the preceding code, nn.Module is the base class for all neural network modules in PyTorch, and our network is a subclass of it.

The `forward()` method in this class represents the forward pass of the network. This is the computation that the network performs when transforming inputs into outputs. Here's a step-by-step explanation:

- The `forward()` method takes an input tensor `x`. This tensor represents the input data. Its shape should be compatible with the network's layers. In this case, as the first linear layer (`self.fc1`) expects `10` input features, the last dimension of `x` should be `10`.

- The input tensor is first passed through a linear transformation, represented by `self.fc1`. This object is an instance of PyTorch's `nn.Linear` class, and it performs a linear transformation that involves multiplying the input data with a weight matrix and adding a bias vector. As defined in the `__init__()` method, this layer transforms the 10D space to a 5D space using a linear transformation. This reduction is often seen as the neural network "learning" or "extracting" features from the input data.

- The output of the first layer is then passed through a **rectified linear unit** (**ReLU**) activation function using `torch.relu()`. This is a simple non-linearity that replaces negative values in the tensor with zeros. This allows the neural network to model more complex relationships between the inputs and the outputs.

- The output from the `ReLU()` function is then passed through another linear transformation, `self.fc2`. As before, this object is an instance of PyTorch's `nn.Linear` class. This layer reduces the dimensionality of the tensor from 5 (the output size of the previous layer) to 1 (the desired output size).

Finally, the output of the second linear layer is returned by the `forward()` method. This output can then be used for various purposes, such as computing a loss for training the network, or as the final output in an inference task (that is when the network is used for prediction).

How it works...

To train the network, we need a dataset to train on, a loss function, and an optimizer.

Let's use the same synthetic dataset that we defined for our previous example:

```
X = torch.randn(100, 10)
Y = torch.randn(100, 1)
```

We can use the **mean squared error** (**MSE**) loss for our task, which is a common loss function for regression problems. PyTorch provides a built-in implementation of this loss function:

```
loss_fn = nn.MSELoss()
```

We will use **stochastic gradient descent** (**SGD**) as our optimizer. SGD is a type of iterative method for optimizing the objective function:

```
optimizer = torch.optim.SGD(net.parameters(), lr=0.01)
```

Now we can train our network. We'll do this for `100` epochs:

```
for epoch in range(100):
    output = net(X)
    loss = loss_fn(output, Y)
    optimizer.zero_grad()
    loss.backward()
    optimizer.step()
    print(f'Epoch {epoch+1}, Loss: {loss.item()}')
```

In each epoch, we perform a forward pass, compute the loss, perform a backward pass to calculate gradients, and then update our weights.

You have now trained a simple feedforward neural network using `PyTorch`. In the upcoming sections, we will dive deeper into more complex network architectures and their applications in time series analysis.

Training a recurrent neural network

Recurrent Neural Networks (**RNNs**) are a class of neural networks that are especially effective for tasks involving sequential data, such as time series forecasting and natural language processing.

Getting ready

RNNs use sequential information by having hidden layers capable of passing information from one step in the sequence to the next.

How to do it...

Similar to the feedforward network, we begin by defining our RNN class. For simplicity, let's define a single-layer RNN:

```
class RNN(nn.Module):
    def __init__(self, input_size, hidden_size, output_size):
        super(RNN, self).__init__()
        self.hidden_size = hidden_size
        self.rnn = nn.RNN(input_size, hidden_size, batch_first=True)
        self.fc = nn.Linear(hidden_size, output_size)

    def forward(self, x):
        h0 = torch.zeros(1, x.size(0), self.hidden_size).to(x.device)
        out, _ = self.rnn(x, h0)   # get RNN output
        out = self.fc(out[:, -1, :])
        return out
```

```
rnn = RNN(10, 20, 1)
print(rnn)
```

Here, `input_size` is the number of input features per time step, `hidden_size` is the number of neurons in the hidden layer, and `output_size` is the number of output features. In the `forward()` method, we pass the input `x` and the initial hidden state `h0` to the recurrent layer. The RNN returns the output and the final hidden state, which we ignore for now. We then take the last output of the sequence (`out[:, -1, :]`) and pass it through a fully connected layer to get our final output. The hidden states act as the memory of the network, encoding the temporal context of the inputs up to the current time step, which is why this type of neural network is useful for sequential data.

Let's note some details we used in our code in this example:

- `x.device`: This refers to the device where the `x` tensor is located. In PyTorch, tensors can be on the CPU or a GPU, and `.device` is a property that tells you where the tensor currently resides. This is particularly important when you are running computations on a GPU, as all inputs to a computation must be on the same device. In the line of code `h0 = torch.zeros(1, x.size(0), self.hidden_size).to(x.device)`, we're ensuring that the initial hidden state tensor `h0` is on the same device as the `x` input tensor.

- `x.size(0)`: This refers to the size of the `0th` dimension of the tensor `x`. In PyTorch, `size()` returns the shape of the tensor, and `size(0)` gives the size of the first dimension. In the context of this RNN, `x` is expected to be a 3D tensor with shape (`batch_size`, `sequence_length`, `num_features`), so `x.size(0)` would return the batch size.

How it works...

The training process for RNNs is similar to that of feedforward networks. We'll use the same synthetic dataset, loss function (MSE), and optimizer (SGD) from the previous example. However, let's modify the input data to be 3D, as required by the RNN (`batch_size`, `sequence_length`, `num_features`). The three dimensions of the input tensor to an RNN represent the following aspects:

- `batch_size`: This represents the number of sequences in one batch of data. In time series terms, you can think of one sample as one sub-sequence (for example, the sales of the past five days). So, a batch contains multiple such samples or sub-sequences, allowing the model to process and learn from multiple sequences simultaneously.

- `sequence_length`: This is essentially the size of the window you use to look at your data. It specifies the number of time steps included in each input sub-sequence. For instance, if you're predicting today's temperature based on past data, `sequence_length` determines how many days back in the past your model looks at each step.

- `num_features`: This dimension indicates the number of features (variables) in each time step of the data sequence. In the context of time series, a univariate series (such as daily temperature at a single location) has one feature per time step. In contrast, a multivariate series (such as daily temperature, humidity, and wind speed at the same location) has multiple features per time step.

Let's create a synthetic dataset as an example:

```
X = torch.randn(100, 5, 10)
Y = torch.randn(100, 1)
```

Now, we can train our network. We'll do this for 100 epochs:

```
loss_fn = nn.MSELoss()
optimizer = torch.optim.SGD(rnn.parameters(), lr=0.01)
for epoch in range(100):
    output = rnn(X)
    loss = loss_fn(output, Y)
    optimizer.zero_grad()
    loss.backward()
    optimizer.step()
    print(f"Epoch {epoch+1}, Loss: {loss.item()}")
```

Now, we have trained an RNN. This is a big step towards applying these models to real-world time series data, which we will discuss in the next chapter.

Training an LSTM neural network

RNNs suffer from a fundamental problem of "vanishing gradients" where, due to the nature of backpropagation in neural networks, the influence of earlier inputs on the overall error diminishes drastically as the sequence gets longer. This is especially problematic in sequence processing tasks where long-term dependencies exist (i.e., future outputs depend on much earlier inputs).

Getting ready

LSTM networks were introduced to overcome this problem. They use a more complex internal structure for each of their cells compared to RNNs. Specifically, an LSTM has the ability to decide which information to discard or to store based on an internal structure called a cell. This cell uses gates (input, forget, and output gates) to control the flow of information into and out of the cell. This helps maintain and manipulate the "long-term" information, thereby mitigating the vanishing gradient problem.

How to do it...

We begin by defining our LSTM class. For simplicity, we'll define a single-layer LSTM network. Note that PyTorch's LSTM expects inputs to be 3D in the format batch_size, seq_length, and num_features:

```
class LSTM(nn.Module):
    def __init__(self, input_size, hidden_size, output_size):
        super(LSTM, self).__init__()
        self.hidden_size = hidden_size
        self.lstm = nn.LSTM(input_size, hidden_size, batch_first=True)
        self.fc = nn.Linear(hidden_size, output_size)

    def forward(self, x):
        h0 = torch.zeros(1, x.size(0), self.hidden_size).to(x.device)
        c0 = torch.zeros(1, x.size(0), self.hidden_size).to(x.device)

        out, _ = self.lstm(x, (h0, c0))  # get LSTM output
        out = self.fc(out[:, -1, :])

        return out


lstm = LSTM(10, 20, 1) # 10 features, 20 hidden units, 1 output
print(lstm)
```

The forward() method is very similar to the one that we introduced earlier for RNNs. The main difference resides in the fact that in the RNNs' case, we initialized a single hidden state h0, and passed it to the RNN layer along with the input x. In the LSTM, however, you need to initialize both a hidden state h0 and a cell state c0 because of the internal structure of LSTM cells. These states are then passed as a tuple to the LSTM layer along with the input x.

How it works...

The training process for LSTM networks is similar to that of feedforward networks and RNNs. We'll use the same synthetic dataset, loss function (MSE), and optimizer (SGD) from the previous examples:

```
X = torch.randn(100, 5, 10)
Y = torch.randn(100, 1)

loss_fn = nn.MSELoss()
optimizer = torch.optim.SGD(lstm.parameters(), lr=0.01)
```

```
for epoch in range(100):
    output = lstm(X)
    loss = loss_fn(output, Y)

    optimizer.zero_grad()
    loss.backward()
    optimizer.step()

    print(f'Epoch {epoch+1}, Loss: {loss.item()}')
```

Training a convolutional neural network

Convolutional neural networks (**CNNs**) are a class of neural networks particularly effective for tasks involving grid-like input data such as images, audio spectrograms, and even certain types of time series data.

Getting ready

The central idea of CNNs is to apply a convolution operation on the input data with convolutional filters (also known as kernels), which slide over the input data to produce output feature maps.

How to do it...

For simplicity, let's define a single-layer 1D convolutional neural network, which is particularly suited for time series and sequence data. In PyTorch, we can use the nn.Conv1d layer for this:

```
class ConvNet(nn.Module):
    def __init__(self,
        input_size,
        hidden_size,
        output_size,
        kernel_size,
        seq_length):
        super(ConvNet, self).__init__()
        self.conv1 = nn.Conv1d(input_size, hidden_size, kernel_size)

        self.fc = nn.Linear(hidden_size*(seq_length-kernel_size+1),
            output_size)

    def forward(self, x):
        x = x.transpose(1, 2)
        out = torch.relu(self.conv1(x))
        out = out.view(out.size(0), -1)  # flatten the tensor
```

```
        out = self.fc(out)
        return out

convnet = ConvNet(5, 20, 1, 3, 10)
print(convnet)
```

In the `forward` method, we pass the input through a convolutional layer followed by a `ReLU()` activation function and finally pass it through a fully connected layer. The `Conv1d` layer expects an input of shape (`batch_size`, `num_channels`, and `sequence_length`). Here, `num_channels` refers to the number of input channels (equivalent to the number of features in the time series data), and `sequence_length` refers to the number of time steps in each sample.

The `Linear` layer will take the output from the `Conv1d` layer and reduce it to the desired output size. The input to the `Linear` layer is calculated as `hidden_size*(seq_length-kernel_size+1)`, where `hidden_size` is the number of output channels from the `Conv1d` layer, and `seq_length-kernel_size+1` is the output sequence length after the convolution operation.

How it works...

The training process for 1D CNNs is similar to the previous network types. We'll use the same loss function (MSE), and optimizer (SGD), but let's modify the input data to be of size (`batch_size`, `sequence_length`, `num_channels`). Recall that the number of channels is equivalent to the number of features:

```
X = torch.randn(100, 10, 5)
Y = torch.randn(100, 1)
```

Now, we can train our network. We'll do this for 100 epochs:

```
loss_fn = nn.MSELoss()
optimizer = torch.optim.SGD(convnet.parameters(), lr=0.01)
for epoch in range(100):
    output = convnet(X)
    loss = loss_fn(output, Y)
    optimizer.zero_grad()
    loss.backward()
    optimizer.step()
    print(f'Epoch {epoch+1}, Loss: {loss.item()}')
```

In the preceding code, we iterate over each epoch. After each training cycle, we print the error of the model into the console to monitor the training process.

3

Univariate Time Series Forecasting

In this chapter, we'll develop deep learning models to tackle univariate time series forecasting problems. We'll touch on several aspects of time series preprocessing, such as preparing a time series for supervised learning and dealing with conditions such as trend or seasonality.

We'll cover different types of models, including simple baselines such as the naïve or historical mean method. We'll provide a brief background on a popular forecasting technique, **autoregressive integrated moving average (ARIMA)**. Then, we'll explain how to create a forecasting model using different types of deep learning methods. These include feedforward neural networks, **long short-term memory (LSTM)**, **gated recurrent units (GRU)**, Stacked **LSTM**, and **convolutional neural networks (CNNs)**. You will also learn how to deal with common problems that arise in time series modeling; for example, how to deal with trend using first differences, and how to stabilize the variance using a logarithm transformation. By the end of this chapter, you will be able to solve a univariate time series forecasting problem.

This chapter will guide you through the following recipes:

- Building simple forecasting models
- Univariate forecasting with ARIMA
- Preparing a time series for supervised learning
- Univariate forecasting with a feedforward neural network
- Univariate forecasting with an LSTM
- Univariate forecasting with a GRU
- Univariate forecasting with a Stacked LSTM
- Combining an LSTM with multiple fully connected layers
- Univariate forecasting with a CNN

- Handling trend – taking first differences

- Handling seasonality – seasonal dummies and a Fourier series

- Handling seasonality – seasonal differencing

- Handling seasonality – seasonal decomposition

- Handling non-constant variance – log transformation

Technical requirements

Before diving into univariate time series forecasting problems, we need to ensure that we have the appropriate software and libraries installed on our system. Here, we'll go over the main technical requirements for implementing the procedures described in this chapter:

- We will primarily need Python 3.9 or a later version, `pip` or Anaconda, PyTorch, and CUDA (optional). You can check the *Installing PyTorch* recipe from the previous chapter for more information on these.

- NumPy (1.26.3) and pandas (2.1.4): Both these `Python` libraries provide several methods for data manipulation and analysis.

- `statsmodels` (0.14.1): This library implements several statistical methods, including a few useful time series analysis techniques.

- `scikit-learn` (1.4.0): `scikit-learn` is a popular `Python` library for statistical learning. It contains several methods to solve different tasks, such as classification, regression, and clustering.

- `sktime` (0.26.0): A Python library that provides a framework for tackling several problems involving time series.

You can install these libraries using `pip`, Python's package manager. For example, to install `scikit-learn`, you would run the following code:

```
pip install -U scikit-learn
```

The code for this chapter can be found at the following GitHub URL: `https://github.com/PacktPublishing/Deep-Learning-for-Time-Series-Data-Cookbook`.

Building simple forecasting models

Before diving into more complex methods, let's get started with some simple forecasting models: the naive, seasonal naive, and mean models.

Getting ready

In this chapter, we focus on forecasting problems involving univariate time series. Let's start by loading one of the datasets we explored in *Chapter 1*:

```python
import pandas as pd
serie = pd.read_csv(
    "assets/datasets/time_series_solar.csv",
    parse_dates=["Datetime"],
    index_col="Datetime",
)['Incoming Solar']
```

In the preceding code, `series` is a pandas `Series` object that contains the univariate time series.

How to do it...

We can now forecast our time series using the three following methods:

- **Naive**: The simplest forecasting method is the naive approach. This method assumes that the next observation is the same as the last one. In `Python`, it could be implemented as simply as the following:

  ```python
  series.shift(1)
  ```

- **Seasonal naive**: This approach assumes that the future observation will be similar to the one observed in the previous observation from the same season. For example, the forecast for the next summer uses the data from the previous summer. If your season is of length m, in `Python`, this can be done as follows:

  ```python
  m = 12
  series.shift(m)
  ```

- **Mean**: The historical mean model, on the other hand, takes the average of all past observations as the forecast. This can be simply done in `Python` as follows:

  ```python
  series.expanding().mean()
  ```

These three methods are useful baselines to benchmark the performance of other, more complex, forecasting solutions.

How it works...

Each of these simple models makes an assumption about the time series data:

- The naive model assumes that the series is random and that each observation is independent of the previous ones

- The seasonal naive model adds a little complexity by recognizing patterns at fixed intervals or "seasons"

- The mean model assumes that the series oscillates around a constant mean, and future values will regress to this mean

There's more...

While these simple models might seem overly basic, they serve two critical purposes:

- **Baselines**: Simple models such as these are often used as baselines for more sophisticated models. If a complex model cannot outperform these simple methods, it suggests that the complex model might be flawed or that the time series data does not contain predictable patterns.

- **Understanding data**: These models can also help us understand our data. If time series data can be well forecasted by a naive or mean model, it suggests that the data may be random or fluctuate around a constant mean.

Implementing simple forecasting models such as naive, seasonal naive, and historical mean models can be quite straightforward, but it may be beneficial to leverage existing libraries that provide off-the-shelf implementations of these models. These libraries not only simplify the implementation but also often come with additional features such as built-in model validation, optimization, and other utilities.

Here are two examples of libraries that provide these models:

- GluonTS: GluonTS is a `Python` library focused on probabilistic models for time series. Among other models, there is an implementation of the seasonal naive model, which can be found at the following link: `https://ts.gluon.ai/dev/api/gluonts/gluonts.model.seasonal_naive.html`.

- `sktime`: This library provides a framework to develop different types of models with time series data. This includes a `NaiveForecaster()` method, which implements several baselines. You can read more about this method at the following URL: `https://www.sktime.net/en/stable/api_reference/auto_generated/sktime.forecasting.naive.NaiveForecaster.html`.

- PyTorch Forecasting: This library focuses on developing state-of-the-art time series forecasting models with neural networks for both real-world cases and research. PyTorch Forecasting provides a baseline model class, which uses the last known target value as the prediction. This class can be found at the following link: `https://pytorch-forecasting.readthedocs.io/en/stable/api/pytorch_forecasting.models.baseline.Baseline.html`.

The preceding libraries can be a great starting point when you are working on a forecasting task. They not only provide implementations of simple forecasting models but also contain many other sophisticated models and utilities that can help streamline the process of developing and validating time series forecasting models.

In the next recipes, we will see how these assumptions can be relaxed or extended to build more complex models.

Univariate forecasting with ARIMA

ARIMA is a univariate time series forecasting method based on two components: an autoregression part and a moving average part. In autoregression, a **lag** refers to a previous point or points in the time series data that are used to predict future values. For instance, if we're using a lag of one, we'd use the value observed in the previous time step to model a given observation. The moving average part uses past errors to model the future observations of the time series.

Getting ready

To work with the ARIMA model, you'll need to install the `statsmodels` Python package if it's not already installed. You can install it using `pip`:

```
pip install -U statsmodels
```

For this recipe, we'll use the same dataset as in the previous recipe.

How to do it...

In Python, you can use the ARIMA model from the `statsmodels` library. Here's a basic example of how to fit an ARIMA model:

```python
import pandas as pd
from statsmodels.tsa.arima.model import ARIMA

series = pd.read_csv(
    "assets/datasets/time_series_solar.csv",
    parse_dates=["Datetime"],
    index_col="Datetime",
)['Incoming Solar']
```

```
model = ARIMA(series, order=(1, 1, 1), freq='H')
model_fit = model.fit()
forecasts = model_fit.predict(start=0, end=5, typ='levels')
```

How it works...

ARIMA models explain a time series based on its past values. They combine aspects of **autoregressive (AR)** models, **integrated (I)** models, and **moving average (MA)** models:

- The AR part involves a regression where the next value of the time series is modeled based on the previous p lags.

- ARIMA is defined for stationary data, so it may be necessary to preprocess the data before modeling. This is done by the I part, which represents the number of differencing operations (d) required to make the series stationary.

- The MA component is another regression where the next value of the series is modeled based on the past q errors.

The order of these operations is represented as a tuple (p, d, q). The best combination depends on the input data. In this example, we used a (1, 1, 1) order as an example.

A prediction is made for the next six observations into the future using the model_fit.predict() function. The start and end indices for the prediction are set to 0 and 5, respectively. The typ='levels' parameter is used to return the predicted values directly rather than differenced values.

There's more...

Determining the ARIMA model's correct order (p, d, q) can be challenging. This often involves checking the **autocorrelation function (ACF)** and the **partial autocorrelation function (PACF)** plots. As we saw in *Chapter 1*, the ACF measures the correlation of a time series and its lagged version. For example, an ACF of lag 2 measures the correlation between a time series and its values in two time periods in the past. On the other hand, the PACF measures autocorrelation while controlling for previous lags. This means a PACF at lag 2 measures the correlation between a series and its values two time periods ago but with the linear dependence of the one time period lag removed. You can learn more about this at the following URL: https://otexts.com/fpp3/acf.html. By examining the ACF and PACF plots, we can better understand the underlying patterns of a time series and thus make more accurate predictions.

Also, the ARIMA model assumes that the time series is stationary, which might not always be true. Thus, it may be necessary to use transformations such as differencing or the log to make the time series stationary before fitting the ARIMA model.

The **seasonal ARIMA** model is commonly used for non-stationary time series with a seasonal component. This model adds a set of parameters to model the seasonal components of the time series specifically.

Note that there are automated ways to tune the parameters of ARIMA. One popular approach is to use the `pmdarima` library's `auto_arima()` function. Another useful implementation is the one available in the `statsforecast` package. You can check it out at the following URL: `https://nixtlaverse.nixtla.io/statsforecast/index.html`.

Besides ARIMA, you can also explore exponential smoothing methods, which is another popular classical approach to forecasting. The implementation of exponential smoothing approaches is also available in `statsmodels` or `statsforecast`, for example.

Preparing a time series for supervised learning

In this recipe, we turn our attention to machine learning approaches to forecasting. We start by describing the process of transforming a time series from a sequence of values into a format suitable for supervised learning.

Getting ready

Supervised learning involves a dataset with explanatory variables (input) and a target variable (output). A time series comprises a sequence of values with an associated timestamp. Therefore, we need to restructure the time series for supervised learning. A common approach to do this is using a sliding window. Each value of the series is based on the recent past values before it (also called lags).

To prepare for this section, you need to have your time series data available in a `pandas` DataFrame and have the `pandas` and NumPy libraries installed. If not, you can install them using `pip`:

```
pip install -U pandas numpy
```

We also load the univariate time series into the Python session:

```
series = pd.read_csv(
    "assets/datasets/time_series_solar.csv",
    parse_dates=["Datetime"],
    index_col="Datetime",
)['Incoming Solar']
```

How to do it...

The following Python function takes a univariate time series and the window size as input and returns the input (X) and output (y) for a supervised learning problem:

```
import pandas as pd

def series_to_supervised(data, n_in=1, n_out=1, dropnan=True):
    n_vars = 1 if len(data.shape) == 1 else data.shape[1]
```

```
    df = pd.DataFrame(data)
    cols, names = list(), list()

    for i in range(n_in, 0, -1):
        cols.append(df.shift(i))
        names += [('var%d(t-%d)' % (j + 1, i)) for j in range(n_vars)]

     for i in range(0, n_out):
        cols.append(df.shift(-i))
        if i == 0:
            names += [('var%d(t)' % (j + 1)) for j in range(n_vars)]
        else:
            names += [('var%d(t+%d)' % (j + 1, i)) for j in range(n_
vars)]

    agg = pd.concat(cols, axis=1)
    agg.columns = names
    if dropnan:
        agg.dropna(inplace=True)
     return agg

data = series_to_supervised(series, 3)
print(data)
```

The series_to_supervised() function is the heart of this script, which takes in four arguments: the time series data, the number of lag observations (n_in), the number of observations as output (n_out), and whether to drop rows with NaN values (dropnan):

1. The function begins by checking the data type and preparing an empty list for columns (cols) and their names (names). It then creates the input sequence (t-n, ..., t-1) by shifting the DataFrame and appending these columns to cols, and the corresponding column names to names.

2. The function continues to create the forecast sequence t, t+1 ..., t+n similarly, again appending these to cols and names. Then, it aggregates all columns into a new DataFrame (agg), assigns the column names, and optionally drops rows with NaN values.

3. The script then loads a time series dataset about solar radiation (time_series_solar. csv) into a DataFrame (df), extracts the Incoming Solar column into a NumPy array (values), and transforms this array into a supervised learning dataset with three lag observations using the series_to_supervised() function.

4. Finally, it prints the transformed data, which consists of sequences of lagged observations as input and the corresponding future observations as output. This format is ready for any supervised learning algorithm.

How it works...

In supervised learning, the goal is to train a model to learn the relationship between input variables and a target variable. Nevertheless, this type of structure is not immediately available when dealing with time series data. The data is typically a sequence of observations (for example, temperature and stock prices) made over time. Thus, we must transform this time series data into a suitable format for supervised learning. This is what the series_to_supervised() function does.

The transformation process involves creating lagged versions of the original time series data using a sliding window approach. This is done by shifting the time series data by a certain number of steps (denoted by n_in in the code) to create the input features. These lagged observations serve as the explanatory variables (input), with the idea that past values influence future ones in many real-world time series.

The target variable (output) is created by shifting the time series in the opposite direction by a number of steps (forecasting horizon) denoted by n_out. This means that for each input sequence, we have the corresponding future values that the model should predict.

For example, suppose we were to prepare a univariate time series for a simple forecasting task using a sliding window of size 3. In that case, we might transform the series [1, 2, 3, 4, 5, 6] into the following supervised learning dataset:

input (t-3, t-2, t-1)	output (t)
1, 2, 3	4
2, 3, 4	5
3, 4, 5	6

Table 3.1: Example of transforming a time series into a supervised learning dataset

The series_to_supervised() function takes as input a sequence of observations, n_in, which specifies the number of lag observations as input, n_out, which specifies the number of observations as output, and a boolean argument dropnan to remove rows with NaN values. It returns a DataFrame suitable for supervised learning.

The function works by iterating over the input data a specified number of times, each time shifting the data and appending it to a list (cols). The list is then concatenated into a DataFrame and the columns are renamed appropriately. If dropnan=True, any rows with missing values are dropped.

There's more...

The window size, which represents how many past time steps we should use to predict future ones, depends on the specific problem and the nature of the time series. A too-small window might not capture important patterns, while a too-large one might include irrelevant information. Testing different window sizes and comparing model performance is a common way to select an appropriate window size.

Univariate forecasting with a feedforward neural network

This recipe walks you through the process of building a feedforward neural network for forecasting with univariate time series.

Getting ready

Having transformed the time series data into an appropriate format for supervised learning, we are now ready to employ it for training a feedforward neural network. We strategically decided to resample the dataset, transitioning from hourly to daily data. This optimization significantly accelerates our training processes:

```
series = series.resample('D').sum()
```

How to do it...

Here are the steps for building and evaluting a feedforward neural network using PyTorch:

1. We begin by splitting the data into training and testing and normalizing them. It's important to note that the scaler should be fitted on the training set and used to transform both the training and test sets:

    ```
    import pandas as pd
    from sklearn.model_selection import train_test_split
    from sklearn.preprocessing import MinMaxScaler

    scaler = MinMaxScaler(feature_range=(-1, 1))
    train, test = train_test_split(data, test_size=0.2,
        shuffle=False)
    train = scaler.fit_transform(train)
    test = scaler.transform(test)

    X_train, y_train = train[:, :-1], train[:, -1]
    X_test, y_test = test[:, :-1], test[:, -1]
    ```

```
X_train = torch.from_numpy(X_train).type(torch.Tensor)
X_test = torch.from_numpy(X_test).type(torch.Tensor)
y_train = torch.from_numpy(y_train).type(torch.Tensor).view(-1)
y_test = torch.from_numpy(y_test).type(torch.Tensor).view(-1)
```

2. Then, we create a simple feedforward neural network with one hidden layer using PyTorch. input_dim represents the number of lags, which is often referred to as the lookback window. hidden_dim is the number of hidden units in the hidden layer of the neural network. Finally, output_dim is the forecasting horizon, which is set to 1 in the following example. We use a ReLU() activation function, which we described in the *Training a feedforward neural network* recipe from the previous chapter:

```
class FeedForwardNN(nn.Module):
    def __init__(self, input_dim, hidden_dim, output_dim):
        super(FeedForwardNN, self).__init__()
        self.fc1 = nn.Linear(input_dim, hidden_dim)
        self.fc2 = nn.Linear(hidden_dim, output_dim)
        self.activation = nn.ReLU()

    def forward(self, x):
        out = self.activation(self.fc1(x))
        out = self.fc2(out)
        return out

model = FeedForwardNN(input_dim=X_train.shape[1],
                      hidden_dim=32,
                      output_dim=1)
```

3. Next, we define the loss function and the optimizer and train the model:

```
loss_fn = nn.MSELoss()
optimizer = torch.optim.Adam(model.parameters(), lr=0.001)
epochs = 200
for epoch in range(epochs):
    model.train()
    optimizer.zero_grad()
    out = model(X_train).reshape(-1,)
    loss = loss_fn(out, y_train)
    loss.backward()
    optimizer.step()
    if epoch % 10 == 0:
        print(f"Epoch: {epoch}, Loss: {loss.item()}")
```

4.   Finally, we evaluate the model on the test set:

```
model.eval()
y_pred = model(X_test).reshape(-1,)
test_loss = loss_fn(y_pred, y_test)
print(f"Test Loss: {test_loss.item()}")
```

How it works...

This script starts by dividing the data into training and testing sets. `MinMaxScaler` is used to scale the features to between `-1` and `1`. It's important to note that we fit the scaler only on the training set to avoid data leakage.

Next, we define a simple feedforward neural network model with one hidden layer. The `FeedForwardNN` class extends `nn.Module`, which is the base class for all neural network modules in PyTorch. The class constructor defines the layers of the network, and the `forward` method specifies how forward propagation is done.

The model is then trained using the mean squared error loss function and the `Adam` optimizer. The model parameters are updated over multiple epochs.

Finally, the model is evaluated on the testing set, and the loss of this unseen data measures how well the model generalizes beyond the training data.

There's more...

This is a simple example of how a feedforward neural network can be used for time series forecasting. There are several ways you can improve this model:

- You can experiment with different network architectures, for example, by adding more layers or changing the number of neurons in the hidden layer. You can also try different activation functions, optimizers, and learning rates.

- It might be beneficial to use a more sophisticated method for preparing the training and testing sets; for example, using a rolling-window validation strategy.

- Another improvement can be using early stopping to prevent overfitting. We'll learn about this technique in the next chapter.

- Last but not least, advanced models such as **recurrent neural networks** (**RNNs**) and LSTM networks are specifically designed for sequence data and can give better results for time series forecasting.

Univariate forecasting with an LSTM

This recipe walks you through the process of building an LSTM neural network for forecasting with univariate time series.

Getting ready

As we saw in *Chapter 2*, LSTM networks, a variant of RNNs, have gained substantial attention for their performance on time series and sequence data. LSTM networks are particularly suited for this task because they can effectively capture long-term temporal dependencies in the input data due to their inherent memory cells.

This section will extend our univariate time series forecasting to LSTM networks using PyTorch. So, we continue with the objects created in the previous recipe (*Univariate forecasting with a feedforward neural network*).

How to do it...

We will use the same train and test sets from the previous section. For an LSTM, we must reshape the input data to 3D. As we explored in the previous chapter, the three dimensions of the input tensor to LSTMs represent the following aspects:

- **Samples**: One sub-sequence (for example, the past five lags) is one sample. A batch is a set of samples.

- **Time steps**: The window size; how many observations we use from the past at each point.

- **Features**: The number of variables used in the model. Univariate time series always contain a single feature.

The following code transforms the input explanatory variables into a 3D format:

```
X_train = X_train.view([X_train.shape[0], X_train.shape[1], 1])
X_test = X_test.view([X_test.shape[0], X_test.shape[1], 1])
```

In the preceding lines of code, `X_train.shape[0]` and `X_test.shape[0]` represent the number of samples (that is, the number of sequences), and `X_train.shape[1]` and `X_test.shape[1]` represent the number of time steps (the window size). The last dimension in the reshape operation, which is set to 1, represents the number of features. We only have one feature in our univariate time series, so we set it to 1. If we had a multivariate time series, this value would correspond to the number of variables in the data.

The `view()` function in PyTorch is used to reshape a `tensor` object. It's equivalent to the `reshape()` function in NumPy and allows us to restructure our data to match the input shape that our LSTM model requires. Reshaping the data this way ensures that the LSTM model receives the data in the expected format. This is crucial for its ability to model the temporal dependencies in our time series data effectively.

Then, we define the LSTM model:

```
class LSTM(nn.Module):
    def __init__(self, input_dim, hidden_dim, num_layers, output_dim):
        super(LSTM, self).__init__()
        self.hidden_dim = hidden_dim
        self.num_layers = num_layers
        self.lstm = nn.LSTM(input_dim, hidden_dim, num_layers,
            batch_first=True)
        self.fc = nn.Linear(hidden_dim, output_dim)
    def forward(self, x):
        h0 = torch.zeros(self.num_layers, x.size(0),
            self.hidden_dim).requires_grad_()
        c0 = torch.zeros(self.num_layers, x.size(0),
            self.hidden_dim).requires_grad_()
        out, (hn, cn) = self.lstm(x, (h0.detach(), c0.detach()))
        out = self.fc(out[:, -1, :])
        return out


model = LSTM(input_dim=1,
            hidden_dim=32,
            output_dim=1,
            num_layers=1)
```

Note that, for the LSTM, the `input_dim` input dimension is 1, which is the number of variables in the time series. This aspect is different from the `input_dim` argument we passed to the feedforward neural network in the previous recipe. In that case, this parameter was set to 3, which denoted the number of lags or features.

We now proceed to train the model:

```
epochs = 200
for epoch in range(epochs):
    model.train()
    optimizer.zero_grad()
    out = model(X_train).reshape(-1,)
    loss = loss_fn(out, y_train)
    loss.backward()
    optimizer.step()
```

```
    if epoch % 10 == 0:
        print(f"Epoch: {epoch}, Loss: {loss.item()}")
```

Finally, we evaluate the model:

```
model.eval()
y_pred = model(X_test)
test_loss = loss_fn(y_pred, y_test)
print(f"Test Loss: {test_loss.item()}")
```

How it works...

In the first step, we reshape our training and testing sets to match the input shape that LSTM expects, i.e., batch_size, sequence_length, and number_of_features.

The LSTM class inherits from nn.Module, which means it is a custom neural network in PyTorch. The LSTM model has an LSTM layer with a specified number of hidden dimensions and layers, followed by a fully connected (linear) layer that outputs the final prediction.

The forward() function defines the forward pass of the LSTM model. We first initialize the hidden states (h0) and cell states (c0) of LSTM with zeros. Then, we pass the input data and initial states into the LSTM layer, which returns the LSTM outputs and the final hidden and cell states. Note that we only use the final time-step output of the LSTM to pass into the fully connected layer to produce the output.

We then instantiate the model, define the loss() function as the **mean squared error** (MSE), and use the Adam optimizer for training the network.

During training, we first set the model into training mode, reset the gradients, perform the forward pass, calculate the loss, perform back-propagation via loss.backward, and then perform a single optimization step.

Finally, we evaluate the model on the test data and print the test loss. Note that we did not do any hyperparameter tuning, which is a very important step when training neural networks. We'll learn about this process in the next chapter.

There's more...

LSTM models are especially effective for time series forecasting due to their ability to capture long-term dependencies. However, their performance can significantly depend on the choice of hyperparameters. Hence, it may be useful to perform hyperparameter tuning to find the optimal configuration. Some important hyperparameters to consider are the number of hidden dimensions, the number of LSTM layers, and the learning rate.

It's also important to remember that LSTMs, like all deep learning models, may be prone to overfitting if the model complexity is too high. Techniques such as dropout, early stopping, or regularization (L1, L2) can be used to prevent overfitting.

Furthermore, advanced variants of LSTMs such as bidirectional LSTMs, or other types of RNNs such as GRUs can also be used to improve performance possibly.

Lastly, while LSTMs are powerful, they may not always be the best choice due to their computational and memory requirements, especially for very large datasets or complex models. In these cases, simpler models or other types of neural networks may be more suitable.

Univariate forecasting with a GRU

This recipe walks you through the process of building a GRU neural network for forecasting with univariate time series.

Getting ready

Now that we have seen how LSTMs can be used for univariate time series forecasting, let's now shift our attention to another type of RNN architecture known as GRU. GRUs, like LSTMs, are designed to capture long-term dependencies in sequence data effectively but do so with a slightly different and less complex internal structure. This often makes them faster to train.

For this section, we will use the same training and testing sets as in the previous sections. Again, the input data should be reshaped into a 3D tensor with dimensions representing observations, time steps, and features respectively:

```
X_train = X_train.view([X_train.shape[0], X_train.shape[1], 1])
X_test = X_test.view([X_test.shape[0], X_test.shape[1], 1])
```

How to do it...

Let's start constructing a GRU network with the help of the following steps:

1. We start by constructing a GRU network in PyTorch:

    ```
    class GRUNet(nn.Module):
        def init(self, input_dim, hidden_dim, output_dim=1,
            num_layers=2):
            super(GRUNet, self).init()
            self.hidden_dim = hidden_dim
            self.num_layers = num_layers
            self.gru = nn.GRU(input_dim, hidden_dim, num_layers,
                batch_first=True)
            self.fc = nn.Linear(hidden_dim, output_dim)
    ```

```
        def forward(self, x):
        h0 = torch.zeros(self.num_layers, x.size(0),
            self.hidden_dim).to(x.device)
        out, _ = self.gru(x, h0)
        out = self.fc(out[:, -1, :])
        return out

model = GRUNet(input_dim=1,
            hidden_dim=32,
            output_dim=1,
            num_layers=1)
```

2.   Like before, we define our `loss` function and `optimizer`:

```
loss_fn = nn.MSELoss()
optimizer = torch.optim.Adam(model.parameters(), lr=0.01)
```

3.   We train our model:

```
epochs = 200
for epoch in range(epochs):
    model.train()
    optimizer.zero_grad()
    out = model(X_train).reshape(-1,)
    loss = loss_fn(out, y_train)
    loss.backward()
    optimizer.step()
    if epoch % 10 == 0:
        print(f"Epoch: {epoch}, Loss: {loss.item()}")
```

4.   Finally, we evaluate our model:

```
model.eval()
y_pred = model(X_test).reshape(-1,)
test_loss = loss_fn(y_pred, y_test)
print(f"Test Loss: {test_loss.item()}")
```

How it works...

Similar to the LSTM, the GRU also requires 3D input data. We begin by reshaping our input data accordingly. Next, we define our GRU model. This model contains a GRU layer and a linear layer. The initial hidden state for the GRU is defined and initialized with zeros.

We then define our `loss()` function and optimizer and train our model. The model's output from the last time step is used for predictions. Finally, we evaluate our model on the test set and print the test loss.

There's more...

There are many ways to improve this model:

- Experimenting with different GRU architectures or varying the number of GRU layers may yield better results

- Using a different loss function or optimizer could also potentially improve model performance

- Implementing early stopping or other regularization techniques can help prevent overfitting

- Applying more sophisticated data preparation techniques, such as sequence padding or truncation, can better equip the model to handle sequences of varying lengths

- More advanced models, such as the sequence-to-sequence model or the transformer, may provide better results for more complex time series forecasting tasks

Univariate forecasting with a Stacked LSTM

This recipe walks you through the process of building an LSTM neural network with multiple layers for forecasting with univariate time series.

Getting ready

For complex time series prediction problems, one LSTM layer may not be sufficient. In this case, we can use a stacked LSTM, which is essentially multiple layers of LSTM stacked one on top of the other. This can provide a higher level of input abstraction and may lead to improved prediction performance.

We will continue to use the same reshaped train and test sets from the previous recipe:

```
X_train = X_train.view([X_train.shape[0], X_train.shape[1], 1])
X_test = X_test.view([X_test.shape[0], X_test.shape[1], 1])
```

We also use the LSTM neural network defined in the *Univariate forecasting with an LSTM* recipe:

```
class LSTM(nn.Module):
    def __init__(self, input_dim, hidden_dim, num_layers, output_dim):
        super(LSTM, self).__init__()
        self.hidden_dim = hidden_dim
        self.num_layers = num_layers
        self.lstm = nn.LSTM(input_dim, hidden_dim, num_layers,
            batch_first=True)
        self.fc = nn.Linear(hidden_dim, output_dim)

    def forward(self, x):
        h0 = torch.zeros(self.num_layers, x.size(0),
            self.hidden_dim).requires_grad_()
```

```
        c0 = torch.zeros(self.num_layers, x.size(0),
            self.hidden_dim).requires_grad_()
        out, (hn, cn) = self.lstm(x, (h0.detach(), c0.detach()))
        out = self.fc(out[:, -1, :])
        return out
```

We'll use these elements to train a stacked LSTM model.

How to do it...

To construct a stacked LSTM in PyTorch, we need to call the LSTM class with the input num_layers=2, like so:

```
model = LSTM(input_dim=1, hidden_dim=32, output_dim=1, num_layers=2)
```

The rest of the training process is quite similar to what we did in the preceding recipes. We define our loss function and optimizer:

```
loss_fn = nn.MSELoss()
optimizer = torch.optim.Adam(model.parameters(), lr=0.001)
```

We train the model:

```
epochs = 200
for epoch in range(epochs):
    model.train()
    optimizer.zero_grad()
    out = model(X_train).reshape(-1,)
    loss = loss_fn(out, y_train)
    loss.backward()
    optimizer.step()
    if epoch % 10 == 0:
        print(f"Epoch: {epoch}, Loss: {loss.item()}")
```

Finally, we evaluate our model:

```
model.eval()
y_pred = model(X_test).reshape(-1,)
test_loss = loss_fn(y_pred, y_test)
print(f"Test Loss: {test_loss.item()}")
```

How it works...

The setup for the stacked LSTM model is similar to the single-layer LSTM model. The major difference lies in the LSTM layer, where we specify that we want more than one LSTM layer. This is accomplished by setting num_layers to 2 or more.

The forward pass for the stacked LSTM is identical to that of the single-layer LSTM. We initialize the hidden state h0 and cell state c0 with zeros, pass the input and the initial states into the LSTM layers, and then use the output from the final time step for our predictions.

The test set loss is again closely aligned with previous results. Several factors could contribute to this observation. It could be a result of limited data or the fact that the expressiveness of the data may not benefit from the complexity of our model. Additionally, we have not conducted any hyperparameter optimization, which could potentially enhance the model's performance. In subsequent sections, we will delve deeper into these aspects, exploring potential solutions and strategies for further improvement.

Combining an LSTM with multiple fully connected layers

Sometimes, it may be valuable to combine different types of neural networks in a single model. In this recipe, you'll learn how to combine an LSTM module with a fully connected layer that is the basis of feedforward neural networks.

Getting ready

In this section, we'll use a hybrid model that combines an LSTM layer with multiple fully connected (also known as dense) layers. This allows us to further abstract features from the sequence, and then learn complex mappings to the output space.

We continue using the reshaped train and test sets from the previous sections.

How to do it...

To construct this hybrid model in PyTorch, we add two fully connected layers after the LSTM layer:

```
class HybridLSTM(nn.Module):
    def __init__(self, input_dim, hidden_dim,
        output_dim=1, num_layers=1):
        super(HybridLSTM, self).__init__()
        self.hidden_dim = hidden_dim
        self.num_layers = num_layers
        self.lstm = nn.LSTM(input_dim, hidden_dim,
            num_layers, batch_first=True)
        self.fc1 = nn.Linear(hidden_dim, 50)
        self.fc2 = nn.Linear(50, output_dim)

    def forward(self, x):
        h0 = torch.zeros(self.num_layers, x.size(0),
            self.hidden_dim).to(x.device)
        c0 = torch.zeros(self.num_layers, x.size(0),
```

```
        self.hidden_dim).to(x.device)
    out, _ = self.lstm(x, (h0, c0))
    out = F.relu(self.fc1(out[:, -1, :]))
    out = self.fc2(out)
    return out

model = HybridLSTM(input_dim=1, hidden_dim=32, output_dim=1,
    num_layers=1)
```

We define our loss function and `optimizer`:

```
loss_fn = nn.MSELoss()
optimizer = torch.optim.Adam(model.parameters(), lr=0.01)
```

We train and evaluate our model similarly to the previous recipes.

How it works...

The setup for the hybrid LSTM model involves an LSTM layer followed by two fully connected layers. After passing through the LSTM layer, the output of the final time step is processed by the fully connected layers. Using the ReLU() activation function between these layers introduces non-linearities, allowing our model to capture more complex relationships in the data.

Note that the output from an LSTM layer is a tensor of shape (batch_size, seq_length, hidden_dim). This is because LSTM, by default, outputs the hidden states for each time step in the sequence for each item in the batch.

In this specific model, we're interested only in the last time step's hidden state to feed into the fully connected layers. We achieve this with out[:, -1, :], effectively selecting the last time step's hidden state for each sequence in the batch. The result is a tensor of shape (batch_size, hidden_dim).

The reshaped output is then passed through the first fully connected (linear) layer with the self.fc1(out[:, -1, :]) function call. This layer has 50 neurons, so the output shape changes to (batch_size, 50).

After applying the ReLU() activation function, this output is then passed to the second fully connected layer self.fc2(out), which has a size equal to output_dim, reducing the tensor to the shape (batch_size, output_dim). This is the final output of the model.

Remember that the hidden dimension (hidden_dim) is a hyperparameter of the LSTM and can be chosen freely. The number of neurons in the first fully connected layer (50, in this case) is also a hyperparameter and can be modified to suit the specific task better.

There's more...

When working with hybrid models, consider the following tips:

- Vary the number of fully connected layers and their sizes to explore different model complexities.
- Different activation functions in the fully connected layers may lead to varied performance.
- As the complexity of the model increases, so does the computational cost. Be sure to balance complexity and computational efficiency.

Univariate forecasting with a CNN

Now, we turn our attention to convolutional neural networks that have also shown promising results with time series data. Let's learn how these methods can be used for univariate time series forecasting.

Getting ready

CNNs are commonly used in problems involving images, but they can also be applied to time series forecasting tasks. By treating time series data as a "sequence image," CNNs can extract local features and dependencies from the data. To implement this, we'll need to prepare our time series data similarly to how we did for LSTM models.

How to do it...

Let's define a simple CNN model in PyTorch. For this example, we will use a single convolutional layer followed by a fully connected layer:

```python
class CNNTimeseries(nn.Module):
    def __init__(self, input_dim, output_dim=1):
        super(CNNTimeseries, self).__init__()
        self.conv1 = nn.Conv1d(in_channels=input_dim,
                               out_channels=64,
                               kernel_size=3,
                               stride=1,
                               padding=1)
        self.fc = nn.Linear(in_features=64,
                            out_features=output_dim)
    def forward(self, x):
        x = F.relu(self.conv1(x))
        x = x.view(x.size(0), -1)
        x = self.fc(x)
        return x

model = CNNTimeseries(input_dim=3, output_dim=1)
```

We train and evaluate our model similarly to the previous sections.

How it works...

The CNN model is based on convolutional layers. These are designed to extract local features directly from the input data. These features are then passed to one or more fully connected layers that model the future values of the time series. The training stage of this type of neural network is similar to others, such as the LSTM.

Let's go through our neural network architecture. It has the following features:

- An input layer, which accepts time series data of shape (`batch_size, sequence_length, number_of_features`). For univariate time series forecasting, `number_of_features` is 1.

- A convolutional layer with 64 filters and a kernel size of 3, defined in PyTorch as `self.conv1 = nn.Conv1d(in_channels=1, out_channels=64, kernel_size=3)`.

- A fully connected (or linear) layer that maps the output of the convolutional layer to our prediction

Let's see how these layers transform the data:

- **Input layer**: The initial shape of our input data would be (`batch_size, sequence_length, 1`).

- `Conv1d`: A 1D convolution is performed over the time series data. The kernel slides over the sequence, computing the dot product of the weights and the input. After this convolution operation, the shape of our data is (`batch_size, out_channels, sequence_length-kernel_size+1`), or in this case, (`batch_size, 64, sequence_length-3+1`).

- **Fully connected layer**: To pass our data into the fully connected layer, we need to flatten our data into two dimensions: (`batch_size, remaining_dims`). `remaining_dims` is calculated by multiplying the remaining dimensions of the tensor (64 and `sequence_length-2` in our case). The resulting shape would be (`batch_size, 64 * (sequence_length-2)`). We can achieve this by using the `view()` function in PyTorch as follows: `x = x.view(x.size(0), -1)`.

Now, `x` is ready to be fed into the fully connected layer, `self.fc = nn.Linear(64 * (sequence_length-2), output_dim)`, where `output_dim` is the dimensionality of the output space, 1 for univariate time series prediction. The output of this layer is of shape (`batch_size, output_dim`), or (`batch_size, 1`), and these are our final predictions.

This way, we can see how the tensor shapes are handled and transformed as they pass through each network layer. Understanding this process is crucial for troubleshooting and designing your own architectures.

There's more...

CNNs can be extended in several ways:

- Multiple convolutional layers can be stacked to form a deeper network
- Pooling layers can be added after convolutional layers to reduce dimensionality and computational cost
- Dropout or other regularization techniques can be applied to prevent overfitting
- The model could be extended to a ConvLSTM, which combines the strengths of CNNs and LSTMs for handling spatial and temporal dependencies

Handling trend – taking first differences

In *Chapter 1*, we learned about different time series patterns such as trend or seasonality. This recipe describes the process of dealing with trend in time series before training a deep neural network.

Getting ready

As we learned in *Chapter 1*, trend is the long-term change in the time series. When the average value of the time series changes, this means that the data is not stationary. Non-stationary time series are more difficult to model, so it's important to transform the data into a stationary series.

Trend is usually removed from the time series by taking the first differences until the data becomes stationary.

First, let's start by splitting the time series into training and testing sets:

```
from sklearn.model_selection import train_test_split

train, test = train_test_split(series, test_size=0.2, shuffle=False)
```

We leave the last 20% of observations for testing.

How to do it...

There are two ways we can compute the difference between consecutive observations using pandas:

1. Let's begin with the standard approach using the diff() method:

    ```
    train.diff(periods=1)
    test.diff(periods=1)
    ```

The `periods` argument details the number of steps used to compute the differences. In this case, `periods=1` means that we compute the difference between consecutive observations, also known as first differences. As an example, setting the number of periods to 7 would compute the difference between each observation and the observation captured 7 time steps before it. In the case of a daily time series, this can be an effective way of removing seasonality. But more on that later.

Another way to difference a time series is using the `shift()` method:

```
train_shifted = train.shift(periods=1)
train_diff = train - train_shifted
test_shifted = test.shift(periods=1)
test_diff = test - test_shifted
```

2. We created a second time series that is shifted by the desired number of periods (in this case, 1). Then, we subtract this series from the original one to get a differenced series.

Differencing stabilizes the level of the series. Still, we can normalize the data into a common value range:

```
scaler = MinMaxScaler(feature_range=(-1, 1))
train_diffnorm = scaler.fit_transform(
    train_diff.values.reshape(-1, 1))
test_diffnorm = scaler.transform(test_diff.values.reshape(-1,1))
```

3. Finally, we transform the time series for supervised learning using the `series_to_supervised()` function as in the previous recipes:

```
train_df = series_to_supervised(train_diffnorm, n_in=3).values
test_df = series_to_supervised(test_diffnorm, n_in=3).values
```

4. The model training phase will remain the same as in the previous recipes:

```
X_train, y_train = train_df[:, :-1], train_df[:, -1]
X_test, y_test = test_df[:, :-1], test_df[:, -1]
X_train = torch.from_numpy(X_train).type(torch.Tensor)
X_test = torch.from_numpy(X_test).type(torch.Tensor)
y_train = torch.from_numpy(y_train).type(torch.Tensor).view(-1)
y_test = torch.from_numpy(y_test).type(torch.Tensor).view(-1)
X_train = X_train.view([X_train.shape[0], X_train.shape[1], 1])
X_test = X_test.view([X_test.shape[0], X_test.shape[1], 1])

model = LSTM(input_dim=1, hidden_dim=32, output_dim=1,
    num_layers=2)
loss_fn = nn.MSELoss()
optimizer = torch.optim.Adam(model.parameters(), lr=0.001)
epochs = 200
```

```
for epoch in range(epochs):
    model.train()
    optimizer.zero_grad()
    out = model(X_train).reshape(-1, )
    loss = loss_fn(out, y_train)
    loss.backward()
    optimizer.step()
    if epoch % 10 == 0:
        print(f"Epoch: {epoch}, Loss: {loss.item()}")
```

5. But our job is not done yet. The preceding neural network is trained on differenced data. So, the predictions are also differenced:

```
model.eval()
y_pred = model(X_test).reshape(-1, )
```

6. We next need to revert the data transformation processes to get the forecasts in the time series' original scale

7. First, we denormalize the time series:

```
y_pred_np = y_pred.detach().numpy().reshape(-1, 1)
y_diff = scaler.inverse_transform(y_pred_np).flatten()
```

8. Then, we revert the differencing operation by adding back the shifted time series:

```
y_orig_scale = y_diff + test_shifted.values[4:]
```

In the preceding code, we skip the first three values as they were used during the transformation process by the `series_to_supervised()` function.

How it works...

Differencing works by stabilizing the level of the time series, thus making it stationary. Instead of modeling the actual values of the series, the neural network models the series of changes; how the time series changes from one time step to another. The raw forecasts that come out of the neural network represent the predicted changes. We need to revert the differencing process to get the forecasts at their original scale.

There's more...

You can also deal with trend by including the time information in the input data. An explanatory variable that denotes the step at which each observation is collected. For example, the first observation has a value of 1, and the second one has a value of 2. This approach is effective if the trend is deterministic and we do not expect it to change. Differencing provides a more general way of dealing with trends.

Handling seasonality – seasonal dummies and Fourier series

In this recipe, we'll describe how to deal with seasonality in time series using seasonal dummy variables and a Fourier series.

Getting ready

Seasonality represents repeatable patterns that recur over a given period, such as every year. Seasonality is an important piece of time series, and it is important to capture it. The consensus in the literature is that neural networks cannot capture seasonal effects optimally. The best way to model seasonality is by feature engineering or data transformation. One way to handle seasonality is to add extra information that captures the periodicity of patterns. This can be done with seasonal dummies or a Fourier series.

We start by preparing the data using the `series_to_supervised()` function:

```
train, test = train_test_split(series, test_size=0.2, shuffle=False)
scaler = MinMaxScaler(feature_range=(-1, 1))
train_norm = scaler.fit_transform(
    train.values.reshape(-1, 1)).flatten()

train_norm = pd.Series(train_norm, index=train.index)
test_norm = scaler.transform(test.values.reshape(-1, 1)).flatten()
test_norm = pd.Series(test_norm, index=test.index)
train_df = series_to_supervised(train_norm, 3)
test_df = series_to_supervised(test_norm, 3)
```

In this recipe, we'll skip the trend removal part for simplicity and focus on modeling seasonality. So, the `train_df` and `test_df` objects contain the lagged values of the training and testing sets.

How to do it...

Both seasonal dummy variables and a Fourier series can be added to the input data as additional explanatory variables. Let's start by exploring seasonal dummies.

Seasonal dummies

Seasonal dummies are binary variables that describe the period of each observation. For example, whether a given value is collected on a Monday.

To build seasonal dummies, we first get the period information of each point. This can be done with the `DateTimeFeatures` class from `sktime` as follows:

```
from sktime.transformations.series.date import DateTimeFeatures

date_features = DateTimeFeatures(ts_freq='D',
    keep_original_columns=False, feature_scope='efficient')
train_dates = date_features.fit_transform(train_df.iloc[:, -1])
```

The main argument for `DateTimeFeatures` is `ts_freq`, which we set to D. This means that we're telling this method that our data is in a daily granularity. Then, we use the training set to fit a `DateTimeFeatures` object by passing it the observations of the first lags of this data (`train_df.iloc[:, -1]`). This results in a `pandas` DataFrame that contains the information detailed in the following table:

Datetime	year	quarter_of_year	month_of_year	week_of_year	day_of_year	day_of_month	day_of_week
2007-10-04	2007	4	10	40	277	4	3
2007-10-05	2007	4	10	40	278	5	4
2007-10-06	2007	4	10	40	279	6	5
2007-10-07	2007	4	10	40	280	7	6
2007-10-08	2007	4	10	41	281	8	0

Table 3.2: Information about the period of each observation

For simplicity, we'll continue this recipe by using the information about the day of the week and month of the year. We get these columns with the following code:

```
train_dates = train_dates[['month_of_year', 'day_of_week']]
```

Then, we convert this data into binary variables using a one-hot encoding approach from `sklearn` (`OneHotEncoder`):

```
from sklearn.preprocessing import OneHotEncoder

encoder = OneHotEncoder(drop='first', sparse=False)
encoded_train = encoder.fit_transform(train_dates)
train_dummies = pd.DataFrame(encoded_train,
    columns=encoder.get_feature_names_out(),dtype=int)
```

This leads to a set of seasonal dummy variables that are shown in the following table:

Datetime	2007-10-04	2007-10-05	2007-10-06	2007-10-07	2007-10-08
month_of_year_2	0	0	0	0	0
month_of_year_3	0	0	0	0	0
month_of_year_4	0	0	0	0	0
month_of_year_5	0	0	0	0	0
month_of_year_6	0	0	0	0	0
month_of_year_7	0	0	0	0	0
month_of_year_8	0	0	0	0	0
month_of_year_9	0	0	0	0	0
month_of_year_10	1	1	1	1	1
month_of_year_11	0	0	0	0	0
month_of_year_12	0	0	0	0	0
day_of_week_1	0	0	0	0	0
day_of_week_2	0	0	0	0	0
day_of_week_3	1	0	0	0	0
day_of_week_4	0	1	0	0	0
day_of_week_5	0	0	1	0	0
day_of_week_6	0	0	0	1	0

Table 3.3: Information about the period of each observation as binary variables

We repeat this process using the test set:

```
test_dates = date_features.transform(test_df.iloc[:, -1])
test_dates = test_dates[['month_of_year', 'day_of_week']]
test_encoded_feats = encoder.transform(test_dates)
test_dummies = pd.DataFrame(test_encoded_feats,
                    columns=encoder.get_feature_names_out(),
                    dtype=int)
```

Note that we fit `DateTimeFeatures` and `OneHotEncoder` on the training data (using the `fit_transform()` method). With the test set, we can use the `transform()` method from the respective object.

A Fourier series

A Fourier series is made up of deterministic sine and cosine waves. The oscillations of these waves enable seasonality to be modeled as a repeating pattern.

We can compute Fourier-based features using sktime as follows:

```
from sktime.transformations.series.fourier import FourierFeatures
fourier = FourierFeatures(sp_list=[365.25],
                          fourier_terms_list=[2],
                          keep_original_columns=False)
train_fourier = fourier.fit_transform(train_df.iloc[:, -1])
test_fourier = fourier.transform(test_df.iloc[:, -1])
```

We use the FourierFeatures transformer to extract Fourier features. There are two main parameters to this operator:

- sp_list: The periodicity of the data. In this example, we set this parameter to 365.25, which captures yearly variations.

- fourier_terms_list: The number of Fourier waves for each sine and cosine function. We set this parameter to 2, which means we compute 2 sine series plus 2 cosine series.

Modeling

After extracting seasonal dummies and the Fourier series, we add the extra variables to the datasets:

```
X_train = np.hstack([X_train, train_dummies, train_fourier])
X_test = np.hstack([X_test, test_dummies, test_fourier])
```

The np.hstack() function is used to merge multiple arrays horizontally (column-wise). In this case, we merge the seasonal dummies and the Fourier series with the lagged features computed using the series_to_supervised() function.

Finally, we feed this data to a neural network as we did in previous recipes:

```
X_train = torch.from_numpy(X_train).type(torch.Tensor)
X_test = torch.from_numpy(X_test).type(torch.Tensor)
y_train = torch.from_numpy(y_train).type(torch.Tensor).view(-1)
y_test = torch.from_numpy(y_test).type(torch.Tensor).view(-1)
X_train = X_train.view([X_train.shape[0], X_train.shape[1], 1])
X_test = X_test.view([X_test.shape[0], X_test.shape[1], 1])

model = LSTM(input_dim=1, hidden_dim=32, output_dim=1, num_layers=2)
loss_fn = nn.MSELoss()
optimizer = torch.optim.Adam(model.parameters(), lr=0.001)
epochs = 200
```

```
for epoch in range(epochs):
    model.train()
    optimizer.zero_grad()
    out = model(X_train).reshape(-1, )
    loss = loss_fn(out, y_train)
    loss.backward()
    optimizer.step()
    if epoch % 10 == 0:
        print(f"Epoch: {epoch}, Loss: {loss.item()}")

model.eval()
y_pred = model(X_test).reshape(-1, )
test_loss = loss_fn(y_pred, y_test)
y_pred_np = y_pred.detach().numpy().reshape(-1, 1)
y_pred_orig = scaler.inverse_transform(y_pred_np).flatten()
```

When utilizing seasonal dummies or a Fourier series, there is no need to perform any additional transformations after the inference step. In the previous code, we reversed the normalization process to obtain the forecasts in their original scale.

How it works...

Seasonal dummies and the Fourier series are variables that capture the recurrence of seasonal patterns. These work as explanatory variables that are added to the input data. The cyclical nature of the Fourier series is shown in the following figure:

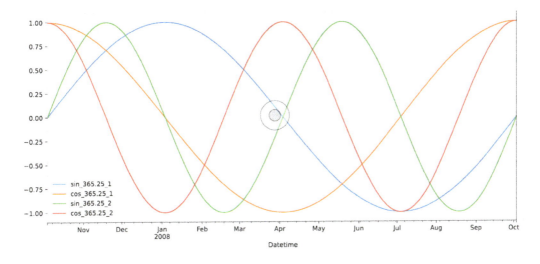

Figure 3.1: Fourier deterministic series that capture seasonality

Note that this process is independent of the neural network used for training. In this recipe, we resorted to a TCN but we could have picked any learning algorithm for multiple regression.

There's more...

An alternative to the Fourier series or seasonal dummies is repeating basis functions. Instead of using trigonometric series, seasonality is modeled using radial basis functions. These are implemented in the `sklego` Python package. You can check out the documentation at the following link: `https://scikit-lego.netlify.app/api/preprocessing.html#sklego.preprocessing.RepeatingBasisFunction`.

Sometimes, a time series can exhibit seasonality at multiple periods. For example, the example daily time series can show repeating patterns not only every month but also every year. In this recipe, we computed seasonal dummies that provide information about different periods, namely the month and day of the week. But you can also do this with a Fourier series by passing multiple periods. Here's how you could capture weekly and yearly seasonality with a Fourier series:

```
fourier = FourierFeatures(sp_list=[7, 365.25],
                          fourier_terms_list=[2, 2],
                          keep_original_columns=False)
```

The preceding code would compute `four` Fourier series for each period (`two` sine and `two` cosine waves for each).

Another important recurrent phenomenon in time series is holidays, some of which move year after year (for example, Easter). A common way to model these events is by using binary dummy variables.

Handling seasonality – seasonal differencing

In this recipe, we show how differencing can be used to model seasonal patterns in time series.

Getting ready

We've learned to use first differences to remove the trend from time series. Differencing can also work for seasonality. But, instead of taking the difference between consecutive observations, for each point, you subtract the value of the previous observation from the same season. For example, suppose you're modeling monthly data. You perform seasonal differencing by subtracting the value of February of the previous year from the value of February of the current year.

The process is similar to what we did with first differences to remove the trend. Let's start by loading the data:

```
time_series = df["Incoming Solar"]
train, test = train_test_split(time_series, test_size=0.2,
shuffle=False)
```

In this recipe, we'll use seasonal differencing to remove yearly seasonality.

How to do it...

We resort to the `shift()` method to apply the differencing operation:

```
periods = 365
train_shifted = train.shift(periods=periods)
train_diff = train - train_shifted
test_shifted = test.shift(periods=periods)
test_diff = test - test_shifted
scaler = MinMaxScaler(feature_range=(-1, 1))
train_diffnorm = scaler.fit_transform(train_diff.values.reshape(-1,1))
test_diffnorm = scaler.transform(test_diff.values.reshape(-1, 1))
train_df = series_to_supervised(train_diffnorm, 3).values
test_df = series_to_supervised(test_diffnorm, 3).values
```

After differencing the series, we transformed it for supervised learning using `series_to_supervised`. Then, we can train a neural network with the differenced data:

```
X_train, y_train = train_df[:, :-1], train_df[:, -1]
X_test, y_test = test_df[:, :-1], test_df[:, -1]
X_train = torch.from_numpy(X_train).type(torch.Tensor)
X_test = torch.from_numpy(X_test).type(torch.Tensor)
y_train = torch.from_numpy(y_train).type(torch.Tensor).view(-1)
y_test = torch.from_numpy(y_test).type(torch.Tensor).view(-1)
X_train = X_train.view([X_train.shape[0], X_train.shape[1], 1])
X_test = X_test.view([X_test.shape[0], X_test.shape[1], 1])

model = LSTM(input_dim=1, hidden_dim=32, output_dim=1, num_layers=2)
loss_fn = nn.MSELoss()
optimizer = torch.optim.Adam(model.parameters(), lr=0.001)
epochs = 200

for epoch in range(epochs):
    model.train()
    optimizer.zero_grad()
    out = model(X_train).reshape(-1, )
    loss = loss_fn(out, y_train)
    loss.backward()
    optimizer.step()
    if epoch % 10 == 0:
        print(f"Epoch: {epoch}, Loss: {loss.item()}")
```

In this case, we need to revert the differencing operation to get the forecasts in the original scale of the time series. We do that as follows:

```
model.eval()
y_pred = model(X_test).reshape(-1, )
y_diff = scaler.inverse_transform(
    y_pred.detach().numpy().reshape(-1, 1)).flatten()
y_original = y_diff + test_shifted.values[(periods+3):]
```

Essentially, we add back the shifted test series to the denormalized predictions.

How it works...

Seasonal differencing removes periodic variations, thus stabilizing the level of the series and making it stationary.

Seasonal differencing is particularly effective when the seasonal patterns change in magnitude and periodicity. In such cases, it's usually a better approach than seasonal dummies or a Fourier series.

Handling seasonality – seasonal decomposition

This recipe describes yet another approach to modeling seasonality, this time using a time series decomposition approach.

Getting ready

We learned about time series decomposition methods in *Chapter 1*. Decomposition methods aim at extracting the individual parts that make up a time series.

We can use this approach to deal with seasonality. The idea is to separate the seasonal component from the rest (trend plus residuals). We can use a deep neural network to model the seasonally adjusted series. Then, we use a simple model to forecast the seasonal component.

Again, we'll start with the daily solar radiation time series. This time, we won't split training and testing to show how the forecasts are obtained in practice.

How to do it...

We start by decomposing the time series using STL. We learned about this method in *Chapter 1*:

```
from statsmodels.tsa.api import STL
series_decomp = STL(series, period=365).fit()
seas_adj = series - series_decomp.seasonal
```

The seasonally adjusted series and the seasonal component are shown in the following figure:

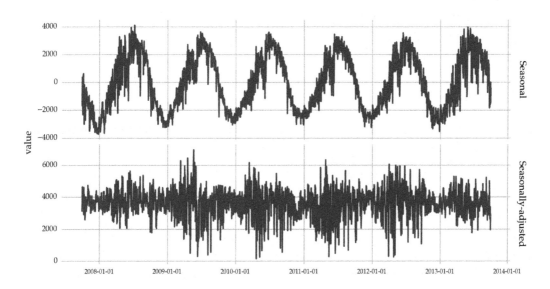

Figure 3.2: Seasonal part and the remaining seasonally adjusted series

Then, we use an LSTM to model the seasonally adjusted series. We'll use a process similar to what we did before in previous recipes:

```
scaler = MinMaxScaler(feature_range=(-1, 1))
train_norm = scaler.fit_transform(
    seas_adj.values.reshape(-1, 1)).flatten()
train_norm = pd.Series(train_norm, index=time_series.index)
train_df = series_to_supervised(train_norm, 3)
X_train, y_train = train_df.values[:, :-1], train_df.values[:, -1]

X_train = torch.from_numpy(X_train).type(torch.Tensor)
y_train = torch.from_numpy(y_train).type(torch.Tensor).view(-1)

X_train = X_train.view([X_train.shape[0], X_train.shape[1], 1])

model = LSTM(input_dim=1, hidden_dim=32, output_dim=1, num_layers=2)

loss_fn = nn.MSELoss()
optimizer = torch.optim.Adam(model.parameters(), lr=0.001)

epochs = 200
```

```
for epoch in range(epochs):
    model.train()
    optimizer.zero_grad()

    out = model(X_train).reshape(-1, )
    loss = loss_fn(out, y_train)
    loss.backward()
    optimizer.step()
```

The preceding code trains the LSTM on the seasonally adjusted series. Now, we use it to forecast the next 14 days of data:

```
latest_obs = train_norm.tail(3)
latest_obs = latest_obs.values.reshape(1, 3, -1)
latest_obs_t = torch.from_numpy(latest_obs).type(torch.Tensor)

model.eval()
y_pred = model(latest_obs_t).reshape(-1, ).detach().numpy()
y_denorm = scaler.inverse_transform(y_pred.reshape(-1,1)).flatten()
```

This is what we see in the preceding code:

1. We get the latest three lags from the time series and structure it as the input data

2. We use the model to predict the next value of the series

3. Then we denormalize the forecast using the scaler object

Now, we need to forecast the seasonal component. This is usually done with a seasonal naive method. In this recipe, we'll use the implementation available in the sktime package:

```
from sktime.forecasting.naive import NaiveForecaster

seas_forecaster = NaiveForecaster(stra'egy='last', sp=365)
seas_forecaster.fit(series_decomp.seasonal)
seas_preds = seas_forecaster.predict(fh=[1])
```

The NaiveForecaster object fits with the seasonal component. The idea of this method is to predict future observations using the previous known value from the same season.

Finally, we get the final forecast by adding the two predictions:

```
preds = y_denorm + seas_preds
```

This addition reverts the decomposition process carried out before, and we get the forecast in the original series scale.

How it works...

Modeling seasonality with a decomposition approach involves removing the seasonal part and modeling the seasonally adjusted time series with a neural network. Another simpler model is used to forecast the future of the seasonal part.

This process is different than when using seasonal dummies, a Fourier series, or seasonal differencing. Seasonal dummies or a Fourier series work as extra input variables for the neural network to model. In the case of decomposition or differencing, the time series is transformed before modeling. This means that we need to revert these transformations after making the predictions with the neural network. With decomposition, this means adding the forecasts of the seasonal part. Differencing is also reverted by adding back the previous values from the same season.

Handling non-constant variance – log transformation

We've learned how to deal with changes in the level of the time series that occur due to either trend or seasonal patterns. In this recipe, we'll deal with changes in the variance of time series.

Getting ready

We've learned in *Chapter 1* that some time series are heteroscedastic, which means that the variance changes over time. Non-constant variance is problematic as it makes the learning process more difficult.

Let's start by splitting the solar radiation time series into training and testing sets:

```
train, test = train_test_split(time_series, test_size=0.2,
    shuffle=False)
```

Again, we leave the last 20% of observations for testing.

How to do it...

We'll show how to stabilize the variance of a time series using the logarithm transformation and a Box-Cox power transformation.

Log transformation

In *Chapter 1*, we defined the `LogTransformation` class that applies the logarithm to a time series:

```
import numpy as np

class LogTransformation:

    @staticmethod
    def transform(x):
        xt = np.sign(x) * np.log(np.abs(x) + 1)
        return xt

    @staticmethod
    def inverse_transform(xt):
        x = np.sign(xt) * (np.exp(np.abs(xt)) - 1)
        return x
```

You can apply the transformation as follows:

```
train_log = LogTransformation.transform(train)
test_log = LogTransformation.transform(test)
```

The `train_log` and `test_log` objects are the transformed datasets with a stabilized variance.

Box-Cox transformation

The logarithm is often an effective approach to stabilize the variance, and is a particular instance of the Box-Cox method. You can apply this method using the `boxcox()` function from `scipy`:

```
from scipy import stats

train_bc, bc_lambda = stats.boxcox(train)
train_bc = pd.Series(train_bc, index=train.index)
```

The Box-Cox method relies on a `lambda` parameter (`bc_lambda`), which we estimate using the training set. Then, we use it to transform the test set as well:

```
test_bc = stats.boxcox(test, lmbda=bc_lambda)
test_bc = pd.Series(test_bc, index=test.index)
```

After transforming the data using either the logarithm or the Box-Cox transformation, we train a neural network.

Modeling

The training process is identical to what we did in the previous recipes. We'll continue the recipe using the transformed series with the logarithm (but the process would be the same for the Box-Cox case):

```
scaler = MinMaxScaler(feature_range=(-1, 1))

train_norm = scaler.fit_transform(train_log.values.reshape(-1, 1))
test_norm = scaler.transform(test_log.values.reshape(-1, 1))

train_df = series_to_supervised(train_norm, 3).values
test_df = series_to_supervised(test_norm, 3).values

X_train, y_train = train_df[:, :-1], train_df[:, -1]
X_test, y_test = test_df[:, :-1], test_df[:, -1]

X_train = torch.from_numpy(X_train).type(torch.Tensor)
X_test = torch.from_numpy(X_test).type(torch.Tensor)
y_train = torch.from_numpy(y_train).type(torch.Tensor).view(-1)
y_test = torch.from_numpy(y_test).type(torch.Tensor).view(-1)

X_train = X_train.view([X_train.shape[0], X_train.shape[1], 1])
X_test = X_test.view([X_test.shape[0], X_test.shape[1], 1])

model = LSTM(input_dim=1, hidden_dim=32, output_dim=1, num_layers=2)

loss_fn = nn.MSELoss()
optimizer = torch.optim.Adam(model.parameters(), lr=0.001)

epochs = 200

for epoch in range(epochs):
    model.train()
    optimizer.zero_grad()

    out = model(X_train).reshape(-1, )
    loss = loss_fn(out, y_train)
    loss.backward()
    optimizer.step()
```

After training, we run the model on the test set. The predictions need to be reverted to the original scale of the time series. This is done with the following code:

```
model.eval()
y_pred = model(X_test).reshape(-1, )
y_pred_np = y_pred.detach().numpy().reshape(-1, 1)
y_pred_denorm = scaler.inverse_transform(y_pred_np).flatten()
y_pred_orig = LogTransformation.inverse_transform(y_pred_denorm)
```

After denormalizing the predictions, we also use the `inverse_transform()` method to revert the log transformation. With the Box-Cox transformation, this process could be done as follows:

```
from scipy.special import inv_boxcox

y_pred_orig = inv_boxcox(y_pred_denorm, bc_lambda)
```

In the preceding code, we pass the transformed predictions and the `bc_lambda` transformation parameter to get the forecasts in the original scale.

How it works...

The process carried out in this recipe attempts to mitigate the problem of non-constant variance. Both the logarithm transformation and the Box-Cox method can be used to stabilize the variance. These methods also bring the data closer to a `Normal` distribution. This type of transformation benefits the training of neural networks as it helps avoid saturation areas in the optimization process.

The transformation methods work directly on the input data, so they are agnostic to the learning algorithm. The models work with transformed data, which means that the forecasts need to be transformed back to the original scale of the time series.

4

Forecasting with PyTorch Lightning

In this chapter, we'll build forecasting models using PyTorch Lightning. We'll touch on several aspects of this framework, such as creating a data module to handle data preprocessing or creating a `LightningModel` structure that encapsulates the training process of neural networks. We'll also explore **TensorBoard** to monitor the training process of neural networks. Then, we'll describe a few metrics for evaluating deep neural networks for forecasting, such as **Mean Absolute Scaled Error (MASE)** and **Symmetric Mean Absolute Percentage Error (SMAPE)**. In this chapter, we'll focus on multivariate time series, which contain more than one variable.

This chapter will guide you through the following recipes:

- Preparing a multivariate time series for supervised learning
- Training a linear regression model for forecasting with a multivariate time series
- Feedforward neural networks for multivariate time series forecasting
- LSTM neural networks for multivariate time series forecasting
- Evaluating deep neural networks for forecasting
- Monitoring the training process using Tensorboard
- Using callbacks – `EarlyStopping`

Technical requirements

In this chapter, we'll leverage the following Python libraries, all of which you can install using `pip`:

- PyTorch Lightning (2.1.4)
- PyTorch Forecasting (1.0.0)
- `torch` (2.2.0)
- `ray` (2.9.2)
- `numpy` (1.26.3)
- `pandas` (2.1.4)
- `scikit-learn` (1.4.0)
- `sktime` (0.26.0)

The code for this chapter can be found in this book's GitHub repository: `https://github.com/PacktPublishing/Deep-Learning-for-Time-Series-Data-Cookbook`.

Preparing a multivariate time series for supervised learning

The first recipe of this chapter addresses the problem of preparing a multivariate time series for supervised learning. We'll show how the sliding window method we used in the previous chapter can be extended to solve this task. Then, we'll demonstrate how to prepare a time series using `TimeSeriesDataSet`, a PyTorch Forecasting class that handles the preprocessing steps of time series.

Getting ready

We'll use the same time series we analyzed in *Chapter 1*. We'll need to load the dataset with `pandas` using the following code:

```
import pandas as pd

data = pd.read_csv('assets/daily_multivariate_timeseries.csv',
                   parse_dates=['Datetime'],
                   index_col='Datetime')
```

The following figure shows a sample of the time series. Please note that the axes have been transposed for visualization purposes:

datetime	2007-10-01	2007-10-02	2007-10-03	2007-10-04	2007-10-05	2007-10-06	2007-10-07	2007-10-08
Incoming Solar	1381.50	3953.20	3098.10	2213.90	1338.80	3671.50	4193.70	4213.80
Wind Dir	281.58	173.42	263.88	209.23	234.41	248.38	238.13	159.58
Snow Depth	0.00	0.00	0.00	0.00	0.00	0.00	0.00	0.00
Wind Speed	0.60	0.60	0.76	0.59	0.80	0.80	0.65	0.63
Dewpoint	1.15	-0.70	0.54	-0.75	-2.56	-4.52	-0.40	-2.58
Precipitation	6.40	0.10	0.00	0.00	0.00	0.00	0.00	0.00
Vapor Pressure	666.96	577.33	636.25	574.96	494.71	420.38	593.67	494.75
Relative Humidity	0.83	0.67	0.61	0.70	0.76	0.68	0.70	0.50
Air Temp	9.40	15.00	10.90	10.20	5.20	7.70	14.20	20.60

Figure 4.1: Sample of a multivariate time series. The variables of the
series are shown on the x axis for visualization purposes

The preceding dataset contains nine variables related to meteorological conditions. As we did in *Chapter 3*, the goal is to forecast the next solar radiation values. We'll use the lags of the extra available variables as input explanatory variables. In the next chapter, you will learn how to prepare a multivariate time series for cases where you want to forecast several variables.

How to do it...

We'll transform a multivariate time series for supervised learning. First, we'll describe how to do this using the sliding window approach that we used in *Chapter 3*. Then, we'll show how this process can be simplified with the `TimeSeriesDataSet` data structure, which is based on PyTorch.

Using a sliding window

In the previous chapter, we used a sliding window approach to transform a univariate time series from a sequence into a matrix format. Preparing a multivariate time series for supervised learning requires a similar process: we apply the sliding window technique to each variable and then combine the results. This process can be carried out as follows:

```
TARGET = 'Incoming Solar'
N_LAGS = 7
HORIZON = 1
input_data = []
output_data = []
for i in range(N_LAGS, data.shape[0]-HORIZON+1):
    input_data.append(data.iloc[i - N_LAGS:i].values)
```

```
    output_data.append(data.iloc[i:(i+HORIZON)][TARGET])

input_data, output_data = np.array(input_data), np.array(output_data)
```

The preceding code follows these steps:

1. First, we define the number of lags and forecasting horizon. We set the number of lags to 7 (N_LAGS=7), the forecasting horizon to 1 (HORIZON=1), and the target variable to Incoming Solar.

2. Then, we iterate over each time step in the multivariate time series. At each point, we retrieve the previous N_LAGS, add these to the input_data, and add the next value of solar radiation to the output data. This means we'll use the past 7 values of each variable to forecast the next value of solar radiation.

3. Finally, we transform the input and output data from a Python list into a NumPy array structure.

output_data is a one-dimensional vector that represents the future value of solar radiation. input_data has 3 dimensions: the first dimension refers to the number of samples, the second is the number of lags, and the third is the number of variables in the series.

Using the TimeSeriesDataSet class

So far, we've been using a sliding window method to preprocess time series for supervised learning. This function and other preprocessing tasks that are required for training a neural network are automated by the TimeSeriesDataSet class, which is available in the PyTorch Forecasting library.

TimeSeriesDataSet provides a simple and useful way of preparing and passing data to models. Let's see how this structure can be used to handle multivariate time series. First, we need to shape the time series in a pandas DataFrame structure with three main pieces of information:

*   group_id: A column that identifies the name of a time series. If the dataset contains a single time series, this column will show a constant value. Some datasets involve multiple time series that can be distinguished by this variable.

*   time_index: This stores the time at which a value is captured by a given series.

*   **Other variables**: Extra variables that store the value of the time series. A multivariate time series contains several variables.

Our time series already contains several variables. Now, we need to add information about time_index and group_id, which can be done as follows:

```
mvtseries['group_id'] = 0
mvtseries['time_index'] = np.arange(mvtseries.shape[0])
```

The value of `group_id` is constantly 0 since we're working with a single time series. We use 0 arbitrarily. You can use any name that suits you. We use the `np.arange()` function to create this time series' `time_index`. This creates a variable that gives 0 for the first observation, 1 for the second observation, and so on.

Then, we must create an instance of the `TimeSeriesDataSet` class, as follows:

```
dataset = TimeSeriesDataSet(
    data=mvtseries,
    group_ids=["group_id"],
    target="Incoming Solar",
    time_idx="time_index",
    max_encoder_length=7,
    max_prediction_length=1,
    time_varying_unknown_reals=['Incoming Solar',
                                'Wind Dir',
                                'Snow Depth',
                                'Wind Speed',
                                'Dewpoint',
                                'Precipitation',
                                'Vapor Pressure',
                                'Relative Humidity',
                                'Air Temp'],
)
```

We can transform a `TimeSeriesDataSet` dataset into a `DataLoader` class as follows:

```
data_loader = dataset.to_dataloader(batch_size=1, shuffle=False)
```

`DataLoader` is used to pass observations to a model. Here's an example of what an observation looks like:

```
x, y = next(iter(data_loader))
x['encoder_cont']
y
```

We use the `next()` and `iter()` methods to get an observation from the data loader. This observation is stored as x and y, which represent the input and output data, respectively. The main input is the `encoder_cont` item, which denotes the 7 lags of each variable. This data is a PyTorch tensor with the shape (1, 7, 9) representing (batch size, number of lags, number of variables). The batch size is a parameter that represents the number of samples used in each training iteration of a neural network. The output data is a float that represents the next value of the solar radiation variable.

How it works...

The `TimeSeriesDataSet` constructor requires a few parameters:

- `data`: A time series dataset with the three elements described earlier
- `group_ids`: The column in `data` that identifies each time series in the dataset
- `target`: The column in `data` that we want to forecast (target variable)
- `time_idx`: The column in `data` that contains the time information of each observation
- `max_encoder_length`: The number of lags used to build the auto-regressive model
- `max_prediction_length`: The forecasting horizon – that is, how many future time steps should be predicted
- `time_varying_unknown_reals`: A list of columns in `data` that describes which numeric variables vary over time

There are other parameters related to `time_varying_unknown_reals`. This particular input details all numeric observations whose future is unknown to the user, such as the variables we want to forecast. Yet, in some cases, we know the future value of an observation, such as the price of a product. This type of variable should be included in the `time_varying_known_reals` input. There are also the `time_varying_known_categoricals` and `time_varying_unknown_categoricals` inputs, which can be used for categorical variables instead of numeric ones.

Regarding the forecasting task, the transformation we carried out in this recipe is the basis of a type of modeling called **Auto-Regressive Distributed Lags** (**ARDL**). ARDL is an extension of auto-regression that also includes the lags of exogenous variables as input.

Training a linear regression model for forecasting with a multivariate time series

In this recipe, we'll use PyTorch to train a linear regression model as our first forecasting model fit on a multivariate time series. We'll show you how to use `TimeSeriesDataSet` to handle the preprocessing steps for training the model and passing data to it.

Getting ready

We'll start this recipe with the `mvtseries` dataset that we used in the previous recipe:

```
import pandas as pd

mvtseries = pd.read_csv('assets/daily_multivariate_timeseries.csv',
```

```
                    parse_dates=['datetime'],
                    index_col='datetime')
```

Now, let's see how we can use this dataset to train a PyTorch model.

How to do it...

In the following code, we'll describe the necessary steps to prepare the time series and build a linear regression model:

1. We start by preprocessing the time series. This includes creating the group identifier and time index columns:

    ```
    mvtseries["target"] = mvtseries["Incoming Solar"]
    mvtseries["time_index"] = np.arange(mvtseries.shape[0])
    mvtseries["group_id"] = 0
    ```

2. Then, we must split the data into different partitions. For this recipe, we'll only keep the training indices:

    ```
    time_indices = data["time_index"].values

    train_indices, _ = train_test_split(
        time_indices,
        test_size=test_size,
        shuffle=False)

    train_indices, _ = train_test_split(train_indices,
                                        test_size=0.1,
                                        shuffle=False)

    train_df = data.loc[data["time_index"].isin(train_indices)]
     train_df_mod = train_df.copy()
    ```

3. Then, we must standardize the time series using the `StandardScaler` operator:

    ```
    target_scaler = StandardScaler()
    target_scaler.fit(train_df_mod[["target"]])
    train_df_mod["target"] = target_scaler.transform
        (train_df_mod[["target"]])
    train_df_mod = train_df_mod.drop("Incoming Solar", axis=1)
     feature_names = [
        col for col in data.columns
        if col != "target" and col != "Incoming Solar"
    ]
    ```

4. The preprocessed time series is passed onto a `TimeSeriesDataSet` instance:

```
training_dataset = TimeSeriesDataSet(
    train_df_mod,
    time_idx="time_index",
    target="target",
    group_ids=["group_id"],
    max_encoder_length=n_lags,
    max_prediction_length=horizon,
    time_varying_unknown_reals=feature_names,
    scalers={name: StandardScaler()
            for name in feature_names},
)


loader = training_dataset.to_dataloader(batch_size=batch_size,
                                        shuffle=False)
```

The `TimeSeriesDataSet` object is transformed into a data loader that can be used to pass batches of samples to a model. This is done using the `to_dataloader()` method. We encapsulate all these data preparation steps into a single function called `create_training_set`. You can check out the function's source in this book's GitHub repository.

5. Next, we call the `create_training_set()` function to create the training dataset:

```
N_LAGS = 7
HORIZON = 1
BATCH_SIZE = 10

data_loader = create_training_set(
    data=mvtseries,
    n_lags=N_LAGS,
    horizon=HORIZON,
    batch_size=BATCH_SIZE,
    test_size=0.3
)
```

6. Then, we must define the linear regression model using PyTorch, as follows:

```
import torch
from torch import nn

class LinearRegressionModel(nn.Module):
    def __init__(self, input_dim, output_dim):
        super(LinearRegressionModel, self).__init__()
        self.linear = nn.Linear(input_dim, output_dim)
```

```
    def forward(self, X):
        X = X.view(X.size(0), -1)
        return self.linear(X)
```

Here, we define a class called `LinearRegressionModel` that implements the multiple linear regression model. It contains a single linear transformation layer (`nn.Linear`). This class takes the input and output sizes as input, which are the second dimension of the `train_input` and `train_output` objects, respectively. We created the model by calling the class with these parameters.

7. Now, we will create an instance of this model, as follows:

```
    num_vars = mvtseries.shape[1] + 1
    model = LinearRegressionModel(N_LAGS * num_vars, HORIZON)
```

`num_vars` contains the number of variables in the time series. Then, we define the input of the model to `num_vars` times `N_LAGS` and the output to the forecasting horizon.

8. We can perform the training process using the following code:

```
    criterion = nn.MSELoss()
    optimizer = torch.optim.Adam(model.parameters(), lr=0.001)
    num_epochs = 10
    for epoch in range(num_epochs):
        for batch in data_loader:
            x, y = batch
            X = x["encoder_cont"].squeeze(-1)
            y_pred = model(X)
            y_pred = y_pred.squeeze(1)
            y_actual = y[0].squeeze(1)
            loss = criterion(y_pred, y_actual)
            loss.backward()
            optimizer.step()
            optimizer.zero_grad()
        print(f"epoch: {epoch + 1}, loss = {loss.item():.4f}")
```

Here, we set the learning rate to `0.001` and the optimizer to Adam. Adam is a popular alternative to approaches such as SGD that has better converge characteristics.

At each training epoch, we get the lags of each batch from the data loader and process them with the model. Note that each batch is reshaped into a two-dimensional format that is required by a linear model. This is done in the `forward()` method of the `LinearRegressionModel` class.

How it works...

We used the `TimeSeriesDataSet` class to handle the data preparation process for us. Then, we converted the dataset into a `DataLoader` class using the `to_dataloader()` method. This data loader provides batches of data to the model. Although we did not define it explicitly, each batch follows an autoregressive way of modeling. The input is based on the past few observations of the time series, and the output represents the future observations.

We implement the linear regression model as a class so that it follows the same structure as in the previous chapter. We could create the model with `model = nn.Linear(input_size, output_size)` for simplicity.

Feedforward neural networks for multivariate time series forecasting

In this recipe, we'll return our attention to deep neural networks. We'll show you how to build a forecasting model for multivariate time series using a deep feedforward neural network. We'll describe how to couple the `DataModule` class with `TimeSeriesDataSet` to encapsulate the data preprocessing steps. We'll also place the `PyTorch` models within a `LightningModule` structure, which standardizes the training process of neural networks.

Getting ready

We'll continue to use the multivariate time series related to solar radiation forecasting:

```
import pandas as pd

mvtseries = pd.read_csv('assets/daily_multivariate_timeseries.csv',
                        parse_dates=['datetime'],
                        index_col='datetime')
n_vars = mvtseries.shape[1]
```

In this recipe, we'll use a data module from `pytorch_lightning` to handle data preprocessing. Data modules are classes that contain all the steps for preprocessing data and sharing it with models. Here is the basic structure of a data module:

```
import lightning.pytorch as pl

class ExampleDataModule(pl.LightningDataModule):
    def __init__(self,
                 data: pd.DataFrame,
                 batch_size: int):
        super().__init__()
```

```
        self.data = data
        self.batch_size = batch_size

    def setup(self, stage=None):
        pass

    def train_dataloader(self):
        pass

    def val_dataloader(self):
        pass

    def test_dataloader(self):
        pass

    def predict_dataloader(self):
        pass
```

All data modules inherit from the `LightningDataModule` class. There are a few key methods that we need to implement:

- `setup()`: This method includes all the main data preprocessing steps
- `train_dataloader()`, `val_dataloader()`, `test_dataloader()`, and `predict_dataloader()`: These are a set of methods that get the data loader for the respective dataset (training, validation, testing, and prediction)

Besides a `DataModule` class, we'll also leverage the `LightningModule` class to encapsulate all the model processes. These modules have the following structure:

```
class ExampleModel(pl.LightningModule):
    def __init__(self):
        super().__init__()
        self.network = ...

    def forward(self, x):
        pass

    def training_step(self, batch, batch_idx):
        pass

    def validation_step(self, batch, batch_idx):
        pass

    def test_step(self, batch, batch_idx):
```

```
        pass

    def predict_step(self, batch, batch_idx, dataloader_idx=0):
        pass

    def configure_optimizers(self):
        pass
```

Let's take a closer look at `ExampleModel`:

- We define any necessary neural network elements in the attributes of the class (such as `self.network`)
- The `forward()` method defines how the elements of the network interact and model the time series
- `training_step`, `validation_step`, and `testing_step` describe the training, validation, and testing processes of the network, respectively
- `predict_step` details the process of getting the latest observations and making a forecast, mimicking a deployment scenario
- Finally, the `configure_optimizers()` method details the optimization setup for the network

Let's see how we can create a data module to preprocess a multivariate time series, and how it couples with `TimeSeriesDataSet`. Then, we'll implement a `LightningModule` structure to handle the training and testing process of a feedforward neural network.

How to do it...

The following code shows how to define the data module to handle the preprocessing steps. First, let's look at the class constructor:

```
from pytorch_forecasting import TimeSeriesDataSet
from sklearn.model_selection import train_test_split
from sklearn.preprocessing import StandardScaler

class MultivariateSeriesDataModule(pl.LightningDataModule):
    def __init__(
            self,
            data: pd.DataFrame,
            n_lags: int,
            horizon: int,
            test_size: float,
            batch_size: int
    ):
```

```
        super().__init__()
        self.data = data
        self.feature_names =
            [col for col in data.columns if col != "Incoming Solar"]
        self.batch_size = batch_size
        self.test_size = test_size
        self.n_lags = n_lags
        self.horizon = horizon
        self.target_scaler = StandardScaler()
        self.training = None
        self.validation = None
        self.test = None
        self.predict_set = None
```

In the constructor, we define all the necessary elements for data preparation, such as the number of lags, forecasting horizon, and datasets. This includes the initialization of the `target_scaler` attribute, which is used to standardize the value of the time series.

Then, we create the `setup()` method, which includes the data preprocessing logic:

```
def setup(self, stage=None):
    self.preprocess_data()
    train_indices, val_indices, test_indices = self.split_data()
    train_df = self.data.loc
        [self.data["time_index"].isin(train_indices)]
    val_df = self.data.loc[self.data["time_index"].isin(val_indices)]
    test_df = self.data.loc
        [self.data["time_index"].isin(test_indices)]
     self.target_scaler.fit(train_df[["target"]])
    self.scale_target(train_df, train_df.index)
    self.scale_target(val_df, val_df.index)
    self.scale_target(test_df, test_df.index)
    train_df = train_df.drop("Incoming Solar", axis=1)
    val_df = val_df.drop("Incoming Solar", axis=1)
    test_df = test_df.drop("Incoming Solar", axis=1)
    self.training = TimeSeriesDataSet(
        train_df,
        time_idx="time_index",
        target="target",
        group_ids=["group_id"],
        max_encoder_length=self.n_lags,
        max_prediction_length=self.horizon,
        time_varying_unknown_reals=self.feature_names,
```

```
        scalers={name: StandardScaler() for name in
            self.feature_names},
    )
    self.validation = TimeSeriesDataSet.from_dataset
        (self.training, val_df)
    self.test = TimeSeriesDataSet.from_dataset(self.training, test_df)
    self.predict_set = TimeSeriesDataSet.from_dataset(
    self.training, self.data, predict=True)
```

Some of the methods, such as `self.preprocess_data()`, have been omitted for conciseness. You can find their source in this book's GitHub repository.

Finally, we must build the data loaders that are responsible for passing data to models:

```
def train_dataloader(self):
    return self.training.to_dataloader
        (batch_size=self.batch_size, shuffle=False)

def val_dataloader(self):
    return self.validation.to_dataloader
        (batch_size=self.batch_size, shuffle=False)

def test_dataloader(self):
    return self.test.to_dataloader
        (batch_size=self.batch_size, shuffle=False)

def predict_dataloader(self):
    return self.predict_set.to_dataloader
        (batch_size=1, shuffle=False)
```

Let's take a closer look at this data module:

- The data preprocessing steps are carried out in the `setup()` method. This includes transforming the time series by including the `time_index` and `group_id` variables, as well as training, validation, and testing splits. The datasets are structured with a `TimeSeriesDataSet` class. Note that we only need to define a `TimeSeriesDataSet` instance for one of the datasets. We can use the `from_dataset()` method to set up an existing `TimeSeriesDataSet` instance for another dataset.

- The information for the preprocessing steps can be passed in the constructor of the `DataModule` class, such as the number of lags (n_lags) or forecasting `horizon`.

- The data loaders can be obtained by using the `to_dataloader()` method on the respective dataset.

Then, we can design the neural network architecture. We will create a class named `FeedForwardNet` that implements a feedforward neural network with three layers:

```
import torch
from torch import nn

class FeedForwardNet(nn.Module):
    def __init__(self, input_size, output_size):
        super().__init__()
        self.net = nn.Sequential(
            nn.Linear(input_size, 16),
            nn.ReLU(),
            nn.Linear(16, 8),
            nn.ReLU(),
            nn.Linear(8, output_size),
        )

    def forward(self, X):
        X = X.view(X.size(0), -1)
        return self.net(X)
```

The network architecture is defined in the `self.net` attribute. The layers of the network are stacked on top of each other with the `nn.Sequential` container:

- The first layer receives the input data with a size of `input_size`. It is a linear transformation (`nn.Linear`) that contains `16` units with a `ReLU()` activation function (`nn.ReLU`).

- The results are passed into the second layer of the same linear type and activation function. This layer contains 8 units.

- The final layer is also a linear transformation of the inputs coming from the previous one. Its size is the same as `output_size`, which in the case of a time series refers to the forecasting horizon.

Then, we insert this neural network within a `LightningModule` model class. First, let's look at the class constructor and the `forward()` method:

```
from pytorch_forecasting.models import BaseModel

class FeedForwardModel(BaseModel):
    def __init__(self, input_dim: int, output_dim: int):
        self.save_hyperparameters()
        super().__init__()
        self.network = FeedForwardNet(
            input_size=input_dim,
            output_size=output_dim,
```

```
        )
        self.train_loss_history = []
        self.val_loss_history = []
        self.train_loss_sum = 0.0
        self.val_loss_sum = 0.0
        self.train_batch_count = 0
        self.val_batch_count = 0

    def forward(self, x):
        network_input = x["encoder_cont"].squeeze(-1)
        prediction = self.network(network_input)
        output = self.to_network_output(prediction=prediction)
        return output
```

The constructor stores the network elements, while the `forward()` method details how these elements interact in the forward pass of the network. The `forward()` method also transforms the output in the original data scale using the `to_network_output()` method. The training step and network optimizer are defined as follows:

```
def training_step(self, batch, batch_idx):
    x, y = batch
    y_pred = self(x).prediction
    y_pred = y_pred.squeeze(1)

    y_actual = y[0].squeeze(1)
    loss = F.mse_loss(y_pred, y_actual)
    self.train_loss_sum += loss.item()
    self.train_batch_count += 1
    self.log("train_loss", loss)
    return loss

def configure_optimizers(self):
    return torch.optim.Adam(self.parameters(), lr=0.01)
```

The `configure_optimizers()` method is where we set up the optimization process. In the training step, we get a batch of samples, pass the input onto the neural network, and then compute the mean squared error using the actual data. Then, we store the error information in different attributes.

The validation and testing steps work similarly to how they do in the training phase:

```
def validation_step(self, batch, batch_idx):
    x, y = batch
    y_pred = self(x).prediction
    y_pred = y_pred.squeeze(1)
```

```
    y_actual = y[0].squeeze(1)
    loss = F.mse_loss(y_pred, y_actual)
    self.val_loss_sum += loss.item()
    self.val_batch_count += 1
    self.log("val_loss", loss)
    return loss


def test_step(self, batch, batch_idx):
    x, y = batch
    y_pred = self(x).prediction
    y_pred = y_pred.squeeze(1)
    y_actual = y[0].squeeze(1)
    loss = F.mse_loss(y_pred, y_actual)
    self.log("test_loss", loss)
```

In the prediction step, we simply pass the input data on to the neural network and get its output in response:

```
def predict_step(self, batch, batch_idx):
    x, y = batch
    y_pred = self(x).prediction
    y_pred = y_pred.squeeze(1)
    return y_pred
```

Let's take a look at the preceding `FeedForwardModel` module:

- The neural network based on `PyTorch` is defined in the `self.network` attribute
- The `forward()` method describes how the neural network processes an instance that it gets from a data loader
- The optimizer is set to `Adam` with a learning rate equal to `0.01`
- Finally, we use the `Trainer` class to train the model:

```
datamodule = MultivariateSeriesDataModule(data=mvtseries,
                                          n_lags=7,
                                          horizon=1,
                                          batch_size=32,
                                          test_size=0.3)
model = FeedForwardModel(input_dim=N_LAGS * n_vars, output_dim=1)
trainer = pl.Trainer(max_epochs=30)
trainer.fit(model, datamodule)
```

The training process runs for 30 epochs. To test the model, we can use the `test()` method from the `Trainer` instance:

```
trainer.test(model=model, datamodule=datamodule)
forecasts = trainer.predict(model=model, datamodule=datamodule)
```

Future observations are forecasted by the `predict()` method. In both cases, we pass both the model and the data module to the `Trainer` instance.

How it works...

The data module encapsulates all the preparation steps. Any specific transformation that you need to perform on the dataset can be included in the `setup()` method. The logic related to the model is handled in the `LightningModule` instance. Using a `DataModule` and `LightningModule` approach provides a modular and tidier way of developing deep learning models.

The `scalers` argument in the `TimeSeriesDataSet` class is used to pass the scaler that should be used to preprocess the explanatory variables of the time series. In this case, we used the following:

```
scalers={name: StandardScaler() for name in self.feature_names}
```

Here, we used `StandardScaler` to transform all explanatory variables into a common value range. We standardized the target variable of the time series using the `self.target_scaler` attribute, which includes a `StandardScaler` operator. We normalized the target variable outside of `TimeSeriesDataSet` to give us more control over the target variable. This can serve as an example of how to carry out transformations that may not be readily available in software packages.

There's more...

We defined the feedforward neural network using the `nn.Sequential` container. Another possible approach is to define each element as its own class attribute and call them in the `forward` method explicitly:

```
class FeedForwardNetAlternative(nn.Module):
    def __init__(self, input_size, output_size):
        super().__init__()
        self.l1 = nn.Linear(input_size, 16)
        self.relu_l1 = nn.ReLU()
        self.l2 = nn.Linear(16, 8)
        self.relu_l2 = nn.ReLU()
        self.l3 = nn.Linear(8, output_size)

    def forward(self, x):
        X = X.view(X.size(0), -1)
```

```
l1_output = self.l1(x)
l1_actf_output = self.relu_l1(l1_output)
l2_output = self.l2(l1_actf_output)
l2_actf_output = self.relu_l2(l2_output)
l3_output = self.l3(l2_actf_output)
return l3_output
```

Both approaches are equivalent. While the first one is tidier, the second one is more versatile.

LSTM neural networks for multivariate time series forecasting

In this recipe, we'll continue the process of building a model to predict the next value of solar radiation using multivariate time series. This time, we'll train an LSTM recurrent neural network to solve this task.

Getting ready

The data setup is similar to what we did in the previous recipe. So, we'll use the same data module we defined there. Now, let's learn how to build an LSTM neural network with a LightningModule class.

How to do it...

The workflow for training an LSTM neural network with PyTorch Lightning is similar, with one small but important detail. For LSTM models, we keep the input data in a three-dimensional structure with a shape of (number of samples, number of lags, number of features). Here's what the module looks like, starting with the constructor and the forward() method:

```
class MultivariateLSTM(pl.LightningModule):
    def __init__(self, input_dim, hidden_dim, num_layers, output_dim):
        super().__init__()
        self.hidden_dim = hidden_dim
        self.lstm = nn.LSTM(input_dim, hidden_dim, num_layers,
            batch_first=True)
        self.fc = nn.Linear(hidden_dim, output_dim)

    def forward(self, x):
        h0 = torch.zeros(self.lstm.num_layers, x.size(0),
            self.hidden_dim).to(self.device)
        c0 = torch.zeros(self.lstm.num_layers, x.size(0),
            self.hidden_dim).to(self.device)
        out, _ = self.lstm(x, (h0, c0))
        out = self.fc(out[:, -1, :])
        return out
```

This time, we don't have to squeeze the inputs for the network into a two-dimensional vector since the LSTM takes a three-dimensional input. The logic behind the LSTM is implemented in the forward() method. The rest of the methods are identical to what we did in the previous recipe. Here's training_step as an example:

```
def training_step(self, batch, batch_idx):
    x, y = batch
    y_pred = self(x['encoder_cont'])
    y_pred = y_pred.squeeze(1)
    loss = F.mse_loss(y_pred, y[0])
    self.log('train_loss', loss)
    return loss
```

You can find the remaining methods in this book's GitHub repository.

After defining the model, we can use it as follows:

```
n_vars = mvtseries.shape[1] - 1

model = MultivariateLSTM(input_dim=n_vars,
                         hidden_dim=10,
                         num_layers=1,
                         output_dim=1)
trainer = pl.Trainer(max_epochs=10)
trainer.fit(model, datamodule)
trainer.test(model, datamodule.test_dataloader())
forecasts = trainer.predict(model=model, datamodule=datamodule)
```

As detailed in the preceding code, PyTorch Lightning makes the testing and predicting processes identical across models.

How it works...

The LSTM is a recurrent neural network architecture that's designed to model sequential data such as time series. This type of network contains a few extra elements relative to feedforward neural networks, such as an extra input dimension or hidden cell states. In this recipe, we stacked two fully connected layers on top of the LSTM layer. LSTM layers are usually passed on to a fully connected layer because the output of the former is an internal state. So, the fully connected layer processes this output in the particular dimension we need.

The class constructor of the LSTM takes four parameters as input – the number of variables in the time series (input_size), the forecasting horizon (output_size), the number of LSTM layers (num_layers), and the number of hidden units in each LSTM layer (hidden_size).

We defined three layers in the `__init__` constructor method. Besides the `LSTM`, we created two fully connected layers, one of which represents the output layer.

The forward pass of the network works like so:

1. Initialize the hidden state (`h0`) and cell state (`c0`) with zeros. This is done by calling the `init_hidden_state()` method.

2. Pass the input data to the LSTM stack. The LSTM returns its output and the hidden and cell states of each LSTM layer.

3. Next, we get the hidden state of the last LSTM layer, which is passed onto a `ReLU()` activation function.

4. The results from `ReLU` are passed to the first fully connected layer, whose output is, once again, transformed with a `ReLU()` activation function. Finally, the output is passed to a linear, fully connected output layer, which provides the forecasts.

This logic is coded in the `forward()` method of the `LightningModule` instance.

There's more...

We created a deep neural network with a single LSTM layer (`num_layers=1`). However, we could increase this value according to our needs. A model with more than one LSTM layer is referred to as a **stacked LSTM** model.

Monitoring the training process using Tensorboard

Training deep learning models often involves tuning numerous hyperparameters, assessing different architectures, and more. To facilitate these tasks, visualization and monitoring tools are essential. `tensorboard` is a powerful tool for tracking and visualizing various metrics during the training process. In this section, we will guide you through integrating `tensorboard` with PyTorch Lightning for monitoring the training process.

Getting ready

Before using `tensorboard` with PyTorch Lightning, you'll need to have `tensorboard` installed. You can install it using the following command:

```
pip install -U tensorboard
```

Once installed, make sure that you are utilizing PyTorch Lightning's built-in `tensorboard` logging capabilities.

How to do it...

Here's how to use `tensorboard` to monitor the training process:

1. First, ensure that `tensorboard` is imported into your script.

2. Next, you'll need to create a `tensorboard` logger and pass it to PyTorch Lightning's `Trainer`:

    ```
    from lightning.pytorch.loggers import TensorBoardLogger
    import lightning.pytorch as pl

    logger = TensorBoardLogger('logs/')
    trainer = pl.Trainer(logger=logger)
    ```

3. You can then start `tensorboard` by running the following command in your terminal:

    ```
    tensorboard --logdir=logs/
    ```

4. Open `tensorboard` in your web browser by navigating to the URL displayed in your terminal; usually, this is `http://localhost:6006`. You'll see real-time updates on various metrics, such as the number of epochs, the train, validation, and test loss, and more.

The following figure shows some plots of the LSTM's performance from the previous recipe. In this case, we can see how the number of epochs, as well as training and validation losses, are evolving:

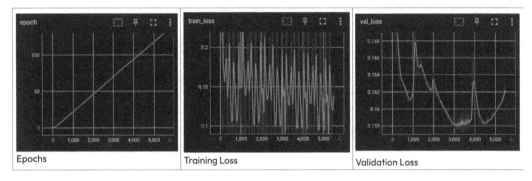

Figure 4.2: Comparison of epochs, training loss, and validation loss

How it works...

`tensorboard` provides visualizations for various training metrics, hyperparameter tuning, model graphs, and more. When integrated with PyTorch Lightning, the following occurs:

- The logger sends the specified metrics to `tensorboard` during training
- `tensorboard` reads the logs and provides interactive visualizations
- Users can monitor various aspects of training in real time

There's more…

Here are some additional details to keep in mind:

- You can log additional information such as images, text, histograms, and more

- By exploring different visualizations, you can gain insights into how your model is performing and make necessary adjustments

- Tensorboard's integration with PyTorch Lightning streamlines the monitoring process, enabling more efficient model development

Using tensorboard with PyTorch Lightning offers a robust solution for monitoring and visualizing the training process, allowing for more informed decision-making in model development.

Evaluating deep neural networks for forecasting

Evaluating the performance of forecasting models is essential to understand how well they generalize to unseen data. Popular metrics include the **Root Mean Squared Error** (**RMSE**), **Mean Absolute Percentage Error** (**MAPE**), **Mean Absolute Scaled Error** (**MASE**), and **Symmetric Mean Absolute Percentage Error** (**SMAPE**), among others. We will implement these metrics in Python and show you how they can be applied to evaluate our model's performance.

Getting ready

We need predictions from our trained model and the corresponding ground truth values to calculate these metrics. Therefore, we must run our model on the test set first to obtain the predictions.

To simplify the implementation, we will use the scikit-learn and sktime libraries since they have useful classes and methods to help us with this task. Since we have not installed sktime yet, let's run the following command:

```
pip install sktime
```

Now, it is time to import the classes and methods for the different evaluation metrics:

```
from sklearn.metrics import mean_squared_error
from sktime.performance_metrics.forecasting
import mean_absolute_scaled_error, MeanAbsolutePercentageError
import numpy as np
```

How to do it...

To evaluate the performance of our model, we must calculate the **RMSE** using the `scikit-learn` library. For **MASE**, **MAPE**, and **SMAPE**, we must leverage the `sktime` library, which offers readily available functions for these metrics.

Here's the code detailing how to calculate these metrics:

```
def mean_absolute_percentage_error(y_true, y_pred):
    y_true, y_pred = np.array(y_true), np.array(y_pred)
    return np.mean(np.abs((y_true - y_pred) / y_true)) * 100

y_pred = model(X_test).detach().numpy()
y_true = y_test.detach().numpy()
rmse_sklearn = np.sqrt(mean_squared_error(y_true, y_pred))
print(f"RMSE (scikit-learn): {rmse_sklearn}")
mape = mean_absolute_percentage_error(y_true, y_pred)
print(f"MAPE: {mape}")
mase_sktime = mean_absolute_scaled_error(y_true, y_pred)
print(f"MASE (sktime): {mase_sktime}")
smape_sktime = symmetric_mean_absolute_percentage_error
    (y_true, y_pred)
 print(f"SMAPE (sktime): {smape_sktime}")
```

How it works...

These metrics each evaluate different aspects of the model's performance:

- **RMSE**: This metric calculates the square root of the average squared differences between the predicted and actual values. It gives a higher penalty for large errors.

- **MASE**: This metric scales the **Mean Absolute Error** (**MAE**) by the MAE of a naive forecast. This makes it easier to interpret, with a MASE value of 1 indicating performance equal to the naive forecast and a MASE value less than 1 indicating better performance than the naive forecast.

- **MAPE**: This metric computes the mean of the absolute percentage difference between the actual and predicted values. It expresses the average absolute error in terms of percentage, which can be useful when you want to understand the relative prediction error.

- **SMAPE**: This metric computes the average absolute percentage error, treating under and over-forecasts equally. It expresses the error as a percentage of the actual values, which can be useful for comparing models and predicting different scales.

There's more...

Remember, the choice of evaluation metric depends on the specific problem and business requirements. For example, if it is more costly to have a model that under-predicts than over-predicts, a metric that treats these two types of errors differently may be more appropriate. Other metrics, such as MAE, can also be used, depending on the problem. Evaluating a model using multiple metrics is always a good idea to gain a more comprehensive understanding of its performance.

Using callbacks – EarlyStopping

Callbacks in PyTorch Lightning are reusable components that allow you to inject custom behavior into various stages of the training, validation, and testing loops. They offer a way to encapsulate functionalities separate from the main training logic, providing a modular and extensible approach to manage auxiliary tasks such as logging metrics, saving checkpoints, early stopping, and more.

By defining a custom class that inherits from PyTorch Lightning's base `Callback` class, you can override specific methods corresponding to different points in the training process, such as `on_epoch_start` or `on_batch_end`. When a trainer is initialized with one or more of these callback objects, the defined behavior is automatically executed at the corresponding stage of the training process. This makes callbacks powerful tools for organizing the training pipeline, adding flexibility without cluttering the main training code.

Getting ready

After defining and training the LSTM model, as described in the previous section, we can further enhance the training process by incorporating a technique called early stopping. This is used to avoid overfitting by halting the training process when a specified metric stops improving. For this purpose, PyTorch Lightning provides an early stopping callback, which we'll be integrating into our existing training code.

How to do it...

To apply early stopping, we'll need to modify our existing PyTorch Lightning `Trainer` by adding the `EarlyStopping` callback. Here's the code to do so:

```
import lightning.pytorch as pl
from lightning.pytorch.callbacks import EarlyStopping

early_stop_callback = EarlyStopping(
    monitor="val_loss",
    min_delta=0.00,
    patience=3,
    verbose=False,
```

```
    mode="min"
)
trainer = pl.Trainer(max_epochs=100,
                    callbacks=[early_stop_callback])
trainer.fit(model, datamodule)
```

In this code snippet, `monitor` is set to the validation loss (`val_loss`), and the training process will stop if this value does not decrease by at least `min_delta` for `patience` consecutive validation epochs.

How it works...

Early stopping is a regularization technique that prevents overfitting in neural networks. It monitors a specified metric (in this case, the validation loss) and halts the training process when this metric stops improving.

Here's how it works in our LSTM model:

- **Monitoring**: Early stopping keeps track of the specified metric (`val_loss`) during the validation phase.

- **Patience**: If the monitored metric does not improve by at least `min_delta` for `patience` consecutive epochs, the training process is halted.

- **Mode**: The `mode` parameter can be set to `min` or `max`, indicating whether the monitored metric should be minimized or maximized. In our case, we want to minimize the validation loss.

By stopping the training process early, we can save time and resources, and also potentially obtain a model that generalizes better to unseen data.

There's more...

Let's look at some further details:

- The early stopping callback is highly configurable, allowing you to tailor its behavior to specific requirements – for example, you can change the `patience` parameter to make the stopping criterion more or less strict

- Early stopping can be combined with other callbacks and techniques, such as model checkpointing, to create a robust and efficient training pipeline

- Utilizing early stopping appropriately can lead to models that perform better on unseen data as it prevents them from fitting too closely to the training data

This `EarlyStopping` callback integrates seamlessly with PyTorch Lightning and our existing LSTM model, demonstrating the extensibility and ease of use of PyTorch Lightning's callback system.

5

Global Forecasting Models

In this chapter, we explore various time series forecasting scenarios and learn how to handle them with deep learning. These scenarios include multi-step and multi-output forecasting tasks, and problems involving multiple time series. We'll cover each of these cases, explaining how to prepare your data, train appropriate neural network models, and validate them.

By the end of this chapter, you should be able to build deep learning forecasting models for different time series datasets. This includes hyperparameter optimization, which is an important stage in model development.

This chapter will guide you through the following recipes:

- Multi-step forecasting with multivariate time series
- Multi-step and multi-output forecasting with multivariate time series
- Preparing multiple time series for a global model
- Training a global LSTM with multiple time series
- Global forecasting models for seasonal time series
- Hyperparameter optimization using Ray Tune

Technical requirements

This chapter requires the following Python libraries:

- numpy (1.26.3)
- pandas (2.0.3)
- scikit-learn (1.4.0)
- sktime (0.26.0)
- torch (2.2.0)

- `pytorch-forecasting` (1.0.0)
- `pytorch-lightning` (2.1.4)
- `gluonts` (0.14.2)
- `ray` (2.9.2)

You can install these libraries in one go using `pip`:

```
pip install -U pandas numpy scikit-learn sktime torch pytorch-
forecasting pytorch-lightning gluonts
```

The recipes in this chapter will follow a design philosophy based on PyTorch Lightning that provides a modular and flexible way of building and deploying PyTorch models. The code for this chapter can be found at the following GitHub URL: `https://github.com/PacktPublishing/Deep-Learning-for-Time-Series-Data-Cookbook`.

Multi-step forecasting with multivariate time series

So far, we've been working on forecasting the next value of a single variable of a time series. Forecasting the value of the next observation is referred to as one-step-ahead forecasting. In this recipe, we'll extend the models we developed in the previous chapter for multi-step-ahead forecasting.

Getting ready

Multi-step ahead forecasting is the process of forecasting several observations in advance. This task is important for reducing the long-term uncertainty of time series.

It turns out that much of the work we did before is also applicable to multi-step forecasting settings. The `TimeSeriesDataSet` class makes it extremely simple to extend the one-step-ahead problem to the multi-step case.

In this recipe, we'll set the forecasting horizon to 7 and the number of lags to `14`:

```
N_LAGS = 7
HORIZON = 14
```

In practice, this means the predictive task is to forecast the next 7 days of solar radiation based on the past 14 days of data.

How to do it...

For multi-step ahead forecasting problems, two things need to be changed:

- One is the output dimension of the neural network model. Instead of 1 (which represents the next value), the output dimension needs to match the number of prediction steps. This is done in the output_dim variable of the model.

- The prediction length of the data module needs to be set to the forecasting horizon. This is done in the max_prediction_length parameter of the TimeSeriesDataSet class.

These two inputs can be passed to the data and model modules as follows:

```
datamodule = MultivariateSeriesDataModule(data=mvtseries,
    n_lags=N_LAGS,
    horizon=HORIZON,
    batch_size=32,
    test_size=0.3)

model = MultivariateLSTM(input_dim=n_vars,
    hidden_dim=32,
    num_layers=1,
    output_dim=HORIZON)
```

Then, the training and testing of the model remain the same:

```
early_stop_callback = EarlyStopping(monitor="val_loss",
    min_delta=1e-4,
    patience=10,
    verbose=False,
    mode="min")

trainer = Trainer(max_epochs=20, callbacks=[early_stop_callback])
trainer.fit(model, datamodule)

trainer.test(model=model, datamodule=datamodule)
```

We trained the model for 20 epochs and then evaluated it in the test set, which is retrieved using the data loader defined in the data module.

How it works...

Traditional supervised machine learning models usually learn from a one-dimensional target variable. In forecasting problems, this variable can be, for example, the value of the time series in the next period. However, multi-step-ahead forecasting problems require the prediction of several values at each time. Deep learning models are naturally multi-output algorithms. So, they can handle several target variables with a single model.

Other approaches for multi-step-ahead forecasting often involve creating several models or reusing the same model for different horizons. However, a multi-output approach is preferable because it enables the capture of dependencies among different horizons. This can lead to better forecasting performance, as has been documented in articles such as the following: Taieb, Souhaib Ben, et al., *A review and comparison of strategies for multi-step ahead time series forecasting based on the NN5 forecasting competition*. Expert systems with applications 39.8 (2012): 7067-7083

There's more...

There are other ways we could use a deep learning neural network for multi-step-ahead forecasting. Three other popular methods are as follows:

- `Recursive`: Training a neural network for one-step-ahead forecasting and using it recursively to get multi-step forecasts

- `Direct`: Training one neural network for each forecasting horizon

- `DirRec`: Training one neural network for each forecasting horizon and feeding the previous forecast as input to the next one

Multi-step and multi-output forecasting with multivariate time series

In this recipe, we'll extend the LSTM model to predict multiple steps of several variables of a multivariate time series.

Getting ready

So far, in this chapter, we have built several models to forecast the future of one particular variable, solar radiation. We used the extra variables in the time series to improve the modeling of solar radiation.

Yet, when working with multivariate time series, we're often interested in forecasting several variables, not just one. A common example occurs when dealing with spatiotemporal data. A spatiotemporal dataset is a particular case of a multivariate time series where a real-world process is observed in different locations. In this type of dataset, the goal is to forecast the future values of all these locations.

Again, we can leverage the fact that neural networks are multi-output algorithms to handle multiple target variables in a single model.

In this recipe, we'll work with the solar radiation dataset, as in previous ones. However, our goal is to forecast the future values of three variables—solar radiation, vapor pressure, and air temperature:

```
N_LAGS = 14
HORIZON = 7
TARGET = ['Incoming Solar', 'Air Temp', 'Vapor Pressure']

mvtseries = pd.read_csv('assets/daily_multivariate_timeseries.csv',
    parse_dates=['datetime'],
    index_col='datetime')
```

Regarding data preparation, the process is similar to what we did before. The difference is that we set the target variable (TARGET) to the preceding list of variables instead of just solar radiation. The TimeSeriesDataSet class and the data module handle all the preprocessing and data sharing for us.

How to do it...

We start by tweaking the data module to handle multiple target variables. In the following code, we make the necessary changes. Let's start by defining the constructor of the module:

```
class MultivariateSeriesDataModule(pl.LightningDataModule):
    def __init__(
            self,
            data: pd.DataFrame,
            target_variables: List[str],
            n_lags: int,
            horizon: int,
            test_size: float = 0.2,
            batch_size: int = 16,
    ):
        super().__init__()
        self.data = data
        self.batch_size = batch_size
        self.test_size = test_size
        self.n_lags = n_lags
        self.horizon = horizon
        self.target_variables = target_variables
        self.target_scaler = {k: MinMaxScaler()
            for k in target_variables}
        self.feature_names = [col for col in data.columns
            if col not in self.target_variables]
```

```
        self.training = None
        self.validation = None
        self.test = None
        self.predict_set = None
        self.setup()
```

The constructor contains a new argument, `target_variables`, which we use to pass the list of target variables. Besides that, we also make a small change to the `self.target_scaler` attribute, which is now a dictionary object that contains a scaler for each target variable. Then, we build the `setup()` method as follows:

```
def setup(self, stage=None):
    self.preprocess_data()
    train_indices, val_indices, test_indices = self.split_data()

    train_df = self.data.loc
        [self.data["time_index"].isin(train_indices)]
    val_df = self.data.loc[self.data["time_index"].isin(val_indices)]
    test_df = self.data.loc
        [self.data["time_index"].isin(test_indices)]

    for c in self.target_variables:
        self.target_scaler[c].fit(train_df[[c]])

    self.scale_target(train_df, train_df.index)
    self.scale_target(val_df, val_df.index)
    self.scale_target(test_df, test_df.index)

    self.training = TimeSeriesDataSet(
        train_df,
        time_idx="time_index",
        target=self.target_variables,
        group_ids=["group_id"],
        max_encoder_length=self.n_lags,
        max_prediction_length=self.horizon,
        time_varying_unknown_reals=self.feature_names +
            self.target_variables,
        scalers={name: MinMaxScaler() for name in self.feature_names},
    )
    self.validation = TimeSeriesDataSet.from_dataset
        (self.training, val_df)
    self.test = TimeSeriesDataSet.from_dataset(self.training, test_df)
```

```
        self.predict_set = TimeSeriesDataSet.from_dataset(
            self.training, self.data, predict=True
        )
```

The main differences from the previous recipe are the following. We pass the list of target variables to the target input of the `TimeSeriesDataSet` class. The scaling process of the target variables is also changed to a `for` loop that iterates over each target variable.

We also update the model module to process multiple target variables. Let's start with the constructor and `forward()` method:

```
class MultiOutputLSTM(LightningModule):
    def __init__(self, input_dim, hidden_dim, num_layers,
        horizon, n_output):
        super().__init__()
        self.n_output = n_output
        self.horizon = horizon
        self.hidden_dim = hidden_dim
        self.input_dim = input_dim
        self.output_dim = int(self.n_output * self.horizon)
        self.lstm = nn.LSTM(input_dim, hidden_dim,
            num_layers, batch_first=True)
        self.fc = nn.Linear(hidden_dim, self.output_dim)

    def forward(self, x):
        h0 = torch.zeros(self.lstm.num_layers, x.size(0),
            self.hidden_dim).to(self.device)
        c0 = torch.zeros(self.lstm.num_layers, x.size(0),
            self.hidden_dim).to(self.device)
        out, _ = self.lstm(x, (h0, c0))
        out = self.fc(out[:, -1, :])
        return out
```

The `forward()` method is the same as in the previous chapter. We store a few more elements in the constructor, such as the forecasting horizon (`self.horizon`), as they are necessary in the following steps:

```
    def training_step(self, batch, batch_idx):
        x, y = batch
        y_pred = self(x['encoder_cont'])
        y_pred = y_pred.unsqueeze(-1).view(-1, self.horizon,
            self.n_output)
        y_pred = [y_pred[:, :, i] for i in range(self.n_output)]
        loss = [F.mse_loss(y_pred[i],
```

```
                    y[0][i]) for i in range(self.n_output)]
            loss = torch.mean(torch.stack(loss))
            self.log('train_loss', loss)
            return loss

    def test_step(self, batch, batch_idx):
        x, y = batch
        y_pred = self(x['encoder_cont'])
        y_pred = y_pred.unsqueeze(-1).view(-1, self.horizon,
            self.n_output)
        y_pred = [y_pred[:, :, i] for i in range(self.n_output)]
        loss = [F.mse_loss(y_pred[i],
            y[0][i]) for i in range(self.n_output)]
        loss = torch.mean(torch.stack(loss))
        self.log('test_loss', loss)

    def predict_step(self, batch, batch_idx, dataloader_idx=0):
        x, y = batch
        y_pred = self(x['encoder_cont'])
        y_pred = y_pred.unsqueeze(-1).view(-1,
            self.horizon, self.n_output)
        y_pred = [y_pred[:, :, i] for i in range(self.n_output)]
        return y_pred

    def configure_optimizers(self):
        return torch.optim.Adam(self.parameters(), lr=0.001)
```

Let's break down the preceding code:

- We add an `n_output` parameter to the constructor, which details the number of target variables (in this example, 3)

- The output dimension is set to the number of target variables times the forecasting horizon (`self.n_output * self.horizon`)

- When processing the data in the training and testing steps, the predictions are reshaped into the appropriate format (batch size, horizon, and number of variables)

- We compute the MSE loss for each target variable, and then take the average across them using `torch.mean(torch.stack(loss))`

Then, the remaining processes are similar to what we did in previous recipes based on PyTorch Lightning:

```
model = MultiOutputLSTM(input_dim=n_vars,
    hidden_dim=32,
    num_layers=1,
```

```
        horizon=HORIZON,
        n_vars=len(TARGET))

datamodule = MultivariateSeriesDataModule(data=mvtseries,
        n_lags=N_LAGS,
        horizon=HORIZON,
        target_variables=TARGET)

early_stop_callback = EarlyStopping(monitor="val_loss",
        min_delta=1e-4,
        patience=10,
        verbose=False,
        mode="min")

trainer = pl.Trainer(max_epochs=20, callbacks=[early_stop_callback])
trainer.fit(model, datamodule)
trainer.test(model=model, datamodule=datamodule)
forecasts = trainer.predict(model=model, datamodule=datamodule)
```

How it works...

The modeling approach used in this recipe follows the idea of **Vector Auto-Regression** (**VAR**). VAR works by modeling the future value of the variables of a multivariate time series as a function of the past values of all these variables. Predicting multiple variables may be relevant in several scenarios, such as spatiotemporal forecasting.

In this recipe, we adapted the VAR principle to a deep learning context, specifically through the use of LSTM networks. Unlike traditional VAR models that linearly project future values based on past observations, our deep learning model captures nonlinear relationships and temporal dependencies across multiple time steps and variables.

To compute the loss() function of our model—essential for training and evaluating its performance—we had to perform some changes in the training_step() and test_step() methods. After the network generates predictions, we segment the output by variable. This segmentation allows us to calculate the MSE loss for each variable separately. These individual losses are then aggregated to form a composite loss measure, which guides the optimization process of the model.

Preparing multiple time series for a global model

Now, it is time to move on to the type of time series problems that involve multiple time series. In this recipe, we will learn the fundamentals of global forecasting models and how they work. We'll also explore how to prepare a dataset that contains multiple time series for forecasting. Again, we leverage the capabilities of the TimeSeriesDataSet and DataModule classes to help us do this.

Getting ready

So far, we've been working with time series problems involving a single dataset. Now, we'll learn about global forecasting models, including the following:

- **Transitioning from local to global models**: Initially, our work with time series forecasting focused on single datasets, where models predict future values based on historical data of one series. These so-called local models are tailored to specific time series, whereas global models involve handling multiple related time series and capturing relevant information across them.

- **Leveraging neural networks**: Neural networks excel in data-rich environments, making them ideal for global forecasting. This is particularly effective in domains such as retail, where understanding the relationships across different product sales can lead to more accurate forecasts.

We'll learn how to build a global forecasting model using a dataset concerning transportation called **NN5**. This dataset was used in a previous forecasting competition and includes 111 different time series.

The data is available in the `gluonts` Python library and can be loaded as follows:

```
N_LAGS = 7
HORIZON = 7
from gluonts.dataset.repository.datasets import get_dataset
dataset = get_dataset('nn5_daily_without_missing', regenerate=False)
```

Here's a sample of five of the time series in the dataset:

	Time Series id: 0	Time Series id: 1	Time Series id: 2	Time Series id: 3	Time Series id: 4
1996-03-18	13.410000	11.550000	5.640000	13.180000	9.780000
1996-03-19	14.730000	13.590000	14.400000	8.450000	10.810000
1996-03-20	20.559999	15.040000	24.420000	19.520000	21.610001
1996-03-21	34.709999	21.570000	28.780001	28.879999	38.520000
1996-03-22	26.629999	19.440001	20.620001	19.469999	24.740000
1996-03-23	16.610001	0.000000	13.800000	0.000000	12.330000
1996-03-24	15.320000	9.720000	11.540000	7.360000	13.000000
1996-03-25	11.610000	12.240000	10.740000	10.830000	11.040000

Figure 5.1: Sample of the NN5 time series dataset

The original source of this dataset is at the following link: https://zenodo.org/records/3889750.

Now, let's build a `DataModule` class to handle the data preprocessing steps.

How to do it...

We'll build a `LightningDataModule` class that handles a dataset with multiple time series and passes them to a model. Here's what it looks like starting with the constructor:

```
import lightning.pytorch as pl

class GlobalDataModule(pl.LightningDataModule):
    def __init__(self,
                 data,
                 n_lags: int,
                 horizon: int,
                 test_size: float,
                 batch_size: int):
        super().__init__()
        self.data = data
        self.batch_size = batch_size
        self.test_size = test_size
        self.n_lags = n_lags
        self.horizon = horizon
        self.training = None
        self.validation = None
        self.test = None
        self.predict_set = None
        self.target_scaler = LocalScaler()
```

Essentially, we store the necessary elements for training and using the model. This includes a `self.target_scaler` attribute based on a `LocalScaler` class.

The main method of the `LocalScaler` class is `transform()`:

```
def transform(self, df: pd.DataFrame):
    df = df.copy()
    df["value"] = LogTransformation.transform(df["value"])
    df_g = df.groupby("group_id")
    scaled_df_l = []
    for g, df_ in df_g:
        df_[["value"]] = self.scalers[g].transform(df_[["value"]])

        scaled_df_l.append(df_)

    scaled_df = pd.concat(scaled_df_l)
    scaled_df = scaled_df.sort_index()
    return scaled_df
```

This method applies two preprocessing operations to the dataset:

- A log transformation to stabilize the variance of the time series

- Standardization of each time series in the dataset

You can extend this class to include any transformation that you need to perform on your dataset. The complete implementation of the `LocalScaler` class is available on the GitHub repository.

Then, we preprocess the data in the `setup()` function:

```
def setup(self, stage=None):
    data_list = list(self.data.train)
    data_list = [pd.Series(ts['target'],
        index=pd.date_range(start=ts['start'].to_timestamp(),
        freq=ts['start'].freq,
        periods=len(ts['target'])))
        for ts in data_list]

    tseries_df = pd.concat(data_list, axis=1)
    tseries_df['time_index'] = np.arange(tseries_df.shape[0])
    ts_df = tseries_df.melt('time_index')
    ts_df = ts_df.rename(columns={'variable': 'group_id'})
    unique_times = ts_df['time_index'].sort_values().unique()
    tr_ind, ts_ind = \
        train_test_split(unique_times,
            test_size=self.test_size,
            shuffle=False)

    tr_ind, vl_ind = \
        train_test_split(tr_ind,
            test_size=0.1,
            shuffle=False)

    training_df = ts_df.loc[ts_df['time_index'].isin(tr_ind), :]
    validation_df = ts_df.loc[ts_df['time_index'].isin(vl_ind), :]
    test_df = ts_df.loc[ts_df['time_index'].isin(ts_ind), :]
    self.target_scaler.fit(training_df)
    training_df = self.target_scaler.transform(training_df)
    validation_df = self.target_scaler.transform(validation_df)
    test_df = self.target_scaler.transform(test_df)

    self.training = TimeSeriesDataSet(
        data=training_df,
        time_idx='time_index',
```

```
            target='value',
            group_ids=['group_id'],
            max_encoder_length=self.n_lags,
            max_prediction_length=self.horizon,
            time_varying_unknown_reals=['value'],
        )

        self.validation = TimeSeriesDataSet.from_dataset
            (self.training, validation_df)
        self.test = TimeSeriesDataSet.from_dataset(self.training, test_df)
        self.predict_set = TimeSeriesDataSet.from_dataset
            (self.training, ts_df, predict=True)
```

In the preceding code, we split the data into training, validation, testing, and prediction sets and set up the respective `TimeSeriesDataSet` instances. Finally, the data loaders are similar to what we've done in previous recipes:

```
    def train_dataloader(self):
        return self.training.to_dataloader(batch_size=self.batch_size,
            shuffle=False)

    def val_dataloader(self):
        return self.validation.to_dataloader
            (batch_size=self.batch_size, shuffle=False)

    def test_dataloader(self):
        return self.test.to_dataloader(batch_size=self.batch_size,
            shuffle=False)

    def predict_dataloader(self):
        return self.predict_set.to_dataloader(batch_size=1,
            shuffle=False)
```

We can call the data module as follows:

```
datamodule = GlobalDataModule(data=dataset,
    n_lags=N_LAGS,
    horizon=HORIZON,
    test_size=0.2,
    batch_size=1)
```

Using this module, each individual series in the dataset will be processed in such a way as to use the last N_LAGS values to predict the next HORIZON observations.

How it works...

Global methods are trained on multiple time series. The idea is that there are common patterns across the different time series. So, a neural network can use observations from these series to train better models.

In the preceding section, we retrieved a dataset involving several time series from the `gluonts` Python library via the `get_dataset()` function. The process of preparing a dataset that contains multiple time series for supervised learning is similar to what we did before. The key input to the `TimeSeriesDataSet` instance is the `group_id` variable that details the entity to which each observation belongs.

The main work happens in the `setup()` method. First, we transform the dataset into a `pandas` DataFrame with a long format. Here's a sample of this data:

time_index	index	group_id	value
0	1996-03-18	Time Series id: 0	13.407029
1	1996-03-19	Time Series id: 0	14.725057
2	1996-03-20	Time Series id: 0	20.564058
3	1996-03-21	Time Series id: 0	34.708050
4	1996-03-22	Time Series id: 0	26.629820
730	1998-03-18	Time Series id: 110	19.108364
731	1998-03-19	Time Series id: 110	25.512888
732	1998-03-20	Time Series id: 110	22.027880
733	1998-03-21	Time Series id: 110	10.678590
734	1998-03-22	Time Series id: 110	7.417149

Figure 5.2: Sample of the NN5 time series dataset in a long format

In this case, the `group_id` column is not constant and details which time series the observation refers to. Since each time series is univariate, there's a single numeric variable called `value`.

Training a global LSTM with multiple time series

In the previous recipe, we learned how to prepare datasets with multiple time series for supervised learning with a global forecasting model. In this recipe, we continue this topic and describe how to train a global LSTM neural network for forecasting.

Getting ready

We'll continue with the same data module we used in the previous recipe:

```
N_LAGS = 7
HORIZON = 7

from gluonts.dataset.repository.datasets import get_dataset, dataset_
names

dataset = get_dataset('nn5_daily_without_missing', regenerate=False)

datamodule = GlobalDataModule(data=dataset,
    n_lags=N_LAGS,
    horizon=HORIZON,
    batch_size=32,
    test_size=0.3)
```

Let's see how to create an LSTM module to handle a data module with multiple time series.

How to do it...

We create a `LightningModule` class that contains the implementation of the LSTM. First, let's look at the class constructor and the `forward()` method:

```
class GlobalLSTM(pl.LightningModule):
    def __init__(self, input_dim, hidden_dim, num_layers, output_dim):
        super().__init__()
        self.hidden_dim = hidden_dim
        self.lstm = nn.LSTM(input_dim, hidden_dim, num_layers,
            batch_first=True)
        self.fc = nn.Linear(hidden_dim, output_dim)

    def forward(self, x):
        h0 = torch.zeros(self.lstm.num_layers, x.size(0),
            self.hidden_dim).to(self.device)
        c0 = torch.zeros(self.lstm.num_layers, x.size(0),
            self.hidden_dim).to(self.device)
```

```
        out, _ = self.lstm(x, (h0, c0))
        out = self.fc(out[:, -1, :])
        return out
```

The logic of the neural network is similar to what we've done for a dataset with a single time series. This is also true for the remaining methods:

```
    def training_step(self, batch, batch_idx):
        x, y = batch
        y_pred = self(x['encoder_cont'])
        loss = F.mse_loss(y_pred, y[0])
        self.log('train_loss', loss)
        return loss

    def validation_step(self, batch, batch_idx):
        x, y = batch
        y_pred = self(x['encoder_cont'])
        loss = F.mse_loss(y_pred, y[0])
        self.log('val_loss', loss)
        return loss

    def test_step(self, batch, batch_idx):
        x, y = batch
        y_pred = self(x['encoder_cont'])
        loss = F.mse_loss(y_pred, y[0])
        self.log('test_loss', loss)

    def predict_step(self, batch, batch_idx, dataloader_idx=0):
        x, y = batch
        y_pred = self(x['encoder_cont'])
        return y_pred

    def configure_optimizers(self):
        return torch.optim.Adam(self.parameters(), lr=0.01)
```

Next, we can call the model and train it as follows:

```
model = GlobalLSTM(input_dim=1,
    hidden_dim=32,
    num_layers=1,
    output_dim=HORIZON)

early_stop_callback = EarlyStopping(monitor="val_loss",
    min_delta=1e-4,
```

```
        patience=10,
        verbose=False,
        mode="min")

trainer = pl.Trainer(max_epochs=20, callbacks=[early_stop_callback])
trainer.fit(model, datamodule)
trainer.test(model=model, datamodule=datamodule)
forecasts = trainer.predict(model=model, datamodule=datamodule)
```

Using the PyTorch Lightning design, the training, testing, and prediction steps are similar to what we did in other recipes based on this framework.

How it works...

As you can see, the `LightningModule` class that contains the LSTM is identical to the one we built for a single multivariate time series. This class only deals with the part of the model definition, so no change is necessary. The main work is done during the data preprocessing stage. So, we only need to change the `setup()` method in the data module to reflect the necessary changes, which were explained in the previous recipe.

We transitioned from a local LSTM model, designed for forecasting a single time series, to a global LSTM model capable of handling multiple time series simultaneously. The main difference lies in how the data is prepared and presented to the model than changes in the neural network architecture itself. Both local and global models utilize the same underlying LSTM structure, characterized by its ability to process sequences of data and predict future values.

In a local LSTM setup, the model's input typically follows the structure [`batch_size, sequence_length, num_features`], with the output shaped to match the forecasting horizon, usually [`batch_size, horizon`]. This setup is straightforward as it deals with data from a single series.

Shifting to a global LSTM model, the approach to input and output configuration remains fundamentally the same in terms of dimensionality. However, the input now aggregates information across multiple time series. It increases the ability of the neural network to learn new patterns and dependencies not just within a single series but across several. Consequently, the output of a global LSTM model is designed to produce forecasts for multiple time series simultaneously, reflecting predictions across the entire dataset.

Global forecasting models for seasonal time series

This recipe shows how to extend a data module to include extra explanatory variables in a `TimeSeriesDataSet` class and a `DataModule` class. We'll use a particular case about seasonal time series.

Getting ready

We load the dataset that we used in the previous recipe:

```
N_LAGS = 7
HORIZON = 7
from gluonts.dataset.repository.datasets import get_dataset
dataset = get_dataset('nn5_daily_without_missing', regenerate=False)
```

This dataset contains time series with a daily granularity. Here, we'll model weekly seasonality using the Fourier series. Unlike what we did in the previous chapter (in the *Handling seasonality: seasonal dummies and Fourier series* recipe), we'll learn how to include these features using the TimeSeriesDataSet framework.

How to do it...

Here's the updated DataModule that includes the Fourier series. We only describe part of the setup() method for brevity. The remaining methods stay the same, and you can check them in the GitHub repository:

```
from sktime.transformations.series.fourier import FourierFeatures
def setup(self, stage=None):
    [...]

    fourier = FourierFeatures(sp_list=[7],
        fourier_terms_list=[2],
        keep_original_columns=False)

    fourier_features = fourier.fit_transform(ts_df['index'])

    ts_df = pd.concat
        ([ts_df, fourier_features], axis=1).drop('index', axis=1)

    [...]

    self.training = TimeSeriesDataSet(
        data=training_df,
        time_idx='time_index',
        target='value',
        group_ids=['group_id'],
        max_encoder_length=self.n_lags,
        max_prediction_length=self.horizon,
        time_varying_unknown_reals=['value'],
        time_varying_known_reals=['sin_7_1', 'cos_7_1',
```

```
                    'sin_7_2', 'cos_7_2']
    )
```

In the `setup()` method, we compute the `Fourier` terms using the date and time information of the dataset. This leads to four deterministic variables: `sin_7_1`, `cos_7_1`, `sin_7_2`, and `cos_7_2`. These are `Fourier` series that we use to model seasonality. After adding them to the dataset using `pd.concat([tseries_long, fourier_features], axis=1)`, we use the `time_varying_known_reals` argument to tell that these features vary over time but in a predictable way.

In the LSTM, we need to update the input dimension to 5 to reflect the number of variables in the dataset (the target variable plus four `Fourier` series). This is done as follows:

```
model = GlobalLSTM(input_dim=5,
        hidden_dim=32,
        num_layers=1,
        output_dim=HORIZON)


datamodule = GlobalDataModuleSeas(data=dataset,
        n_lags=N_LAGS,
        horizon=HORIZON,
        batch_size=128,
        test_size=0.3)

early_stop_callback = EarlyStopping(monitor="val_loss",
        min_delta=1e-4,
        patience=10,
        verbose=False,
        mode="min")

trainer = pl.Trainer(max_epochs=20, callbacks=[early_stop_callback])
trainer.fit(model, datamodule)
trainer.test(model=model, datamodule=datamodule)
forecasts = trainer.predict(model=model, datamodule=datamodule)
```

Again, the training and inference stages are similar to the previous recipe since the only differences here are in the data preprocessing stage handled by the data module.

How it works...

Modeling seasonality with the `Fourier` series involves enriching the dataset with extra variables derived from the Fourier transformation. This approach was implemented in the `setup()` method of the `DataModule` instance, where these variables were incorporated into the `TimeSeriesDataSet` objects.

`Fourier` series decomposition allows us to capture seasonality by breaking down complex periodic patterns into simpler, sinusoidal waves. Each component of the `Fourier` series corresponds to a different frequency, capturing different seasonal cycles within the time series data. This is particularly beneficial for neural networks for several reasons:

- **Feature engineering**: The `Fourier` series acts as automatic feature engineering, creating informative features that directly encode periodic behaviors. This can significantly improve the ability of the model to recognize and predict seasonal patterns, even in complex or noisy data. Since Fourier features are added to the input data, they can work with any neural network algorithm or architecture.

- **Flexibility in modeling complex seasonality**: Real-world time series often exhibit multiple seasonal patterns (e.g., daily, weekly, or yearly). `Fourier` series can model these multiple seasonality levels simultaneously, providing a more nuanced representation of the data that can be difficult to achieve with traditional seasonal decomposition methods.

- **Improved generalization**: By providing a clear, mathematical representation of seasonality, Fourier features help neural networks to generalize better from the observed data to unseen future periods. This reduces the risk of overfitting noise and anomalies in the data, focusing the model's learning on the underlying periodic trends.

There's more...

You can check the following URL to learn how to include extra categorical variables in the dataset (such as holidays): `https://pytorch-forecasting.readthedocs.io/en/stable/tutorials/stallion.html#Load-data`.

Hyperparameter optimization using Ray Tune

Neural networks have hyperparameters that define their structure and learning process. Hyperparameters include the learning rate or the number of hidden layers and units. Different hyperparameter values can affect the learning process and the accuracy of models. Incorrectly chosen values can result in underfitting or overfitting, which decreases the model's performance. So, it's important to optimize the value of hyperparameters to get the most out of deep learning models. In this recipe, we'll explore how to do hyperparameter optimization using Ray Tune, including learning rate, regularization parameters, the number of hidden layers, and so on. The optimization of these parameters is very important to the performance of our models. More often than not, we face poor results in fitting neural network models simply due to poor selection of hyperparameters, which can lead to underfitting or overfitting unseen data.

Getting ready

Before we begin with hyperparameter optimization, we need to install Ray Tune, if it's not already installed. This can be done using the following command:

```
pip install -U 'ray[data,train,tune,serve]'
```

We will use the same data and LSTM model to optimize:

```
class GlobalDataModule(pl.LightningDataModule):
    ...


class GlobalLSTM(pl.LightningModule):
    ...


from ray.train.lightning import RayTrainReportCallback
from ray import tune
from ray.tune.schedulers import ASHAScheduler
from ray.train import RunConfig, ScalingConfig, CheckpointConfig
from ray.train.torch import TorchTrainer
```

In the preceding code, we also made all the necessary imports for this recipe.

How to do it...

Let's discuss how we can implement hyperparameter optimization using Ray Tune:

1. **Define the search space**: First, define the hyperparameter space you want to explore.

2. **Configure Ray Tune**: Initialize the Tune experiment with the desired settings, such as the number of trials, resources, and so on.

3. **Run the optimization**: Execute the experiment by passing the training function and the defined search space.

4. **Analyze the results**: Utilize Ray Tune's tools to analyze the results and identify the best hyperparameters.

Let's start by defining the search space:

```
search_space = {
    "hidden_dim": tune.choice([8, 16, 32]),
    "num_layers": tune.choice([1, 2]),
}
```

In this example, we only optimize two parameters: the number of hidden units and the number of layers in the LSTM neural network.

Then, we define the training cycle within a function:

```
def train_tune(config_hyper):
    hidden_dim = config_hyper["hidden_dim"]
    num_layers = config_hyper["num_layers"]
    model = GlobalLSTM(input_dim=1,
        hidden_dim=hidden_dim,
        output_dim=HORIZON,
        num_layers=num_layers)

    data_module = GlobalDataModule(dataset,
        n_lags=N_LAGS,
        horizon=HORIZON,
        batch_size=128,
        test_size=0.3)
    trainer = Trainer(callbacks=[RayTrainReportCallback()])
    trainer.fit(model, data_module)
```

After defining the training function, we pass it to a `TorchTrainer` class instance, along with the running configuration:

```
scaling_config = ScalingConfig(
    num_workers=2, use_gpu=False,
        resources_per_worker={"CPU": 1, "GPU": 0}
)

run_config = RunConfig(
    checkpoint_config=CheckpointConfig(
        num_to_keep=1,
        checkpoint_score_attribute="val_loss",
        checkpoint_score_order="min",
    ),
)

ray_trainer = TorchTrainer(
    train_tune,
    scaling_config=scaling_config,
    run_config=run_config,
)
```

In the `ScalingConfig` instance, we configured the computational environment, specifying whether the process should run on a GPU or CPU, the number of workers allocated, and the resources per worker. Meanwhile, the `RunConfig` instance is set to define the optimization process, including the metric that should be monitored throughout this process.

Then, we create a `Tuner` instance that combines this information:

```
scheduler = ASHAScheduler(max_t=30, grace_period=1, reduction_
factor=2)

tuner = tune.Tuner(
    ray_trainer,
    param_space={"train_loop_config": search_space},
    tune_config=tune.TuneConfig(
        metric="val_loss",
        mode="min",
        num_samples=10,
        scheduler=scheduler,
    ),
)
```

The `Tuner` instance requires a scheduler as one of its inputs. For this purpose, we utilize `ASHAScheduler`, which employs an **Asynchronous Successive Halving Algorithm** (**ASHA**) to efficiently allocate resources across various configurations. This method helps identify the most effective configuration by iteratively narrowing down the search space based on performance. Ultimately, by running this process, we can determine the optimal configuration:

```
results = tuner.fit()

best_model_conf = \
    results.get_best_result(metric='val_loss', mode='min')
```

In the preceding code, we get the configuration that minimizes the validation loss.

After selecting the best hyperparameters based on the validation loss, we can evaluate the model on the test set. Retrieve the model weights from the checkpoint and load the best hyperparameters from the tuning process. Then, use these parameters to load the model and evaluate it on the test data:

```
path = best_model_conf.get_best_checkpoint(metric='val_loss',
    mode='min').path
config = best_model_conf.config['train_loop_config']

best_model = \
    GlobalLSTM.load_from_checkpoint(checkpoint_path=f'{path}/
        checkpoint.ckpt',
```

```
        **config)

data_module = GlobalDataModule(dataset, n_lags=7, horizon=3)

trainer = Trainer(max_epochs=30)
trainer.test(best_model, datamodule=data_module)
```

In the preceding code, we load the model with the best configuration and test it in the test set defined in the `DataModule` class.

How it works...

Our hyperparameter optimization process involves defining a search space, configuring and executing the optimization, and analyzing the results. The code snippets shared in this section provide a step-by-step guide to integrating Ray Tune into any machine learning workflow, allowing us to explore and find the best hyperparameters for our model:

- The `search_space` dictionary defines the hyperparameter search space

- The `train_tune()` function encapsulates the training process, including model configuration, data preparation, and fitting

- The `ScalingConfig` class defines the computational environment for the optimization process, such as whether to run it on GPU or CPU

- The `RunConfig` class sets up how the optimization is done, such as the metric that should be tracked during this process

- The `ASHAScheduler` class is a scheduler that defines how to select from among different possible configurations

Ray Tune efficiently explores the hyperparameter space using various algorithms such as Random Search, Grid Search, or more advanced methods such as ASHA. It parallelizes trials to utilize available resources effectively, hence speeding up the search process.

There's more...

Ray Tune offers several additional features and advantages. It can integrate with other libraries, making it compatible with popular machine learning frameworks such as PyTorch, TensorFlow, and Scikit-Learn. Moreover, it provides advanced search algorithms such as Bayesian Optimization and Population-Based Training, giving users the flexibility to experiment with different optimization strategies. Lastly, Ray Tune supports visualization tools, allowing users to utilize TensorBoard or custom tools provided by Ray to effectively visualize and analyze the hyperparameter search process.

6

Advanced Deep Learning Architectures for Time Series Forecasting

In previous chapters, we've learned how to create forecasting models using different types of neural networks but, so far, we've worked with basic architectures such as feedforward neural networks or LSTMs. This chapter describes how to build forecasting models with state-of-the-art approaches such as DeepAR or Temporal Fusion Transformers. These have been developed by tech giants such as Google and Amazon and are available in different Python libraries. These advanced deep learning architectures are designed to tackle different types of forecasting problems.

We'll cover the following recipes:

- Interpretable forecasting with N-BEATS
- Optimizing the learning rate with PyTorch Forecasting
- Getting started with GluonTS
- Training a DeepAR model with GluonTS
- Training a Transformer with NeuralForecast
- Training a Temporal Fusion Transformer with GluonTS
- Training an Informer model with NeuralForecast
- Comparing different Transformers with NeuralForecast

By the end of this chapter, you'll be able to train state-of-the-art deep learning forecasting models.

Technical requirements

This chapter requires the following Python libraries:

- `numpy` (1.23.5)
- `pandas` (1.5.3)
- `scikit-learn` (1.2.1)
- `sktime` (0.24.0)
- `torch` (2.0.1)
- `pytorch-forecasting` (1.0.0)
- `pytorch-lightning` (2.1.0)
- `gluonts` (0.13.5)
- `neuralforecast` (1.6.0)

You can install these libraries in one go using `pip`:

```
pip install -U pandas numpy scikit-learn sktime torch pytorch-
forecasting pytorch-lightning gluonts neuralforecast
```

The code for this chapter can be found at the following GitHub URL: `https://github.com/PacktPublishing/Deep-Learning-for-Time-Series-Data-Cookbook`.

Interpretable forecasting with N-BEATS

This recipe introduces **Neural Basis Expansion Analysis for Interpretable Time Series Forecasting (N-BEATS)**, a deep learning method for forecasting problems. We'll show you how to train N-BEATS using PyTorch Forecasting and interpret its output.

Getting ready

N-BEATS is particularly designed for problems involving several univariate time series. So, we'll use the dataset introduced in the previous chapter (check, for example, the *Preparing multiple time series for a global model* recipe):

```
import numpy as np
import pandas as pd
from gluonts.dataset.repository.datasets import get_dataset
from pytorch_forecasting import TimeSeriesDataSet
import lightning.pytorch as pl
from sklearn.model_selection import train_test_split
```

```
dataset = get_dataset('nn5_daily_without_missing', regenerate=False)

N_LAGS = 7
HORIZON = 7

datamodule = GlobalDataModule(data=dataset,
    n_lags=N_LAGS,
    horizon=HORIZON)
```

Our goal is to forecast the next seven values (HORIZON) of a time series based on the past seven lags (N_LAGS).

How to do it...

Let's create the training, validation, and testing datasets:

1. We start by calling the setup() method in the GlobalDataModule class:

    ```
    datamodule.setup()
    ```

2. N-BEATS is available off-the-shelf in PyTorch Forecasting. You can define a model as follows:

    ```
    from pytorch_forecasting import NBeats

    model = NBeats.from_dataset(
        dataset=datamodule.training,
        stack_types=['trend', 'seasonality'],
        num_blocks=[3, 3],
        num_block_layers=[4, 4],
        widths=[256, 2048],
        sharing=[True],
        backcast_loss_ratio=1.0,
    )
    ```

    We create an NBeats instance using the from_dataset() method in the preceding code. The following parameters need to be defined:

*   dataset: The TimeSeriesDataSet instance that contains the training set.

*   stack_types: The mode you want to run N-BEATS on. A trend and seasonality type of stack enables the model to be interpretable, while a ['generic'] setup is usually more accurate.

*   num_blocks: A block is the cornerstone of the N-BEATS model. It contains a set of fully connected layers that model the time series.

- `num_block_layers`: The number of fully connected layers in each block.

- `widths`: The width of the fully connected layers in each block.

- `sharing`: A Boolean parameter that denotes whether the weights are shared blocks per stack. In the interpretable mode, this parameter should be set to `True`.

- `backcast_loss_ratio`: The relevance of the backcast loss in the model. Backcasting (predicting the input sample) is an important mechanism in the training of N-BEATS. This parameter balances the loss of the backcast with the loss of the forecast.

3. After creating the model, you can pass it on to a PyTorch Lightning `Trainer` to train it:

```
import lightning.pytorch as pl
from lightning.pytorch.callbacks import EarlyStopping

early_stop_callback = EarlyStopping(monitor="val_loss",
    min_delta=1e-4,
    patience=10,
    verbose=False,
    mode="min")

trainer = pl.Trainer(
    max_epochs=30,
    accelerator="auto",
    enable_model_summary=True,
    gradient_clip_val=0.01,
    callbacks=[early_stop_callback],
)
```

4. We also include an early stopping callback to guide the training process. The model is trained using the `fit()` method:

```
trainer.fit(
    model,
    train_dataloaders=datamodule.train_dataloader(),
    val_dataloaders=datamodule.val_dataloader(),
)
```

We pass the training data loader to train the model, and the validation data loader for early stopping.

5. After fitting a model, we can evaluate its testing performance and use it to make predictions. Before that, we need to load the model from the saved checkpoint:

```
best_model_path = trainer.checkpoint_callback.best_model_path
best_model = NBeats.load_from_checkpoint(best_model_path)
```

6. You can get the forecasts and respective true values from the test set as follows:

```
predictions = best_model.predict(datamodule.test.to_
dataloader(batch_size=1, shuffle=False))

actuals = torch.cat(
    [y[0] for x, y in iter(
        datamodule.test.to_dataloader(batch_size=1,
            shuffle=False))])
```

7. We estimate the forecasting performance as the average absolute difference between these two quantities (that is, the mean absolute error):

```
(actuals - predictions).abs().mean()
```

Depending on your device, you may need to convert the `predictions` object to a PyTorch tensor object using `predictions.cpu()` before computing the difference specified in the preceding code.

8. The workflow for forecasting new instances is also made quite simple by the data module:

```
forecasts = best_model.predict(datamodule.predict_dataloader())
```

Essentially, the data module gets the latest observations and passes them to the model, which makes the forecasts.

One of the most interesting aspects of N-BEATS is its interpretability components. These can be valuable for inspecting the forecasts, and the driver behind them:

9. We can break down the forecasts into different components and plot them using the `plot_interpretation()` method. To do that, we need to get the raw forecasts beforehand as follows:

```
raw_predictions = best_model.predict
    (datamodule.val_dataloader(),
    mode="raw",
    return_x=True)

best_model.plot_interpretation(x=raw_predictions[1],
    output=raw_predictions[0],
    idx=0)
```

In the preceding code, we call the plot for the first instance of the test set (idx=0). Here's what the plot looks like:

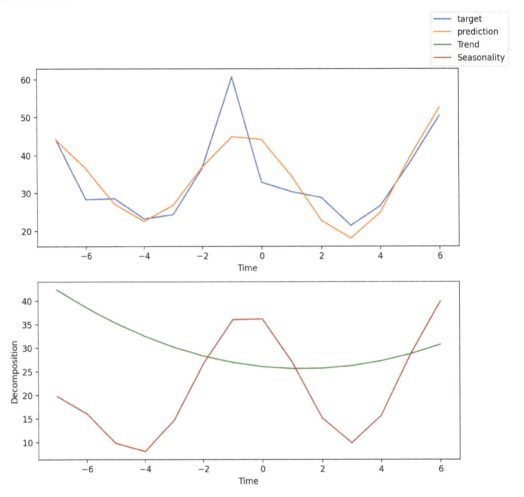

Figure 6.1: Breaking down the N-BEATS forecasts into different parts

The preceding figure shows the trend and seasonality components of the prediction.

How it works...

N-BEATS is based on two main components:

- A double stack of residual connections that involve forecasting and backcasting. Backcasting, in the context of N-BEATS, refers to reconstructing a time series's past values. It helps the model learn better data representations by forcing it to understand the time series structure in both directions.

- A deep stack of densely connected layers.

This combination leads to a model with both high forecasting accuracy and interpretability capabilities.

The workflow for training, evaluating, and using the model follows the framework provided by PyTorch Lightning. The data preparation logic is developed in the data module component, specifically within the `setup()` function. The modeling stage is created in two parts:

1. First, you define the N-BEATS model architecture. In this example, we use the `from_dataset()` method to create an `NBeats` instance based on the input data directly.

2. Then, the training process logic is defined in the `Trainer` instance, including any callback you might need.

Some callbacks, such as early stopping, save the best version of the model in a local file, which you can load after training.

It's important to note that the interpretation step, carried out with the `plot_interpretation` part, is a special feature of N-BEATS that helps practitioners understand the predictions made by the forecasting model. This can also aid in understanding the conditions in which the model is not applicable in practice.

N-BEATS is an important model to have in your forecasting arsenal. For example, in the M5 forecasting competition, which featured a set of demand time series, this model was used in many of the best solutions. You can see more details here: `https://www.sciencedirect.com/science/article/pii/S0169207021001874`.

There's more...

There are a few things you can do to maximize the potential of N-BEATS:

- You can check the PyTorch Forecasting library documentation to get a better sense of how to select the values of each parameter: `https://pytorch-forecasting.readthedocs.io/en/stable/api/pytorch_forecasting.models.nbeats.NBeats.html`.

- Another interesting method is NHiTS, which you can read about at the following link: `https://pytorch-forecasting.readthedocs.io/en/stable/api/pytorch_forecasting.models.nhits.NHiTS.html#pytorch_forecasting.models.nhits.NHiTS`. Its implementation from the PyTorch Forecasting library follows a similar logic to N-BEATS.

- As mentioned before, N-BEATS was developed to handle datasets involving several univariate time series. Yet, it was extended to handle exogenous variables by the N-BEATSx method, which is available in the `neuralforecast` library: `https://nixtla.github.io/neuralforecast/models.nbeatsx.html`.

Regarding interpretability, there are two other approaches you can take besides N-BEATS:

- Use model-agnostic explainers such as TimeShap: `https://github.com/feedzai/timeshap`.

- Use a **Temporal Fusion Transformer** (TFT) deep learning model, which also contains special interpretability operations. You can check an example at the following link: `https://pytorch-forecasting.readthedocs.io/en/stable/tutorials/stallion.html#Interpret-model`.

Optimizing the learning rate with PyTorch Forecasting

In this recipe, we show how to optimize the learning rate of a model based on PyTorch Forecasting.

Getting ready

The learning rate is a cornerstone parameter of all deep learning methods. As the name implies, it controls how quickly the learning process of the network is. In this recipe, we'll use the same setup as the previous recipe:

```
datamodule = GlobalDataModule(data=dataset,
    n_lags=N_LAGS,
    horizon=HORIZON,
    batch_size=32,
    test_size=0.2)

datamodule.setup()
```

We'll also use N-BEATS as an example. However, the process is identical for all models based on PyTorch Forecasting.

How to do it...

The optimization of the learning rate can be carried out using the `Tuner` class from PyTorch Lightning. Here is an example with N-BEATS:

```
from lightning.pytorch.tuner import Tuner
import lightning.pytorch as pl
from pytorch_forecasting import NBeats


trainer = pl.Trainer(accelerator="auto", gradient_clip_val=0.01)
tuner = Tuner(trainer)

model = NBeats.from_dataset(
    dataset=datamodule.training,
    stack_types=['trend', 'seasonality'],
    num_blocks=[3, 3],
    num_block_layers=[4, 4],
    widths=[256, 2048],
    sharing=[True],
    backcast_loss_ratio=1.0,
)
```

In the preceding code, we define a `Tuner` instance as a wrapper of a `Trainer` object. We also define an `NBeats` model as in the previous section. Then, we use the `lr_optim()` method to optimize the learning rate:

```
lr_optim = tuner.lr_find(model,
    train_dataloaders=datamodule.train_dataloader(),
    val_dataloaders=datamodule.val_dataloader(),
    min_lr=1e-5)
```

After this process, we can check which learning rate value is recommended and also inspect the results across the different tested values:

```
lr_optim.suggestion()

fig = lr_optim.plot(show=True, suggest=True)
fig.show()
```

We can visualize the results in the following figure:

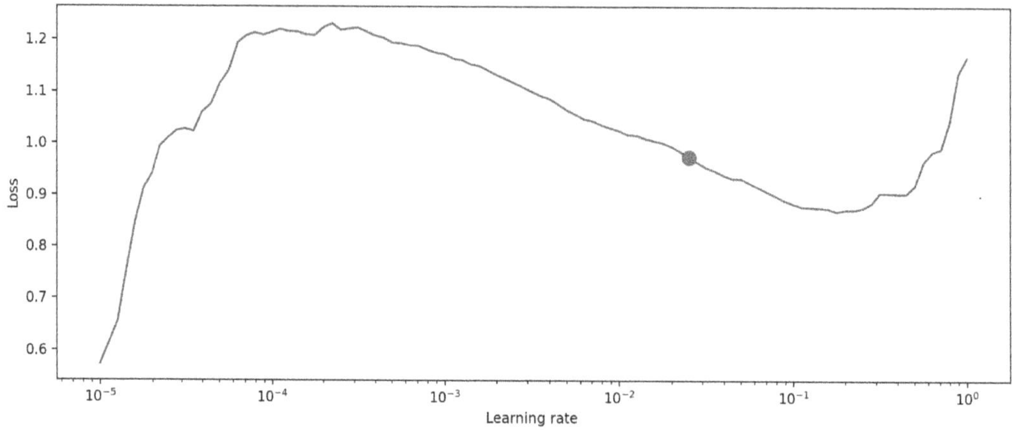

Figure 6.2: Learning rate optimization with PyTorch Forecasting

In this example, the suggested learning rate is about **0.05**.

How it works...

The `lr_find()` method from PyTorch Lightning works by testing different learning rate values and selecting one that minimizes the loss of the model. This method uses the training and validation data loaders to this effect.

It's important to select a sensible value for the learning rate because different values can lead to models with different performances. A large learning rate converges faster but to a sub-optimal solution. However, a small learning rate can take a prohibitively long time to converge.

After the optimization is done, you can create a model using the selected learning rate as we did in the previous recipe.

There's more...

You can learn more about how to get the most out of models such as N-BEATS in the *Tutorials* section of PyTorch Forecasting, which is available at the following link: `https://pytorch-forecasting.readthedocs.io/en/stable/tutorials.html`.

Getting started with GluonTS

GluonTS is a flexible and extensible toolkit for probabilistic time series modeling using PyTorch. The toolkit provides state-of-the-art deep learning architectures specifically designed for time series tasks and an array of utilities for time series data processing, model evaluation, and experimentation.

The main objective of this section is to introduce the essential components of the `gluonts` library, emphasizing its core functionalities, adaptability, and user-friendliness.

Getting ready

To begin our journey, ensure that `gluonts` is installed as well as its backend dependency, `pytorch`:

```
pip install gluonts pytorch
```

With the installations complete, we can now dive into the capabilities of `gluonts`.

How to do it...

We start by accessing a sample dataset provided by the library:

```
from gluonts.dataset.repository.datasets import get_dataset

dataset = get_dataset("nn5_daily_without_missing", regenerate=False)
```

This will load the `nn5_daily_without_missing` dataset, one of the datasets that `gluonts` offers for experimentation.

Its characteristics can be inspected after loading a dataset using the `get_dataset()` function. Each `dataset` object contains metadata that offers insights into the time series frequency, associated features, and other relevant attributes. You can learn a bit more about the dataset by checking the metadata as follows:

```
print(dataset.metadata)
```

To enhance time series data, `gluonts` provides a list of transformers. For instance, the `AddAgeFeature` data transformer adds an `age` feature to the dataset, representing the lifespan of each time series:

```
from gluonts.transform import AddAgeFeature

transformation_with_age = Chain([
    AddAgeFeature(output_field="age",
    target_field="target",
    pred_length=dataset.metadata.prediction_length)
])
```

```
transformed_train_with_age = TransformedDataset(dataset.train,
    transformation_with_age)
```

Data intended for training in gluonts is commonly denoted as a collection of dictionaries, each representing a time series accompanied by potential features:

```
training_data = list(dataset.train)
print(training_data[0])
```

One of the fundamental models in gluonts is the SimpleFeedForwardEstimator model. Here's its setup:

First, the estimator is initialized by determining the prediction length, context length (indicating the number of preceding time steps to consider), and the data frequency, among other parameters:

```
from gluonts.torch.model.simple_feedforward import
SimpleFeedForwardEstimator

estimator_with_age = SimpleFeedForwardEstimator(
    hidden_dimensions=[10],
    prediction_length=dataset.metadata.prediction_length,
    context_length=100,
    trainer_kwargs={'max_epochs': 100}
)
```

To train the model, simply invoke the train() method on the estimator supplying the training data:

```
predictor_with_age = estimator_with_age.train
    (transformed_train_with_age)
```

This process trains the model using the provided data, resulting in a predictor prepared for forecasting. Here's how we can get the prediction from the model:

```
forecast_it_with_age, ts_it_with_age = make_evaluation_predictions(
    dataset=dataset.test,
    predictor=predictor_with_age,
    num_samples=100,
)

forecasts_with_age = list(forecast_it_with_age)
tss_with_age = list(ts_it_with_age)

fig, ax = plt.subplots(2, 1, figsize=(10, 8), sharex=True)

ts_entry_with_age = tss_with_age[0]
ax[0].plot(ts_entry_with_age[-150:].to_timestamp())
```

```
forecasts_with_age[0].plot(show_label=True, ax=ax[0])
ax[0].set_title("Forecast with AddAgeFeature")
ax[0].legend()
```

In the preceding code, predictions can be generated with the `make_evaluation_predictions()` method, which can then be plotted against the actual values. Here's the plot with the forecasts and actual values:

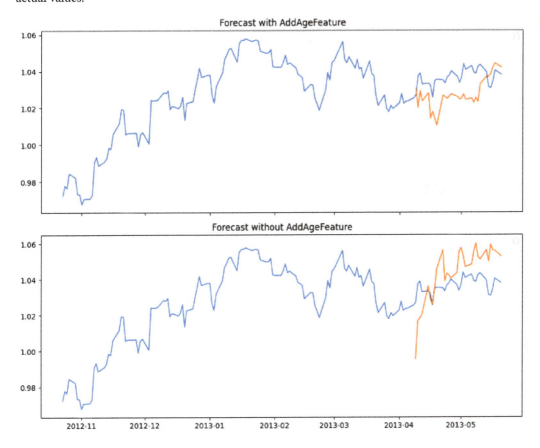

Figure 6.3: Comparative analysis of forecasts with and without AddAgeFeature

In the preceding figure, we show a comparative analysis of the forecasts with and without `AddAgeFeature`. The use of this feature improves forecasting accuracy, which indicates that it's an important variable in this dataset.

How it works...

GluonTS provides a series of built-in features that are useful for time series analysis and forecasting. For example, data transformers allow you to quickly build new features based on the raw dataset. As utilized in our experiment, the `AddAgeFeature` transformer appends an `age` attribute to each time series. The age of a time series can often provide relevant contextual information to the model. A good example where we can find it useful is when working with stocks, where older stocks might exhibit different volatility patterns than newer ones.

Training in GluonTS adopts a dictionary-based structure, where each dictionary corresponds to a time series and includes additional associated features. This structure makes it easier to append, modify, or remove features.

We tested a simple model in our experiment by using the `SimpleFeedForwardEstimator` model. We defined two instances of the model, one that was trained with the `AddAgeFeature` and one without. The model trained with the `age` feature showed better forecasting accuracy, as we can see in *Figure 6.3*. This improvement highlights the importance of feature engineering in time series analysis.

Training a DeepAR model with GluonTS

DeepAR is a state-of-the-art forecasting method that utilizes autoregressive recurrent networks to predict future values of time series data. Amazon introduced it; it was designed for forecasting tasks that can benefit from longer horizons, such as demand forecasting. The method is particularly powerful when there's a need to generate forecasts for multiple related time series.

Getting ready

We'll use the same dataset as in the previous recipe:

```
from gluonts.dataset.repository.datasets import get_dataset
dataset = get_dataset("nn5_daily_without_missing", regenerate=False)
```

Now, let's see how to build a DeepAR model with this data.

How to do it...

We start by formatting the data for training:

1. Let's do this by using the `ListDataset` data structure:

    ```
    from gluonts.dataset.common import ListDataset
    from gluonts.dataset.common import FieldName

    train_ds = ListDataset(
        [
    ```

```
        {FieldName.TARGET: entry["target"],
            FieldName.START: entry["start"]}
        for entry in dataset.train
    ],
    freq=dataset.metadata.freq,
)
```

2. Next, define the DeepAR estimator with the DeepAREstimator class, specifying parameters such as prediction_length (forecasting horizon), context_length (number of lags), and freq (sampling frequency):

```
from gluonts.torch.model.deepar import DeepAREstimator
N_LAGS=7
HORIZON=7

estimator = DeepAREstimator(
    prediction_length=HORIZON,
    context_length=N_LAGS,
    freq=dataset.metadata.freq,
    trainer_kwargs={"max_epochs": 100},
)
```

3. After defining the estimator, train the DeepAR model using the train() method:

```
predictor = estimator.train(train_ds)
```

4. With the trained model, make predictions on your test data and visualize the results:

```
forecast_it, ts_it = make_evaluation_predictions(
    dataset=dataset.test,
    predictor=predictor,
    num_samples=100,
)
forecasts = list(forecast_it)
tss = list(ts_it)

fig, ax = plt.subplots(1, 1, figsize=(10, 6))
ts_entry = tss[0]
ax.plot(ts_entry[-150:].to_timestamp())
forecasts[0].plot(show_label=True, ax=ax, intervals=())
ax.set_title("Forecast with DeepAR")
ax.legend()
plt.tight_layout()
plt.show()
```

Here's the plot of the predictions:

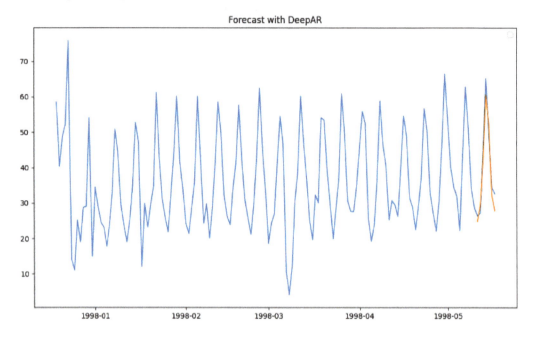

Figure 6.4: Comparison of predictions from DeepAR and the true values from our dataset

The model is able to match the true values closely.

How it works...

DeepAR uses an RNN architecture, often leveraging LSTM units or GRUs to model time series data.

The `context_length` parameter is crucial as it determines how many past observations the model will consider as its context when making a prediction. For instance, if you set `context_length` to 7, the model will use the last week's data to forecast future values.

Conversely, the `prediction_length` parameter defines the horizon, (i.e., how many steps the model should predict into the future). In the given code, we've used a horizon of one week.

DeepAR also stands out because of its ability to generate probabilistic forecasts. Instead of giving a single-point estimate, it provides a distribution over possible future values, allowing us to understand the uncertainty associated with our predictions.

Finally, when working with multiple related time series, DeepAR exploits the commonalities between the series to make more accurate predictions.

There's more...

DeepAR shines when the following conditions are met:

- You have multiple related time series; DeepAR can use information from all series to improve forecasts.

- Your data has seasonality or recurring patterns.

- You want to generate probabilistic forecasts, which predict a point estimate and provide uncertainty intervals. We will discuss uncertainty estimation in the next chapter.

You can train a single DeepAR model for a global dataset and generate forecasts for all time series in the dataset. On the other hand, for individual time series, DeepAR can be trained on each series separately, although this might be less efficient.

This model could be particularly useful for demand forecasting in retail, stock price prediction, and predicting web traffic, among other applications.

Training a Transformer model with NeuralForecast

Now, we turn our attention to Transformer architectures that have been driving recent advances in various fields of artificial intelligence. In this recipe, we will show you how to train a vanilla Transformer using the NeuralForecast Python library.

Getting ready

Transformers have become a dominant architecture in the deep learning community, especially for **natural language processing** (**NLP**) tasks. Transformers have been adopted for various tasks beyond NLP, including time series forecasting.

Unlike traditional models that analyze time series data point by point in sequence, Transformers evaluate all time steps simultaneously. This approach is similar to observing an entire timeline at once, determining the significance of each moment in relation to others for a specific point in time.

At the core of the Transformer architecture is the **attention mechanism**. This mechanism calculates a weighted sum of input values, or values from previous layers, according to their relevance to a specific input. Unlike RNNs, which process inputs step by step, this allows Transformers to consider all parts of an input sequence simultaneously.

Key components of the Transformer include the following:

- **Self-attention mechanism**: Computes the attention scores for all pairs of input values and then creates a weighted combination of these values based on these scores

- **Multi-head attention**: The model can focus on different input parts for different tasks or reasons by running multiple attention mechanisms in parallel

- **Position-wise feedforward networks**: These apply linear transformations to the output of the attention layer

- **Positional encoding**: Since the Transformer doesn't have any inherent sense of order, positional encodings are added to the input embeddings to provide the model with information about the position of each element in the sequence

Let's see how to train a Transformer model. In this recipe, we'll resort again to the dataset provided in the `gluonts` library. We'll use the Transformer implementation available in the NeuralForecast library. NeuralForecast is a Python library that contains the implementation of several neural networks that are focused on forecasting problems, including several Transformer architectures.

How to do it...

First, let's prepare the dataset for the Transformer model. Unlike sequence-to-sequence models such as RNNs, LSTMs, or GRUs, which process input sequences step by step, Transformers process entire sequences at once. Therefore, how we format and feed data into them can be slightly different:

1. Let's start by loading the dataset and the necessary libraries:

```
from gluonts.dataset.repository.datasets import get_dataset
import pandas as pd
from sklearn.preprocessing import StandardScaler
import matplotlib.pyplot as plt

from neuralforecast.core import NeuralForecast
from neuralforecast.models import VanillaTransformer

dataset = get_dataset("nn5_daily_without_missing",
regenerate=False)

N_LAGS = 7
HORIZON = 7
```

2. Next, convert the dataset into a pandas DataFrame and standardize it. Recall that standardization is key for any deep learning model fitting:

```
data_list = list(dataset.train)

data_list = [
    pd.Series(
        ds["target"],
        index=pd.date_range(
```

```
            start=ds["start"].to_timestamp(),
            freq=ds["start"].freq,
            periods=len(ds["target"]),
        ),
    )
    for ds in data_list
]

tseries_df = pd.concat(data_list, axis=1)
tseries_df[tseries_df.columns] =
    \StandardScaler().fit_transform(tseries_df)
tseries_df = tseries_df.reset_index()

df = tseries_df.melt("index")
df.columns = ["ds", "unique_id", "y"]
df["ds"] = pd.to_datetime(df["ds"])
```

3. With the data ready, we'll train a Transformer model. Unlike the DeepAR model, which uses recurrent architectures, the Transformer will rely on its attention mechanisms to consider various parts of the time series when making predictions:

```
model = [
    VanillaTransformer(
        h=HORIZON,
        input_size=N_LAGS,
        max_steps=100,
        val_check_steps=5,
        early_stop_patience_steps=3,
    ),
]

nf = NeuralForecast(models=model, freq="D")

Y_df = df[df["unique_id"] == 0]
Y_train_df = Y_df.iloc[:-2*HORIZON]
Y_val_df = Y_df.iloc[-2*HORIZON:-HORIZON]
training_df = pd.concat([Y_train_df, Y_val_df])

nf.fit(df=training_df, val_size=HORIZON)
```

4.   Finally, visualize the forecast results:

```
forecasts = nf.predict()

Y_df = df[df["unique_id"] == 0]
Y_hat_df = forecasts[forecasts.index == 0].reset_index()

Y_hat_df = Y_test_df.merge(Y_hat_df, how="outer",
    on=["unique_id", "ds"])
plot_df = pd.
    concat([Y_train_df, Y_val_df, Y_hat_df]).set_index("ds")
plot_df = plot_df.iloc[-150:]

fig, ax = plt.subplots(1, 1, figsize=(20, 7))
plot_df[["y", "VanillaTransformer"]].plot(ax=ax, linewidth=2)

ax.set_title("First Time Series Forecast with Transformer",
fontsize=22)
ax.set_ylabel("Value", fontsize=20)
ax.set_xlabel("Timestamp [t]", fontsize=20)
ax.legend(prop={"size": 15})
ax.grid()

plt.show()
```

The following figure includes the Transformer forecasts and actual values of the time series:

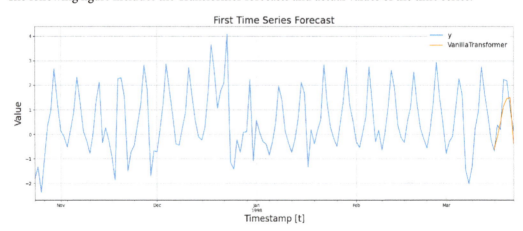

Figure 6.5: Comparison of Transformer predictions and our dataset's true values

How it works...

The `neuralforecast` library requires the data in a specific format. Each observation consists of three pieces of information: the timestamp, the time series identifier, and the corresponding value. We started this recipe by preparing the data in this format. The Transformer is implemented in the `VanillaTransformer` class. We set a few parameters, such as the forecasting horizon, number of training steps, or early stopping related inputs. You can check the complete list of the parameters at the following link: `https://nixtla.github.io/neuralforecast/models.vanillatransformer.html`. The training process is carried out by the `fit()` method in the `NeuralForecast` class instance.

Transformers process time series data by encoding the entire sequence using self-attention mechanisms, capturing dependencies without regard for their distance in the input sequence. This global perspective is particularly valuable when patterns or dependencies exist over long horizons or when the relevance of past data changes dynamically.

Positional encodings are used to ensure that the Transformer recognizes the order of data points. Without them, the model would treat the time series as a bag of values without any inherent order.

The multi-head attention mechanism allows the Transformer to focus on different time steps and features concurrently, making it especially powerful for complex time series with multiple interacting patterns and seasonality.

There's more...

Transformers can be highly effective for time series forecasting due to the following reasons:

- Their ability to capture long-term dependencies in the data
- Scalability with large datasets
- Flexibility in modeling both univariate and multivariate time series

Like other models, Transformers benefit from hyperparameter tuning, such as adjusting the number of attention heads, the size of the model (i.e., the number of layers and the dimension of the embeddings), and the learning rate.

Training a Temporal Fusion Transformer with GluonTS

The TFT is an attention-based architecture developed at Google. It has recurrent layers to learn temporal relationships at different scales combined with self-attention layers for interpretability. TFTs also use variable selection networks for feature selection, gating layers to suppress unnecessary components, and quantile loss as their loss function to produce forecasting intervals.

In this section, we delve into training and performing inference with a TFT model using the GluonTS framework.

Getting ready

Ensure you have the GluonTS library and PyTorch backend installed in your environment. We'll use the `nn5_daily_without_missing` dataset from the GluonTS repository as a working example:

```
from gluonts.dataset.common import ListDataset, FieldName
from gluonts.dataset.repository.datasets import get_dataset

dataset = get_dataset("nn5_daily_without_missing", regenerate=False)

train_ds = ListDataset(
    [
        {FieldName.TARGET: entry["target"], FieldName.START:
entry["start"]}
        for entry in dataset.train
    ],
    freq=dataset.metadata.freq,
)
```

In the following section, we'll train a TFT model with this dataset.

How to do it...

With the dataset in place, let's define the TFT estimator:

1. We'll begin with specifying hyperparameters such as the prediction length, context length, and training frequency:

    ```
    from gluonts.torch.model.tft import
    TemporalFusionTransformerEstimator

    N_LAGS = 7
    HORIZON = 7
    estimator = TemporalFusionTransformerEstimator(
        prediction_length=HORIZON,
        context_length=N_LAGS,
        freq=dataset.metadata.freq,
        trainer_kwargs={"max_epochs": 100},
    )
    ```

2. After defining the estimator, proceed to train the TFT model using the training dataset:

    ```
    predictor = estimator.train(train_ds)
    ```

3. Once trained, we can make predictions using the model. Utilize the make_evaluation_
    predictions() function to accomplish this:

```
from gluonts.evaluation import make_evaluation_predictions
forecast_it, ts_it = make_evaluation_predictions(
    dataset=dataset.test,
    predictor=predictor,
    num_samples=100,
)
```

4. Lastly, we can visualize our forecasts to understand the model's performance:

```
import matplotlib.pyplot as plt

ts_entry = tss[0]
ax.plot(ts_entry[-150:].to_timestamp())
forecasts[0].plot(show_label=True, ax=ax, intervals=())
ax.set_title("Forecast with Temporal Fusion Transformer")
ax.legend()

plt.tight_layout()
plt.show()
```

The following is a comparison of the predictions of the model with the actual values of the dataset.

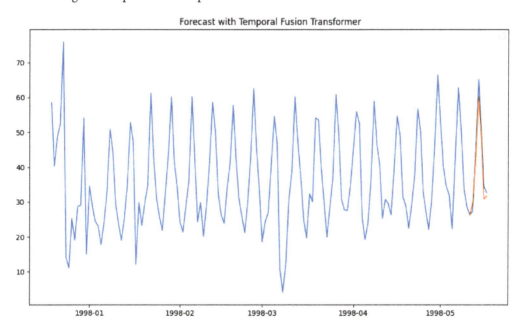

Figure 6.6: Comparison of predictions from a TFT and the true values from our dataset

How it works...

We use the implementation of TFT that is available in `gluonts`. The main parameters are the number of lags (context length) and forecasting horizon. You can also test different values for some of the parameters of the model, such as the number of attention heads (`num_heads`) or the size of the Transformer hidden states (`hidden_dim`). The full list of parameters can be found at the following link: `https://ts.gluon.ai/stable/api/gluonts/gluonts.torch.model.tft.estimator.html`.

TFT fits several use cases due to its complete feature set:

- **Temporal processing**: TFT addresses the challenge of integrating past observations and known future inputs through a sequence-to-sequence model, leveraging LSTM Encoder-Decoders.

- **Attention mechanism**: The model employs attention mechanisms, enabling it to dynamically assign importance to different time steps. This ensures that the model remains focused only on relevant historical data.

- **Gating mechanisms**: TFT architectures leverage gated residual networks that provide flexibility in the modeling process, adapting to the complexity of the data. This adaptability is important for handling diverse datasets, especially smaller or noisier ones.

- **Variable selection networks**: This component is used to determine the relevance of each covariate to the forecast. By weighting the input features' importance, it filters out noise and relies only on significant predictors.

- **Static covariate encoders**: TFT encodes static information into multiple context vectors, enriching the model's input.

- **Quantile prediction**: By forecasting various percentiles at each time step, TFT provides a range of possible outcomes.

- **Interpretable outputs**: Even though TFT is a deep learning model, it provides insights into feature importance, ensuring transparency in predictions.

There's more...

Beyond its architectural innovations, TFT's interpretability makes it a good choice when there is a need to explain how the predictions were produced. Components such as variable network selection and the temporal multi-head attention layer shed light on the importance of different inputs and temporal dynamics, making TFT not just a forecasting tool but also an analytical one.

Training an Informer model with NeuralForecast

In this recipe, we'll explore the `neuralforecast` Python library to train an Informer model, another Transformer-based deep learning approach for forecasting.

Getting ready

Informer is a Transformer method tailored for long-term forecasting – that is, predicting with a large forecasting horizon. The main difference relative to a vanilla Transformer is that Informer provides an improved self-attention mechanism, which significantly reduces the computational requirements to run the model and generate long-sequence predictions.

In this recipe, we'll show you how to train Informer using `neuralforecast`. We'll use the same dataset as in the previous recipes:

```
from gluonts.dataset.repository.datasets import import get_dataset

dataset = get_dataset('nn5_daily_without_missing')
```

How to do it...

This time, instead of creating `DataModule` to handle the data preprocessing, we'll use the typical workflow of the `neuralforecast`-based models:

1. We start by preparing the time series dataset in the specific format expected by the `neuralforecast` methods:

    ```
    import pandas as pd
    from sklearn.preprocessing import StandardScaler

    data_list = list(dataset.train)

    data_list = [pd.Series(ds['target'],
        index=pd.date_range(start=ds['start'].to_timestamp(),
            freq=ds['start'].freq,
            periods=len(ds['target'])))
        for ds in data_list]

    tseries_df = pd.concat(data_list, axis=1)
    tseries_df[tseries_df.columns] = \
        StandardScaler().fit_transform(tseries_df)
    tseries_df = tseries_df.reset_index()

    df = tseries_df.melt('index')
    df.columns = ['ds', 'unique_id', 'y']
    df['ds'] = pd.to_datetime(df['ds'])

    n_time = len(df.ds.unique())
    val_size = int(.2 * n_time)
    ```

2. We transformed the dataset into a pandas DataFrame with three columns: ds, unique_id, and y. These represent the timestamp, the ID of the time series, and the value of the corresponding time series, respectively. In the preceding code, we transformed all the time series into a common value range using a standard scaler from scikit-learn. We also set the validation set size to 20% of the size of the time series. Now, we can set up the Informer model as follows:

```
from neuralforecast.core import NeuralForecast
from neuralforecast.models import Informer

N_LAGS = 7
HORIZON = 7

model = [Informer(h=HORIZON,
    input_size=N_LAGS,
    max_steps=1000,
    val_check_steps=25,
    early_stop_patience_steps=10)]

nf = NeuralForecast(models=model, freq='D')
```

3. We set Informer with a context length (number of lags) of 7 to forecast the next 7 values at each time step. The number of training steps was set to 1000, and we also set up an early stopping mechanism to help the fitting process. These are only a subset of the parameters you can use to set up Informer. You can check out the following link for the complete list of parameters: https://nixtla.github.io/neuralforecast/models.informer.html. The model is passed on to a NeuralForecast class instance, where we also set the frequency of the time series to daily (the D keyword). Then, the training process is done as follows:

```
nf.fit(df=df, val_size=val_size)
```

4. The nf object is used to fit the model and can then be used to make predictions:

```
forecasts = nf.predict()
forecasts.head()
```

The forecasts are structured as a pandas DataFrame, so you can check a sample of the forecasts by using the head() method.

How it works...

The neuralforecast library provides yet another simple framework to train powerful models for time series problems. In this case, we handle the data logic outside of the framework because it handles the passing of the data to models internally.

The `NeuralForecast` class instance takes a list of models as input (in this case, with a single `Informer` instance) and takes care of the training process. This library can be a good solution if you want to use state-of-the-art models off the shelf. The limitation is that it is not as flexible as the base PyTorch ecosystem.

There's more...

In this recipe, we described how to train a particular Transformer model using `neuralforecast`. But, this library contains other Transformers that you can try, including the following:

- Vanilla Transformer
- TFT
- Autoformer
- PatchTST

You can check the complete list of models at the following link: `https://nixtla.github.io/neuralforecast/core.html`.

Comparing different Transformers with NeuralForecast

NeuralForecast contains several deep learning methods that you can use to tackle time series problems. In this recipe, we'll walk you through the process of comparing different Transformer-based models using `neuralforecast`.

Getting ready

We'll use the same dataset as in the previous recipe (the `df` object). We set the validation and test size to 10% of the data size each:

```
val_size = int(.1 * n_time)
test_size = int(.1 * n_time)
```

Now, let's see how to compare different models using `neuralforecast`.

How to do it...

We start by defining the models we want to compare. In this case, we'll compare an Informer model with a vanilla Transformer, which we set up as follows:

```
from neuralforecast.models import Informer, VanillaTransformer

models = [
    Informer(h=HORIZON,
```

```
        input_size=N_LAGS,
        max_steps=1000,
        val_check_steps=10,
        early_stop_patience_steps=15),
    VanillaTransformer(h=HORIZON,
        input_size=N_LAGS,
        max_steps=1000,
        val_check_steps=10,
        early_stop_patience_steps=15),
]
```

The training parameters are set equally for each model. We can use the `NeuralForecast` class to compare different models using the `cross_validation()` method as follows:

```
from neuralforecast.core import NeuralForecast

nf = NeuralForecast(
    models=models,
    freq='D')

cv = nf.cross_validation(df=df,
    val_size=val_size,
    test_size=test_size,
    n_windows=None)
```

The `cv` object is the result of the comparison. Here's a sample of the forecasts of each model in a particular time series:

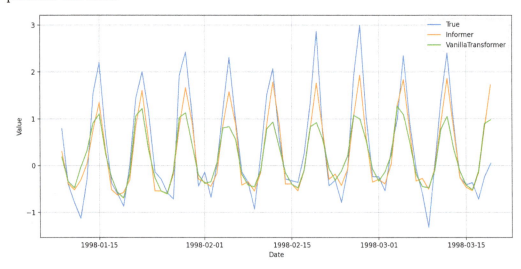

Figure 6.7: Forecasts of two Transformer models in an example time series

The Informer model seems to produce better forecasts, which we can check by computing the mean absolute error:

```
from neuralforecast.losses.numpy import mae

mae_informer = mae(cv['y'], cv['Informer'])
mae_transformer = mae(cv['y'], cv['VanillaTransformer'])
```

The error of Informer is 0.42, which is better than the 0.53 score obtained by `VanillaTransformer`.

How it works...

Under the hood, the `cross_validation()` method works as follows. Each model is trained using the training and validation sets. Then, they are evaluated on testing instances. The forecasting performance on the test set provides a reliable estimate for the performance we expect the models to have when applied in practice. So, you should select the model that maximizes forecasting performance, and retrain it using the whole dataset.

The `neuralforecast` library contains other models that you can compare. You can also compare different configurations of the same method and see which one works best for your data.

7

Probabilistic Time Series Forecasting

In the preceding chapters, we delved into time series problems from a point forecasting perspective. Point forecasting models predict a single value. However, forecasts are inherently uncertain, so it makes sense to quantify the uncertainty around a prediction. This is the goal of probabilistic forecasting, which can be a valuable approach for better-informed decision-making.

In this chapter, we'll focus on three types of probabilistic forecasting settings. We'll delve into exceedance probability forecasting, which helps us estimate the likelihood of a time series surpassing a predefined threshold. We will also deal with prediction intervals, which provide a range of possible values within which a future observation is likely to fall. Finally, we will explore predicted probability forecasting, which offers a probabilistic assessment of individual outcomes, providing a fine-grained perspective of future possibilities.

This chapter covers the following recipes:

- Introduction to exceedance probability forecasting
- Exceedance probability forecasting with an LSTM
- Creating prediction intervals using conformal prediction
- Probabilistic forecasting with an LSTM
- Probabilistic forecasting with DeepAR
- Introduction to Gaussian Processes
- Using Prophet for probabilistic forecasting

Technical requirements

We'll focus on the PyTorch ecosystem in this chapter. Here's the full list of libraries that will be used in this chapter:

- NumPy (1.26.2)
- pandas (2.1.3)
- scikit-learn (1.3.2)
- PyTorch Forecasting (1.0.0)
- PyTorch Lightning (2.1.2)
- torch (2.1.1)
- statsforecast (1.6.0)
- GluonTS (0.14.2)
- gpytorch (1.11)
- prophet (1.1.5)

You can install these libraries using `pip`, Python's package manager. For example, to install `scikit-learn`, you can run the following command:

```
pip install -U scikit-learn
```

The code for this chapter can be found in this book's GitHub repository: https://github.com/PacktPublishing/Deep-Learning-for-Time-Series-Data-Cookbook.

Introduction to exceedance probability forecasting

This recipe introduces exceedance probability forecasting problems. Exceedance events occur when a time series exceeds a predefined threshold in a predefined future period. This problem is relevant when the tails of the time series distribution can have a significant impact on the domain. For example, consider the case of the inflation rate in the economy. Central banks leverage this type of forecast to assess the possibility that the inflation rate will exceed some critical threshold, above which they might consider increasing interest rates.

From a data science perspective, exceedance events are binary problems. Thus, it is common to tackle them using binary probabilistic classification models. One of the challenges is that the class representing the exceedance events is rare, which makes the learning task more difficult.

Getting ready

We'll use a multivariate time series as an example to describe what an exceedance probability task is and why they are relevant. Specifically, we'll use the solar radiation dataset that was used in previous chapters (check, for example, the *Preparing a multivariate time series for supervised learning* recipe from *Chapter 4*).

Let's start by loading the dataset using `pandas`:

```
import pandas as pd

mvtseries = pd.read_csv
    ('assets/data/daily_multivariate_timeseries.csv',
    parse_dates=['datetime'],
    index_col='datetime')
```

Now, let's see how to define an exceedance problem using this time series.

How to do it...

Exceedance probability forecasting is the process of predicting the probability that a time series will exceed a critical threshold in a future period. We'll use a data module from PyTorch Lightning, which can be used to handle all the necessary steps for defining the task.

The main component of this module is the `setup()` method. Most of the steps were already explained in the *Feedforward neural networks for multivariate time series forecasting* recipe. To create an exceedance task, we must start by defining the new binary target variable, as follows:

```
mvtseries['target'] =
    \(mvtseries['Incoming Solar'].diff() < -2000).astype(int)
```

In the preceding code, we use the `diff()` method to compute how the solar radiation values change between consecutive observations. Then, we check whether the total daily solar radiation (in watts/m²) decreases by 2000 from one day to the next. This value was set arbitrarily. The intuition is that this should be a major event that we are interested in predicting. In this case study, such significant decreases in solar radiation mean that power systems will not be able to produce as much solar energy from photovoltaic devices. Therefore, predicting these events promptly allows power systems to generate energy from alternative sources efficiently.

Here's a plot of the differenced series and the selected threshold:

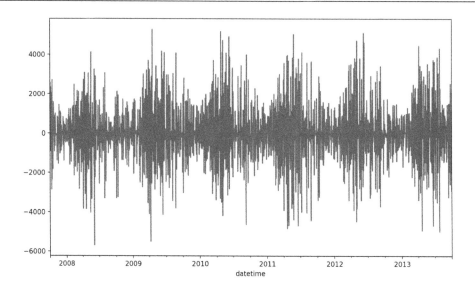

Figure 7.1: Difference in total daily solar radiation in consecutive observations

Afterward, we pass this variable as the target variable in the `TimeSeriesDataSet` instance within the data module. Let's start by loading the required libraries and building the constructor of the data modules:

```python
import numpy as np

from sklearn.model_selection import train_test_split
from sklearn.preprocessing import MinMaxScaler
from pytorch_forecasting import TimeSeriesDataSet
from pytorch_lightning import LightningDataModule

class ExceedanceDataModule(LightningDataModule):
    def __init__(self,
                 data: pd.DataFrame,
                 test_size: float = 0.2,
                 batch_size: int = 1):
        super().__init__()
        self.data = data
        self.var_names = self.data.columns.tolist()
        self.batch_size = batch_size
        self.test_size = test_size
        self.training = None
        self.validation = None
        self.test = None
        self.predict_set = None
```

In the constructor, we store all the elements that are used during the data preprocessing stage. The `setup()` method of the class is implemented in the following code:

```
def setup(self, stage=None):
    self.data['target'] = (
        self.data['Incoming Solar'].diff() < -2000).astype(int)

    self.data['time_index'] = np.arange(self.data.shape[0])
    self.data['group_id'] = 0

    unique_times = self.data['time_index'].sort_values().unique()

    tr_ind, ts_ind = \
        train_test_split(unique_times,
            test_size=self.test_size,
            shuffle=False)

    tr_ind, vl_ind = train_test_split(tr_ind,
            test_size=0.1, shuffle=False)

    training_df = self.data.loc[
        self.data['time_index'].isin(tr_ind), :]
    validation_df = self.data.loc[
        self.data['time_index'].isin(vl_ind), :]
    test_df = self.data.loc[
        self.data['time_index'].isin(ts_ind), :]

    self.training = TimeSeriesDataSet(
        data=training_df,
        time_idx="time_index",
        target="target",
        group_ids=['group_id'],
        max_encoder_length=14,
        max_prediction_length=7,
        time_varying_unknown_reals=self.var_names,
        scalers={k: MinMaxScaler()
                for k in self.var_names
                if k != 'target'}
    )

    self.validation = TimeSeriesDataSet.from_dataset(
        self.training, validation_df)
    self.test = TimeSeriesDataSet.from_dataset(
        self.training, test_df)
```

```
self.predict_set = TimeSeriesDataSet.from_dataset(
    self.training, self.data, predict=True)
```

This function works similarly to a standard auto-regressive pipeline. The crucial difference is that we're setting the target variable to a binary variable that denotes whether there's an exceedance event. We also set up the training, validation, and testing sets to build and evaluate the model. We set the number of lags to 14 (max_encoder_length) and the forecasting horizon to 7 (max_prediction_length).

The remaining methods of the LightningDataModule instance are similar to what we built in the previous chapter (for example, see the *Feedforward neural networks for multivariate time series forecasting* recipe):

```
def train_dataloader(self):
    return self.training.to_dataloader(
        batch_size=self.batch_size, shuffle=False)

def val_dataloader(self):
    return self.validation.to_dataloader(
        batch_size=self.batch_size, shuffle=False)

def test_dataloader(self):
    return self.test.to_dataloader(
        batch_size=self.batch_size, shuffle=False)

def predict_dataloader(self):
    return self.predict_set.to_dataloader(
        batch_size=1, shuffle=False)
```

Here's how to get a single observation using this data module:

```
datamodule = ExceedanceDataModule(data=mvtseries)
datamodule.setup()
x, y = next(iter(datamodule.train_dataloader()))
```

In the preceding code, we create an instance of ExceedanceDataModule, after which we use the iter() and next() methods to get observations from it.

How it works...

Exceedance problems can also be tackled with an auto-regressive approach. So, we can predict the probability of an exceedance event based on the value of recent observations of the time series.

An exceedance probability forecasting problem is a particular type of binary classification task that can be defined using a time series where the events are defined by exceedance. Yet, other types of events can be defined that are not necessarily based on exceedance events, and a probabilistic model can be built accordingly. The required logic is all set in the `setup()` method, which encapsulates all the preprocessing steps.

There's more...

In this recipe, we used a single multivariate time series to describe exceedance tasks. Yet, we remark that our approach can be defined trivially for datasets involving multiple time series using the data module framework.

There is a related problem to exceedance probability forecasting tasks called **time series classification**, in which a given time series has an associated label. We'll learn about this problem in the next chapter.

Exceedance probability forecasting with an LSTM

This recipe describes creating a probabilistic deep learning model to tackle exceedance tasks with a multivariate time series.

Getting ready

We'll continue our example with the solar radiation dataset. Here's the data module that we defined in the previous recipe:

```
N_LAGS = 14
HORIZON = 7

mvtseries = pd.read_csv('assets/daily_multivariate_timeseries.csv',
        parse_dates=['datetime'],
        index_col='datetime')

datamodule = ExceedanceDataModule(data=mvtseries,
        batch_size=64, test_size=0.3)
```

Now, let's see how to create a classifier using an LSTM neural network and PyTorch's `LightningModule`.

How to do it...

We will set up a binary classification using PyTorch Lightning's `LightningModule`. Here's the constructor and the `forward()` method:

```
import torch.nn as nn
import lightning.pytorch as pl


class ExceedanceLSTM(pl.LightningModule):
    def __init__(self, input_dim, hidden_dim, num_layers):
        super().__init__()
        self.hidden_dim = hidden_dim
        self.lstm = nn.LSTM(input_dim, self.hidden_dim,
                    num_layers, batch_first=True)
        self.fc = nn.Linear(self.hidden_dim, 1)

    def forward(self, x):
        h0 = torch.zeros(self.lstm.num_layers, x.size(0),
            self.hidden_dim).to(self.device)
        c0 = torch.zeros(self.lstm.num_layers, x.size(0),
            self.hidden_dim).to(self.device)
        out, _ = self.lstm(x, (h0, c0))
        out = self.fc(out[:, -1, :])
        out = torch.sigmoid(out)

        return out
```

The LSTM architecture is similar to what we learned about in *Chapter 4* – we create an LSTM layer based on PyTorch and set up its configuration regarding the number of layers, number of units, and input dimension (number of time series variables). During the forward pass, the output of the LSTM layer is passed onto a linear layer. In the previous recipes involving predicting the numeric value of future observations, this would be the final layer of the network. Yet, for classification, we add a sigmoid layer (`torch.sigmoid`), which transforms the model's output into a value between 0 and 1.

The training and validation steps of the module are coded as follows:

```
    def training_step(self, batch, batch_idx):
        x, y = batch

        y_bin = (y[0] > 0).any(axis=1).long().type(torch.FloatTensor)
        y_pred = self(x['encoder_cont'])
        loss = F.binary_cross_entropy(y_pred.squeeze(-1), y_bin)
        self.log('train_loss', loss)
```

```
        return loss

    def validation_step(self, batch, batch_idx):
        x, y = batch
        y_bin = (y[0] > 0).any(axis=1).long().type(torch.FloatTensor)
        y_pred = self(x['encoder_cont'])
        loss = F.binary_cross_entropy(y_pred.squeeze(-1), y_bin)
        self.log('val_loss', loss)
        return loss

    def configure_optimizers(self):
        return torch.optim.Adam(self.parameters(), lr=0.001)
```

In the preceding code, the training and validation methods follow similar steps:

1. First, we check if any of the observations in the forecasting horizon is positive (in the y[0] > 0).any(axis=1).long() snippet). In effect, we're building a neural network that models whether there's an exceedance event in any of the next 7 observations.

2. We convert the output of this test into a torch.FloatTensor data structure, which is required for the loss() function to work.

3. Then, we compare the prediction with the actual value using binary cross entropy (F.binary_ cross_entropy), which is used to train the model.

Besides these methods, we also set up the optimizer as Adam with a 0.001 learning rate. Finally, we set up the testing method:

```
    def test_step(self, batch, batch_idx):
        x, y = batch
        y_bin = (y[0] > 0).any(axis=1).long().type(torch.FloatTensor)
        y_pred = self(x['encoder_cont'])
        loss = F.binary_cross_entropy(y_pred.squeeze(-1), y_bin)
        auroc = AUROC(task='binary')
        auc_score = auroc(y_pred, y_bin)

        self.log('test_bce', loss)
        self.log('test_auc', auc_score)
```

In the preceding code, we add the area under the ROC curve as an evaluation metric, which is commonly used to test binary classification models.

Finally, we must train and test the model:

```
model = ExceedanceLSTM(input_dim=10, hidden_dim=32, num_layers=1)

early_stop_callback = EarlyStopping(monitor="val_loss",
                                    min_delta=1e-4,
                                    patience=10,
                                    verbose=False,
                                    mode="min")

trainer = pl.Trainer(
    max_epochs=100,
    accelerator="cpu",
    callbacks=[early_stop_callback]
)

trainer.fit(model, datamodule)
trainer.test(model, datamodule)
```

As you can see, the workflow follows the PyTorch Lightning style, where a `Trainer` instance uses the neural network model and the data module for training and testing.

How it works...

The deep learning models we built in the previous chapters can be extended for classification predictive tasks. In this case, we added a sigmoid layer, which maps the output of the previous layer into a $0-1$ value range. This value can be interpreted as the likelihood of the observations belonging to the positive class, which in our case is the exceedance event.

Classification models are no longer optimized with metrics such as mean squared error. For binary problems, we use binary cross entropy. In the testing phase, we added the area under the ROC curve as a secondary evaluation metric, which is helpful in understanding how the model distinguishes the two classes. The following figure shows the results of the ROC curve:

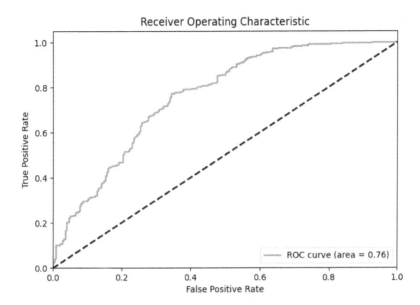

Figure 7.2: Results of the exceedance probability model in a ROC curve

The ROC curve provides a way of visualizing the performance of the probabilistic classifier for different decision thresholds. Results on the diagonal line denote a performance identical to a random guess. As the curve goes toward the top-left corner, it indicates better performance by the model.

Besides these tweaks to the pipeline, the design pattern provided by PyTorch Lightning makes the overall code similar to what we used in previous chapters for building models for point forecasting.

There's more...

We remark that while we are focusing on an LSTM here, other architectures can be used, such as feedforward neural networks or convolutional neural networks.

Creating prediction intervals using conformal prediction

In this recipe, we'll explore how to create prediction intervals. Prediction intervals describe the range of values within which future observations will likely fall with some confidence level. The greater the confidence required, the larger the intervals will be.

In practice, the model predicts not just a single point but a distribution for future observations. Various techniques exist to construct these intervals, including parametric methods that assume a specific distribution of errors and non-parametric methods that use empirical data to estimate intervals.

We'll resort to a conformal prediction approach, which is increasingly popular among data science practitioners.

Getting ready

We'll build prediction intervals for an ARIMA model, which is a popular forecasting approach. Yet, conformal prediction is agnostic to the underlying method and can be applied to other forecasting methods.

Let's start by loading a time series. In this example, we'll work with a univariate time series:

```
import pandas as pd
dataset = pd.read_csv(
    "assets/daily_multivariate_timeseries.csv",
    parse_dates=["datetime"],
)
```

Let's see how to create prediction intervals using this dataset.

How to do it...

The data is split into training and testing sets to fit the ARIMA model. We'll focus on the `statsforecast` Python library, so we need to transform the time series into a `pandas` DataFrame with three columns:

- `ds`: The timestep for the corresponding observation
- `unique_id`: The identifier of the time series, which is constant since we're working with a single time series
- `y`: The value of the observation

This process is done as follows:

```
series = dataset[['Incoming Solar']].reset_index()
series['id'] = 'Solar'
series = series.rename(columns={'index': 'ds', 'Incoming Solar': 'y',
    'id': 'unique_id'})
```

Next, we must split the data into training and testing sets:

```
from sklearn.model_selection import train_test_split
HORIZON = 7
train, test = train_test_split(series, test_size=HORIZON)
```

The test set is composed of the last 7 observations.

Now, we must set up the conformal method using the `ConformalIntervals` class from `statsforecast`. We must also create an ARIMA model and pass the conformal instance to it:

```
from statsforecast.utils import ConformalIntervals
intervals = ConformalIntervals(h=HORIZON)
```

```
models = [
    ARIMA(order=(2, 0, 2),
          season_length=365,
          prediction_intervals=intervals),
]
```

In the preceding code, we set the seasonal length to 365 since our data is daily, and we expect that solar radiation will exhibit a repeating yearly variation.

Finally, we must use the `StatsForecast` class instance to get the forecasts from the model:

```
sf = StatsForecast(
    df=train,
    models=models,
    freq='D',
)

forecasts = sf.forecast(h=HORIZON, level=[95])
```

Here, we set the level of the prediction intervals to 95. This means that we expect that the actual value will be within the respective interval with 95% confidence.

Here's a plot of the prediction interval we obtained:

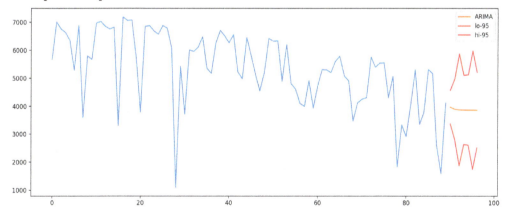

Figure 7.3: ARIMA model forecasts and their respective intervals

How it works...

Conformal prediction involves using a subset of historical data to fit the ARIMA model. Then, another subset is used to calibrate the conformal prediction, typically through calculating nonconformity scores that measure the deviation between the actual observed values and the model's predictions. The calibration step allows a threshold to be determined that corresponds to the desired confidence level (for example, 95%). This threshold is used for future forecasts to construct intervals around the predicted values, providing a range within which the actual values are expected to fall with the specified confidence level.

Conformal prediction helps quantify the uncertainty behind point forecasts by building intervals around these. In this recipe, we trained an ARIMA model and built intervals around its predictions using conformal prediction. We set the confidence level to 95, but we can explore several values at the same time. You can do this by changing the level argument to `level=[80, 95]`, for example.

Overall, this recipe follows a simple train plus testing cycle that uses the `statsforecast` Python library framework.

Probabilistic forecasting with an LSTM

This recipe will walk you through building an LSTM neural network for probabilistic forecasting using PyTorch Lightning.

Getting ready

In this recipe, we'll introduce probabilistic forecasting with LSTM networks. This approach combines the strengths of LSTM models in capturing long-term dependencies within sequential data with the nuanced perspective of probabilistic forecasting. This method goes beyond traditional point estimates by predicting a range of possible future outcomes, each accompanied by a probability. This means that we are incorporating uncertainty into forecasts.

This recipe uses the same dataset that we used in *Chapter 4*, in the *Feedforward neural networks for multivariate time series forecasting* recipe. We'll also use the same data module we created in that recipe, which is called `MultivariateSeriesDataModule`.

Let's explore how to use this data module to build an LSTM model for probabilistic forecasting.

How to do it...

In this subsection, we'll define a probabilistic LSTM model that outputs the predictive mean and standard deviation for each forecasted point of the time series. This technique involves designing the LSTM model to predict parameters that define a probability distribution for future outcomes rather than outputting a single value. The model is usually configured to output parameters of a specific distribution, such as the mean and variance for a Gaussian distribution. These describe the expected value and the spread of future values, respectively:

1. Let's start by defining a callback:

```python
class LossTrackingCallback(Callback):
    def __init__(self):
        self.train_losses = []
        self.val_losses = []

    def on_train_epoch_end(self, trainer, pl_module):
        if trainer.logged_metrics.get("train_loss_epoch"):
            self.train_losses.append(
                trainer.logged_metrics["train_loss_epoch"].
item())

    def on_validation_epoch_end(self, trainer, pl_module):
        if trainer.logged_metrics.get("val_loss_epoch"):
            self.val_losses.append(
                trainer.logged_metrics["val_loss_epoch"].item())
```

The LossTrackingCallback class is used to monitor the training and validation losses throughout the epochs. This is important for diagnosing the learning process of the model, identifying overfitting, and deciding when to stop training.

2. Then, we must build the LSTM model based on PyTorch Lightning's LightningModule class:

```python
class ProbabilisticLSTM(LightningModule):
    def __init__(self, input_size,
                 hidden_size, seq_len,
                 num_layers=2):
        super().__init__()
        self.save_hyperparameters()
        self.lstm = nn.LSTM(input_size, hidden_size,
            num_layers, batch_first=True)
        self.fc_mu = nn.Linear(hidden_size, 1)
        self.fc_sigma = nn.Linear(hidden_size, 1)
        self.hidden_size = hidden_size

        self.softplus = nn.Softplus()

    def forward(self, x):
        lstm_out, _ = self.lstm(x)
        lstm_out = lstm_out[:, -1, :]
        mu = self.fc_mu(lstm_out)
```

```
        sigma = self.softplus(self.fc_sigma(lstm_out))
        return mu, sigma
```

The `ProbabilisticLSTM` class defines the LSTM architecture for our probabilistic forecasts. The class includes layers to compute the predictive mean (`fc_mu`) and standard deviation (`fc_sigma`) of the forecast distribution. The standard deviation is passed through a `Softplus()` activation function to ensure it is always positive, reflecting the nature of standard deviation.

3. The following code implements the training and validation steps, along with the network configuration parameters:

```
    def training_step(self, batch, batch_idx):
        x, y = batch[0]["encoder_cont"], batch[1][0]
        mu, sigma = self.forward(x)
        dist = torch.distributions.Normal(mu, sigma)
        loss = -dist.log_prob(y).mean()
        self.log(
            "train_loss", loss, on_step=True,
            on_epoch=True, prog_bar=True, logger=True
        )
        return {"loss": loss, "log": {"train_loss": loss}}

    def validation_step(self, batch, batch_idx):
        x, y = batch[0]["encoder_cont"], batch[1][0]
        mu, sigma = self.forward(x)
        dist = torch.distributions.Normal(mu, sigma)
        loss = -dist.log_prob(y).mean()
        self.log(
            "val_loss", loss, on_step=True,
            on_epoch=True, prog_bar=True, logger=True
        )
        return {"val_loss": loss}

    def configure_optimizers(self):
        optimizer = optim.Adam(self.parameters(), lr=0.0001)
        scheduler = optim.lr_scheduler.ReduceLROnPlateau(
            optimizer, "min")
        return {
            "optimizer": optimizer,
            "lr_scheduler": scheduler,
            "monitor": "val_loss",
        }
```

4. After defining the model architecture, we initialize the data module and set up training callbacks. As we saw previously, the `EarlyStopping` callback is a valuable tool for preventing overfitting by halting the training process once the model ceases to improve on the validation set. The `ModelCheckpoint` callback ensures that we capture and save the best version of the model based on its validation performance. Together, these callbacks optimize the training process, aiding in developing a robust and well-tuned model:

```
datamodule = ContinuousDataModule(data=mvtseries)
datamodule.setup()

model = ProbabilisticLSTM(
    input_size = input_size, hidden_size=hidden_size,
    seq_len=seq_len
)

early_stop_callback = EarlyStopping(monitor="val_loss",
    patience=5)
checkpoint_callback = ModelCheckpoint(
    dirpath="./model_checkpoint/", save_top_k=1,
    monitor="val_loss"
)

loss_tracking_callback = LossTrackingCallback()

trainer = Trainer(
    max_epochs=100,
    callbacks=[early_stop_callback, checkpoint_callback,
    loss_tracking_callback],
)

trainer.fit(model, datamodule)
```

Using the `Trainer` class from PyTorch Lightning simplifies the training process, handling the complex training loops internally and allowing us to focus on defining the model and its behavior. It increases the code's readability and maintainability, making experimenting with different model configurations easier.

5. After training, assessing the model's performance and visualizing its probabilistic forecasts is very important. The graphical representation of the forecasted means, alongside their uncertainty intervals against the actual values, offers a clear depiction of the model's predictive power and the inherent uncertainty in its predictions. We built a visualization framework to plot the forecasts. You can check the functions at the following link: https://github. com/PacktPublishing/Deep-Learning-for-Time-Series-Data-Cookbook.

The following figure illustrates the true values of our time series in blue, with the forecasted means depicted by the dashed red line:

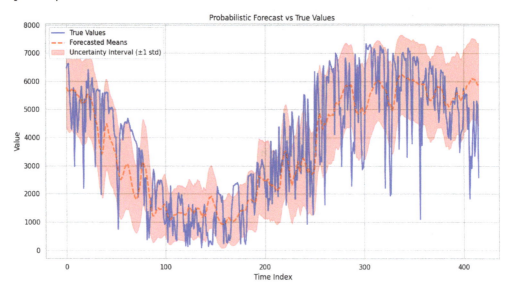

Figure 7.4: Probabilistic forecasts with uncertainty intervals and true values

The shaded area represents the uncertainty interval, calculated as a standard deviation from the forecasted mean. This probabilistic approach to forecasting provides a more comprehensive picture than point estimates as it accounts for the variability and uncertainty inherent in the time series data. The overlap between the uncertainty intervals and the actual values indicates areas where the model has higher confidence in its predictions. Conversely, wider intervals may suggest periods of more significant uncertainty, potentially due to inherent noise in the data or complex underlying dynamics that the model finds more challenging to capture.

Moreover, the following figure provides insights into the training dynamics of our probabilistic LSTM model:

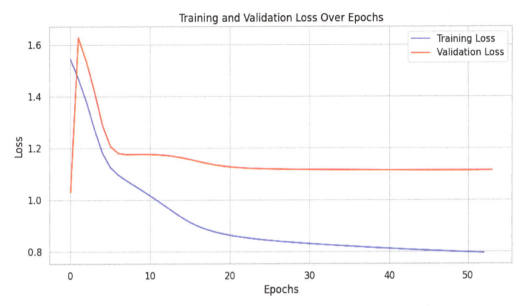

Figure 7.5: Training and validation loss over epochs, demonstrating
the learning progress of the probabilistic LSTM model

The relatively stable and low validation loss suggests that our model generalizes well without overfitting the training data.

How it works...

The probabilistic LSTM model extends beyond traditional point prediction models. Unlike point forecasts, which output a single expected value, this model predicts a full distribution characterized by mean and standard deviation parameters.

This probabilistic approach provides a richer representation by capturing the uncertainty inherent in the data. The mean of the distribution gives the expected value of the forecast, while the standard deviation quantifies the confidence in the prediction, expressing the expected variability around the mean.

To train this model, we use a loss function that differs from those used in point prediction models. Instead of using MSE or MAE, which minimizes the difference between predicted and actual values, the probabilistic LSTM employs a negative log-likelihood loss function. This loss function, often called the probabilistic loss, maximizes the likelihood of the observed data under the predicted distribution.

This probabilistic loss function is particularly suited for uncertainty estimation as it directly penalizes the divergence between the predicted probability distribution and the observed values. When the predicted distribution assigns a high probability to the actual observed values, the negative log-likelihood is low, and thus the loss is low.

Probabilistic forecasting with DeepAR

This time, we'll turn our attention to DeepAR, a state-of-the-art method for probabilistic forecasting. We'll also leverage the neuralforecast framework to exemplify how to apply DeepAR for this task.

Getting ready

We'll continue with the same dataset that we used in the previous recipe.

Since we are using a different Python package, we need to change our preprocessing steps to get the data into a suitable format. Now, each row corresponds to a single observation at a given time for a specific time series. This is similar to what we did in the *Prediction intervals using conformal prediction* recipe:

```python
def load_and_prepare_data(file_path, time_column, series_column,
    aggregation_freq):
    """Load the time series data and prepare it for modeling."""
    dataset = pd.read_csv(file_path, parse_dates=[time_column])
    dataset.set_index(time_column, inplace=True)
    target_series = (
        dataset[series_column].resample(aggregation_freq).mean()
    )
    return target_series


def add_time_features(dataframe, date_column):
    """Add time-related features to the DataFrame."""
    dataframe["week_of_year"] = (
        dataframe[date_column].dt.isocalendar().week.astype(float)
    )
    dataframe["month"] = dataframe[date_column].dt.month.astype(float)
    dataframe["sin_week"] = np.sin(
        2 * np.pi * dataframe["week_of_year"] / 52
    )
    dataframe["cos_week"] = np.cos(
        2 * np.pi * dataframe["week_of_year"] / 52
    )
    dataframe["sin_2week"] = np.sin(
        4 * np.pi * dataframe["week_of_year"] / 52
    )
    dataframe["cos_2week"] = np.cos(
        4 * np.pi * dataframe["week_of_year"] / 52
    )
    dataframe["sin_month"] = np.sin(
        2 * np.pi * dataframe["month"] / 12
    )
```

```python
    dataframe["cos_month"] = np.cos(
        2 * np.pi * dataframe["month"] / 12
    )
    return dataframe

def scale_features(dataframe, feature_columns):
    """Scale features."""
    scaler = MinMaxScaler()
    dataframe[feature_columns] = (
        scaler.fit_transform(dataframe[feature_columns])
    )
    return dataframe, scaler


FILE_PATH = "assets/daily_multivariate_timeseries.csv"
TIME_COLUMN = "datetime"
TARGET_COLUMN = "Incoming Solar"
AGGREGATION_FREQ = "W"

weekly_data = load_and_prepare_data(
    FILE_PATH, TIME_COLUMN, TARGET_COLUMN, AGGREGATION_FREQ
)
weekly_data = (
    weekly_data.reset_index().rename(columns={TARGET_COLUMN: "y"})
)
weekly_data = add_time_features(weekly_data, TIME_COLUMN)

numerical_features = [
    "y",
    "week_of_year",
    "sin_week",
    "cos_week",
    "sin_2week",
    "cos_2week",
    "sin_month",
    "cos_month",
]
features_to_scale = ["y", "week_of_year"]
weekly_data, scaler = scale_features(weekly_data, features_to_scale)
```

In this case, we select the targeted series within the dataset and resample it to a weekly frequency, aggregating the data points using the mean.

Next, we show how to enhance the dataset by adding time-related features. We introduce Fourier series components for the week and month of the year. By incorporating sine and cosine transformations, we capture the cyclical nature of time in our data. Additionally, we scale the target using a `MinMaxScaler`.

Finally, we split our dataset into training and testing sets:

```
def split_data(dataframe, date_column, split_time):
    """Split the data into training and test sets."""
    train = dataframe[dataframe[date_column] <= split_time]
    test = dataframe[dataframe[date_column] > split_time]
    return train, test


SPLIT_TIME = weekly_data["ds"].max() - pd.Timedelta(weeks=52)
train, test = split_data(weekly_data, "ds", SPLIT_TIME)
```

Now, let's see how to build a DeepAR model using neuralforecast.

How to do it...

With the data prepared, we can define and train the DeepAR model. The NeuralForecast class receives a list of models as input. In this case, we only define the DeepAR class. The library provides a straightforward way to specify the architecture and training behavior of the model. After training, we generate forecasts using the predict() method:

```
nf = NeuralForecast(
    models=[
        DeepAR(
            h=52,
            input_size=52,
            lstm_n_layers=3,
            lstm_hidden_size=128,
            trajectory_samples=100,
            loss=DistributionLoss(
                distribution="Normal", level=[80, 90],
                    return_params=False
            ),
            futr_exog_list=[
                "week_of_year",
                "sin_week",
                "cos_week",
                "sin_2week",
                "cos_2week",
                "sin_month",
                "cos_month",
            ],
            learning_rate=0.001,
            max_steps=1000,
            val_check_steps=10,
```

```
            start_padding_enabled=True,
            early_stop_patience_steps=30,
            scaler_type="identity",
            enable_progress_bar=True,
        ),
    ],
    freq="W",
)

nf.fit(df=train, val_size=52)
Y_hat_df = nf.predict(
    futr_df=test[
        [
            "ds",
            "unique_id",
            "week_of_year",
            "sin_week",
            "cos_week",
            "sin_2week",
            "cos_2week",
            "sin_month",
            "cos_month",
        ]
    ]
)
```

The following figure illustrates a probabilistic forecast generated by `DeepAR`:

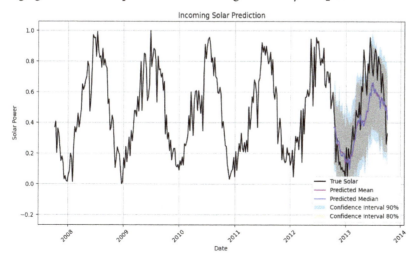

Figure 7.6: DeepAR probabilistic forecast showing the mean prediction and associated uncertainty

The solid line represents the mean prediction, while the shaded region shows the uncertainty bounds for the 80% and 95% confidence intervals. This plot shows the range of likely future values and is more informative than a single predicted value, especially for decision-making under uncertainty.

How it works...

`DeepAR` is a probabilistic forecasting method that generates a probability distribution, such as a normal distribution or a negative binomial distribution, for each future time point. Once again, we are interested in capturing the uncertainty in our predictions rather than just producing point forecasts.

The `DeepAR` model uses an autoregressive recurrent network structure and conditions it on past observations, covariates, and an embedding of the time series. The output is a set of parameters, typically the mean and variance, which define the distribution of future values. During training, the model maximizes the likelihood of the observed data given these parameters.

`DeepAR` is designed to work well with multiple related time series, enabling it to learn complex patterns across similar sequences and improve prediction accuracy by leveraging cross-series information.

Introduction to Gaussian Processes

In this recipe, we'll introduce **Gaussian Processes** (**GP**), a powerful algorithm for probabilistic machine learning.

Getting ready

GP offers a flexible, probabilistic approach to modeling in machine learning. This section introduces the concept of GP and prepares the necessary environment for forecasting using a GP model.

We need to import a new library to be able to fit GP, namely `gpytorch`:

```
import torch
import gpytorch
import numpy as np
import pandas as pd
from sklearn.model_selection import train_test_split
from sklearn.preprocessing import StandardScaler
from pytorch_lightning import LightningDataModule
```

Then, we must read the multivariate time series data and process it, scaling both the features and target variable, as scaled data typically improves GP modeling performance significantly.

How to do it...

We'll use the `gpytorch` library to implement a GP model:

1. The key components in a GP model are the mean and covariance functions, which are defined in the GPModel class:

```
class GPModel(gpytorch.models.ExactGP):
    def init(self, train_x, train_y, likelihood):
        super(GPModel, self).init(train_x, train_y, likelihood)
        self.mean_module = gpytorch.means.ConstantMean()
        self.covar_module = gpytorch.kernels.
ScaleKernel(gpytorch.kernels.RBFKernel()) + gpytorch.kernels.
ScaleKernel(gpytorch.kernels.PeriodicKernel())

    def forward(self, x):
        mean_x = self.mean_module(x)
        covar_x = self.covar_module(x)
        return gpytorch.distributions.MultivariateNormal(
            mean_x, covar_x)
```

2. The model is then trained using the standard PyTorch training loop, optimizing the marginal log-likelihood:

```
likelihood = GaussianLikelihood()
model = GPModel(datamodule.train_x[:, 0], datamodule.train_y,
    likelihood)

model.train()
likelihood.train()

optimizer = torch.optim.Adam(model.parameters(), lr=0.01)

mll = ExactMarginalLogLikelihood(likelihood, model)

training_iter = 100
for i in range(training_iter):
    optimizer.zero_grad()
    output = model(datamodule.train_x[:, 0])
    loss = -mll(output, datamodule.train_y)
    loss.backward()
    optimizer.step()
```

After training, the GP model can make predictions for new data points. The key advantage of GP is its ability to quantify uncertainty in these predictions. The following code snippet demonstrates how predictions are made using a trained GP model:

```
with torch.no_grad(), gpytorch.settings.fast_pred_var():
    observed_pred = likelihood
        (model(datamodule.original_x[:, 0]))
```

Here's a visualization of the fitted values of the model:

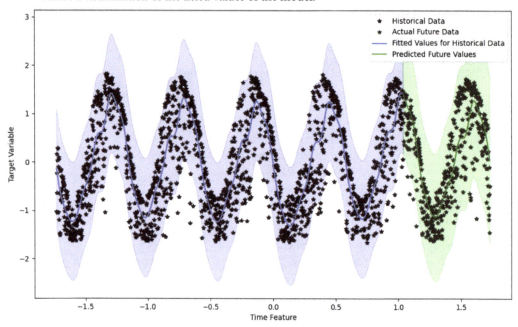

Figure 7.7: A visualization of the GP model's predictions

This preceding figure illustrates the GP model's ability to fit the historical data and forecast future values with quantified uncertainty. The shaded areas around the predictions visually represent the model's forecast confidence, with wider intervals indicating more significant uncertainty.

How it works...

GP offers a sophisticated way to analyze and understand complicated datasets. It differs from typical models because it doesn't rely on a fixed number of parameters to describe data. Instead, GP uses a limitless range of possible functions, which gives it great adaptability to fit any type of data generation process.

GP is a collection of random variables. The key characteristic of these variables in GP is that one variable affects or is related to the values of others. The dependency pattern is governed by the Gaussian distribution. A GP can model a wide variety of functions (for example, nonlinear, noisy, and others). This method is particularly useful in our current setting because it adopts a probabilistic approach to modeling. GP can not only predict the most likely outcome but also quantify the uncertainty of these predictions.

GP is defined by the mean and kernel functions:

- **Mean function**: The baseline expectation for the function's values. It provides a starting point for predictions and is often set to zero.

- **Kernel function**: The core of a GP, this determines the relationship between data points by encoding the function's properties (for example, smoothness, periodicity, and so on). It influences how predictions are made by assessing the similarity among points.

The kernel function is the essential component of a GP model's predictive accuracy, adapting the model to the data's underlying structure. In practice, you can mix different kernels to capture various aspects of the data. For instance, combining a kernel that's good for smooth data with one good for periodic data can help model data with both characteristics.

Training a GP involves fine-tuning specific parameters in the kernel to fit your data best. This is often done using optimization techniques such as gradient descent. Once the GP has been trained, it can predict new data points.

Using Prophet for probabilistic forecasting

In this recipe, we'll show how to use Prophet for probabilistic forecasting.

Getting ready

Prophet is a tool developed by Facebook for forecasting time series data. It's particularly adept at handling data with strong seasonal patterns and irregular events such as holidays. To get started with Prophet, we need to prepare our data and environment.

The process begins with loading and preprocessing the time series data so that it fits the format Prophet requires. Each time series in Prophet must have two columns – ds (the timestamp) and y (the value we wish to predict):

```
import pandas as pd
from prophet import Prophet
import matplotlib.pyplot as plt
from sklearn.model_selection import train_test_split
from sklearn.preprocessing import StandardScaler
```

```
mvtseries = pd.read_csv(
"assets/daily_multivariate_timeseries.csv",
parse_dates=["datetime"],
)


mvtseries['ds'] = mvtseries['datetime']
mvtseries['y'] = mvtseries['Incoming Solar']
```

Now, let's see how to build a Prophet model.

How to do it...

Follow these steps to build a Prophet model:

1. After preprocessing, we must divide the dataset into training and testing sets. Prophet is then used to fit the model on the training data:

    ```
    train_data, test_data = train_test_split(mvtseries,
        test_size=0.2, shuffle=False)
    ```

2. Then, we must create a Prophet instance and train it, as follows:

    ```
    model = Prophet()
    model.fit(train_data[['ds', 'y']])
    ```

3. We can use the model to make future predictions once the model has been trained. This involves creating a future dataframe for the desired forecast period and then using the model to predict the values:

    ```
    future = model.make_future_dataframe(periods=len(test_data))
    forecast = model.predict(future)
    ```

4. Here's how to visualize the forecasts:

    ```
    fig = model.plot(forecast)
    plt.show()
    ```

These forecasts are shown in the following figure:

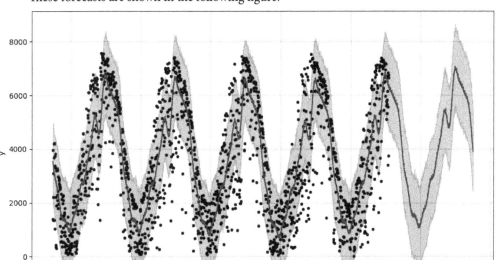

Figure 7.8: Prophet forecast with uncertainty intervals and observed data

In addition to the basic forecasting model, Prophet also provides functionality to dissect and understand various components of the time series. This can be particularly useful for gaining insights into the underlying patterns of the data. Here's how to visualize the forecasts by each component:

```
fig = model.plot_components(forecast)
plt.show()
```

Here's the plot:

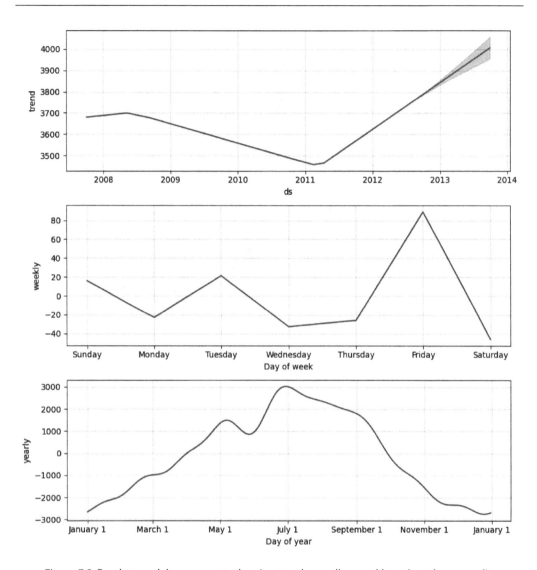

Figure 7.9: Prophet model components showing trend, as well as weekly and yearly seasonality

The top plot illustrates the overall trend in the data over time. Here, we can see a general upward trend, suggesting that the value we predict increases over the years. The middle plot shows the weekly seasonality. This plot indicates how each day of the week affects our forecasting value. For instance, there might be peaks on specific days associated with weekly events or habits. The bottom plot represents yearly seasonality, showing how the time of the year influences the forecast. This could capture increased activity during certain months or seasonal effects.

How it works...

Prophet is an additive model that decomposes the time series into several components: trend, seasonality, and holidays. In this recipe, we used the default parameters of the model. However, you can tweak Prophet with several parameters. Check out the documentation at `https://facebook.github.io/prophet/docs/quick_start.html` for more information.

The `prophet` library requires the data to be framed in a specific format: a `pandas` DataFrame with two columns: `ds` (timestamps) and `y` (the values). Then, the training and inference steps are carried out using a `fit()` method and a `predict()` method, respectively. You can also visualize the predictions by each component, which gives the model a more interpretable characteristic.

There's more...

There's a newer extension of the Prophet model called `NeuralProphet`. It incorporates neural network models for improved forecasting, especially in complex patterns and multiple seasonality scenarios.

8

Deep Learning for Time Series Classification

In this chapter, we'll tackle **time series classification** (**TSC**) problems using deep learning. As the name implies, TSC is a classification task involving time series data. The dataset contains several time series, and each of these has an associated categorical label. This problem is similar to a standard classification task, but the input explanatory variables are time series. We'll explore how to approach this problem using different approaches. Besides using the **K-nearest neighbors** model to tackle this task, we'll also develop different neural networks, such as a **residual neural network** (**ResNet**) and a convolutional neural network.

By the end of this chapter, you'll be able to set up a TSC task using a PyTorch Lightning data module and solve it with different models. You'll also learn how to use the `sktime` Python library to solve this problem.

This chapter contains the following recipes:

- Tackling TSC with K-nearest neighbors
- Building a `DataModule` class for TSC
- Convolutional neural networks for TSC
- ResNets for TSC
- Tackling TSC problems with `sktime`

Technical requirements

We'll focus on the PyTorch Lightning ecosystem to build deep learning models. Besides that, we'll also use scikit-learn to create a baseline. Overall, the list of libraries used in the package is the following:

- scikit-learn (1.3.2)
- pandas (2.1.3)
- NumPy (1.26.2)
- Torch (2.1.1)
- PyTorch Lightning (2.1.2)
- sktime (0.24.1)
- keras-self-attention (0.51.0)

As an example, we'll use the Car dataset from the repository available at the following link: https://www.timeseriesclassification.com. You can learn more about the dataset in the following work:

Thakoor, Ninad, and Jean Gao. *Shape classifier based on generalized probabilistic descent method with hidden Markov descriptor.* Tenth IEEE **International Conference on Computer Vision** (**ICCV**'05) Volume 1. Vol. 1. IEEE, 2005.

The code and datasets used in this chapter can be found at the following GitHub URL: https://github.com/PacktPublishing/Deep-Learning-for-Time-Series-Data-Cookbook.

Tackling TSC with K-nearest neighbors

In this recipe, we'll show you how to tackle TSC tasks using a popular method called K-nearest neighbors. The goal of this recipe is to show you how standard machine-learning models can be used to solve this problem.

Getting ready

First, let's start by loading the data using pandas:

```
import pandas as pd

data_directory = 'assets/datasets/Car'
train = pd.read_table(f'{data_directory}/Car_TRAIN.tsv', header=None)
test = pd.read_table(f'{data_directory}/Car_TEST.tsv', header=None)
```

The dataset is already split into a training and testing set, so we read them separately. Now, let's see how to build a K-nearest neighbor model using this dataset.

How to do it...

Here, we describe the steps necessary for building a time series classifier using scikit-learn:

1. Let's start by splitting the target variable from the explanatory variables:

    ```
    y_train = train.iloc[:, 0]
    y_test = test.iloc[:, 0]
    X_train = train.iloc[:, 1:]
    X_test = test.iloc[:, 1:]
    ```

    The first column of each dataset (index 0) contains the target variable, which we assign to the `y_train` and `y_test` objects for the training and testing sets, respectively. The `X_train` and `X_test` objects contain the input explanatory time series for the corresponding datasets.

    This particular dataset contains four different classes. Here's what the distribution looks like:

    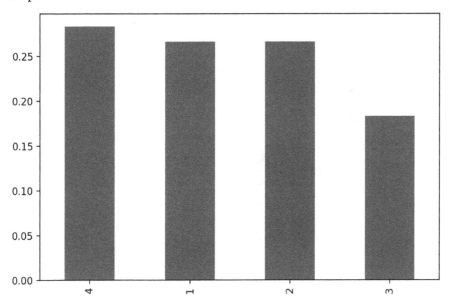

    Figure 8.1: Distribution of the four classes in the dataset

2. Afterward, we need to normalize the time series. We accomplish this using the `MinMaxScaler` method from scikit-learn, which brings all values into a range between 0 and 1:

    ```
    from sklearn.preprocessing import MinMaxScaler

    scaler = MinMaxScaler()

    X_train = scaler.fit_transform(X_train)
    X_test = scaler.transform(X_test)
    ```

In the preceding code, we fit the scaler using the training set, and then use it to transform the data in both datasets.

3. Finally, we're ready to create a K-nearest neighbors classification model:

```
classifier = KNeighborsTimeSeriesClassifier()

classifier.fit(X_train, y_train)

predictions = classifier.predict(X_test)
```

In the preceding code, we create a KNeighborsTimeSeriesClassifier instance that implements K-nearest neighbors and fits it using the training set. Then, we apply this model to the testing set by calling the predict() method.

The following figure shows the confusion matrix concerning the predictions of the K-nearest neighbor model:

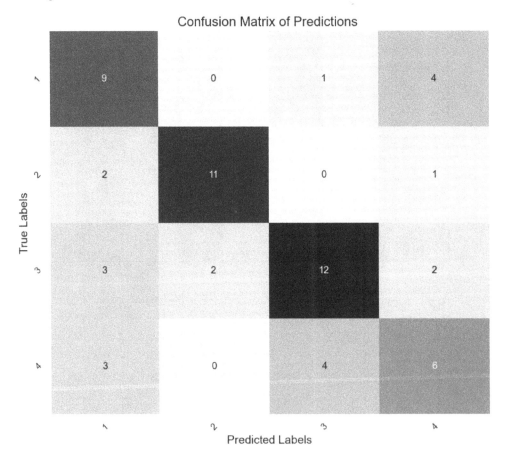

Figure 8.2: Confusion matrix for the predictions of the K-nearest neighbor model

How it works...

TSC problems are like standard classification tasks where the input explanatory variables are time series. So, the process for tackling the problem is similar. After splitting the explanatory variables (X) from the target variable (y), we prepare the explanatory variables using operators such as normalization functions. Then, we can use any classifier to solve this task. In this recipe, we use the K-nearest neighbor model, which is well-known for being a simple yet effective approach for this task.

Note that the normalization step using `MinMaxScaler` is important to bring all observations into a common value range.

There's more...

The `sktime` Python library provides several methods for tackling TSC problems. Here's the link to the documentation: `https://www.sktime.net/en/stable/examples/02_classification.html`.

In this recipe, we used the K-nearest neighbors model using default parameters. For example, we used the Minkowski metric, which may not be the best one. For time series, distance metrics such as dynamic time warping are usually better approaches.

Building a DataModule class for TSC

In this recipe, we return to the PyTorch Lightning framework. We'll build a `DataModule` class to encapsulate the data preprocessing and the passing of observations to models.

Getting ready

Let's load the dataset from the previous recipe:

```
import pandas as pd

data_directory = 'assets/datasets/Car'
train = pd.read_table(f'{data_directory}/Car_TRAIN.tsv', header=None)
test = pd.read_table(f'{data_directory}/Car_TEST.tsv', header=None)
```

Next, we'll build a `DataModule` class to handle this dataset.

How to do it...

In the previous chapters, we used `TimeSeriesDataSet` from PyTorch Forecasting to handle the data preparation for us. This class managed several steps. These include normalization and transformation of the data for supervised learning. However, in TSC, an observation uses the entire time series as input:

1. We'll start creating a simpler variant of `TimeSeriesDataSet` to handle the passing of observations to the model:

    ```
    from torch.utils.data import Dataset

    class TSCDataset(Dataset):
        def __init__(self, X_data, y_data):
            self.X_data = X_data
            self.y_data = y_data

        def __getitem__(self, index):
            return self.X_data[index], self.y_data[index]

        def __len__(self):
            return len(self.X_data)
    ```

    The `__getitem__()` method is used internally to get observations from the dataset and pass them to the model, while the `__len__()` method outputs the size of the dataset.

2. Then, we're ready to build our `LightningDataModule` class. Here's the constructor:

    ```
    from torch.utils.data import Dataset, DataLoader
    import lightning.pytorch as pl
    from sklearn.preprocessing import MinMaxScaler, OneHotEncoder

    class TSCDataModule(pl.LightningDataModule):
        def __init__(self, train_df, test_df, batch_size=1):
            super().__init__()
            self.train_df = train_df
            self.test_df = test_df
            self.batch_size = batch_size

            self.scaler = MinMaxScaler()
            self.encoder = OneHotEncoder(categories='auto',
                sparse_output=False)

            self.train = None
            self.validation = None
            self.test = None
    ```

TSCDataModule contains the self.train, self.validation, and self.test dataset attributes that will be filled with the setup() method. Besides that, the constructor also sets up the normalization method based on MinMaxScaler and the one-hot encoder called OneHotEncoder. We use the one-hot encoder to transform the target variable into a set of binary variables. This process is necessary for the training of neural networks.

3. Then, the setup() method is implemented as follows:

```python
def setup(self, stage=None):
    y_train = self.encoder.fit_transform(
        self.train_df.iloc[:, 0].values.reshape(-1, 1)
    )
    y_test = self.encoder.transform(
        self.test_df.iloc[:,0].values.reshape(-1, 1))

    X_train = train.iloc[:, 1:]
    X_test = test.iloc[:, 1:]

    X_train = self.scaler.fit_transform(X_train)
    X_test = self.scaler.transform(X_test)

    X_train, X_val, y_train, y_val = train_test_split(
        X_train, y_train, test_size=0.2, stratify=y_train
    )

    X_train, X_val, X_test = [
        torch.tensor(arr, dtype=torch.float).unsqueeze(1)
        for arr in [X_train, X_val, X_test]
    ]
    y_train, y_val, y_test = [
        torch.tensor(arr, dtype=torch.long)
        for arr in [y_train, y_val, y_test]
    ]

    self.train = TSCDataset(X_train, y_train)
    self.validation = TSCDataset(X_val, y_val)
    self.test = TSCDataset(X_test, y_test)
```

In the preceding code, we use the encoder to transform the target variable and do the same using the normalization method with the explanatory variables. Then, we create a validation set based on the training instances. We also cast the data objects as torch data structures using the torch.tensor() method. Finally, we create the TSCDataset instances based on the training, validation, and testing sets.

4. We create the data loader methods using the `DataLoader` class directly on the respective dataset:

```
def train_dataloader(self):
    return DataLoader(self.train,
        batch_size=self.batch_size)


def val_dataloader(self):
    return DataLoader(self.validation,
        batch_size=self.batch_size)


def test_dataloader(self):
    return DataLoader(self.test, batch_size=self.batch_size)
```

5. Finally, here's an example of how to get an observation using this data module:

```
datamodule = TSCDataModule(train_df=train, test_df=test)
datamodule.setup()
x, y = next(iter(datamodule.train_dataloader()))
```

In the next recipe, we'll learn how to build a classification model using this data module.

How it works...

We created a `DataModule` class tailored for TSC classification problems. We encapsulated the data logic within the `setup()` method, thus enabling us to use the PyTorch Lightning ecosystem to build deep learning models.

In this case, TSC problems do not involve autoregression. So, we created a simple variant of the `TimeSeriesDataSet` class to handle the process of passing the data to models.

Convolutional neural networks for TSC

In this recipe, we'll walk you through building a convolutional neural network to tackle TSC problems. We'll use the `DataModule` class created in the previous recipe to do this.

Getting ready

We start again by importing the dataset used in the previous recipe:

```
import pandas as pd


data_directory = 'assets/datasets/Car'
train = pd.read_table(f'{data_directory}/Car_TRAIN.tsv', header=None)
test = pd.read_table(f'{data_directory}/Car_TEST.tsv', header=None)
```

```
datamodule = TSCDataModule(train_df=train,
                           test_df=test,
                           batch_size=8)
```

We also create an instance of the `TSCDataModule` data module we defined in the previous recipe. Let's see how to create a convolutional neural network classifier to handle this task.

How to do it...

Here, we will walk you through the steps of building a convolutional neural network for TSC problems using PyTorch:

1. Let's start by creating the neural network based on PyTorch:

    ```python
    from torch import nn

    class ConvolutionalTSC(nn.Module):
        def __init__(self, input_dim, output_dim=1):
            super(ConvolutionalTSC, self).__init__()

            self.conv1 = nn.Conv1d(in_channels=input_dim,
                                   out_channels=64,
                                   kernel_size=3,
                                   stride=1,
                                   padding=1)

            self.conv2 = nn.Conv1d(in_channels=64,
                                   out_channels=32,
                                   kernel_size=3,
                                   stride=1,
                                   padding=1)

            self.conv3 = nn.Conv1d(in_channels=32,
                                   out_channels=16,
                                   kernel_size=3,
                                   stride=1,
                                   padding=1)

            self.maxp = nn.MaxPool1d(kernel_size=3)

            self.fc1 = nn.Linear(in_features=336, out_features=32)
            self.fc2 = nn.Linear(in_features=32,
                out_features=output_dim)
    ```

```
      def forward(self, x):
          x = F.relu(self.conv1(x))
          x = self.maxp(x)
          x = F.relu(self.conv2(x))
          x = self.maxp(x)
          x = F.relu(self.conv3(x))
          x = self.maxp(x)
          x = x.view(x.size(0), -1)
          x = self.fc1(x)
          x = self.fc2(x)
          return x
```

2. We then wrap this model within a `LightningModule` class from PyTorch Lightning called `TSCCnnModel`:

```
import torch.nn.functional as F
import lightning.pytorch as pl

class TSCCnnModel(pl.LightningModule):
    def __init__(self, output_dim):
        super().__init__()
        self.network = ConvolutionalTSC(
            input_dim=1,
            output_dim=output_dim,
        )

    def forward(self, x):
        x = x.type(torch.FloatTensor)
        return self.network(x)
```

This module also contains the usual training, validation, and testing steps. These are implemented as follows:

```
    def training_step(self, batch, batch_idx):
        x, y = batch
        y_pred = self.forward(x)
        loss = F.cross_entropy(y_pred,
            y.type(torch.FloatTensor))
        self.log('train_loss', loss)
        return loss

    def validation_step(self, batch, batch_idx):
        x, y = batch
        y_pred = self(x)
        loss = F.cross_entropy(y_pred,
```

```
        y.type(torch.FloatTensor))
    self.log('val_loss', loss)
    return loss

def test_step(self, batch, batch_idx):
    x, y = batch
    y_pred = self(x)
    loss = F.cross_entropy(y_pred,
        y.type(torch.FloatTensor))
    self.log('test_loss', loss)

def configure_optimizers(self):
    return torch.optim.Adam(self.parameters(), lr=0.01)
```

These steps are similar to those developed for forecasting problems, but in this case, we use cross entropy as the `loss()` function.

3. We are now ready to train the model, which we do with a `Trainer` instance as follows:

```
import lightning.pytorch as pl
from lightning.pytorch.callbacks import EarlyStopping

model = TSCCnnModel(output_dim=4)

early_stop_callback = EarlyStopping(monitor="val_loss",
    min_delta=1e-4,
    patience=10,
    verbose=False,
    mode="min")

trainer = pl.Trainer(
    max_epochs=30,
    accelerator='cpu',
    log_every_n_steps=2,
    enable_model_summary=True,
    callbacks=[early_stop_callback],
)

trainer.fit(model, datamodule)
```

In the preceding code, we set the output dimension to 4 when creating an instance of the `TSCCnnModel` class, which represents the number of classes in the dataset. We also set up an early stopping callback to drive the training process of the network.

How it works...

Convolutional neural networks have been successfully applied to TSC problems. In this recipe, we explored developing a classifier based on PyTorch Lightning's `LightningModule`. We create a `ConvolutionalTSC` class that extends the `nn.Module` class. In the constructor of this class, we define the layers of the network: three convolutional layers (`conv1`, `conv2`, and `conv3`), and two densely connected layers (`fc1` and `fc2`). The `forward()` method details how these layers are composed together. Then, the convolutional layers stack on top of each other, and a max pooling operation (`MaxPool1d`) is applied after each convolution. Finally, we stack two densely connected layers, where the last one is the output layer.

The following figure shows the confusion matrix for the convolution neural network:

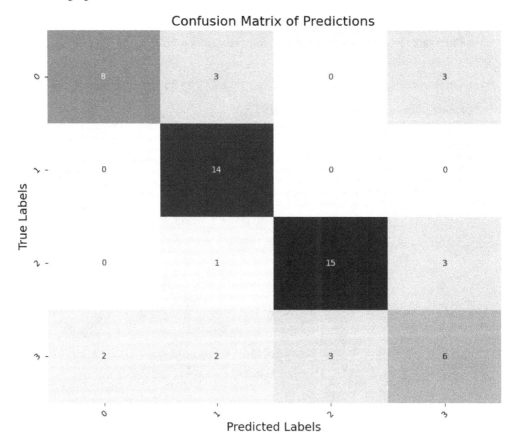

Figure 8.3: Confusion matrix for the convolutional neural network

The results obtained with the neural network are better than those when using the K-nearest neighbor model.

The workflow of this model follows the same logic as other recipes based on PyTorch Lightning. The main difference to take into account is that we're dealing with a classification problem. So, we need to set a loss function that deals with this problem. Cross-entropy is the usual go-to function to train neural networks for classification tasks. The output dimension of the neural network is also set according to the number of classes. Essentially, there's an output unit for each class in the dataset.

ResNets for TSC

This recipe shows you how to train a ResNet for TSC tasks. ResNets are a type of deep neural network architecture widely used in computer vision problems, such as image classification or object detection. Here, you'll learn how to use them for modeling time series data.

Getting ready

We'll continue with the same dataset and data module as in the previous recipe:

```
import pandas as pd
data_directory = 'assets/datasets/Car'

train = pd.read_table(f'{data_directory}/Car_TRAIN.tsv', header=None)
test = pd.read_table(f'{data_directory}/Car_TEST.tsv', header=None)

datamodule = TSCDataModule(train_df=train,
    test_df=test,
    batch_size=8)
```

Let's see how to build a ResNet and train it with PyTorch Lightning.

How to do it...

In this section, we describe the process of creating a ResNet for TSC tasks:

1. Let's start by creating a ResNet using nn.Module from the torch library:

    ```
    class ResidualNeuralNetworkModel(nn.Module):
        def __init__(self,
                        in_channels: int,
                        out_channels: int = 64,
                        num_classes: int = 1):
            super().__init__()

            self.input_args = {
    ```

```
            'in_channels': in_channels,
            'num_classes': num_classes
        }

        self.layers = nn.Sequential(*[
            ResNNBlock(in_channels=in_channels,
                out_channels=out_channels),
            ResNNBlock(in_channels=out_channels,
                out_channels=out_channels * 2),
            ResNNBlock(in_channels=out_channels * 2,
                out_channels=out_channels * 2),
        ])

        self.fc = nn.Linear(mid_channels * 2, num_classes)

    def forward(self, x):
        x = self.layers(x)
        return self.fc(x.mean(dim=-1))
```

Then, we wrap `ResidualNeuralNetworkModel` with `pl.LightningModule`:

```
class TSCResNet(pl.LightningModule):
    def __init__(self, output_dim):
        super().__init__()

        self.resnet = \
            ResidualNeuralNetworkModel(in_channels=1,
                num_pred_classes=output_dim)

    def forward(self, x):
        out = self.resnet.forward(x)

        return out
```

2. The training, validation, and testing steps are implemented identically to in the previous recipe:

```
    def training_step(self, batch, batch_idx):
        x, y = batch
        x = x.type(torch.FloatTensor)
        y = y.type(torch.FloatTensor)
        y_pred = self.forward(x)
        loss = F.cross_entropy(y_pred, y)
        self.log('train_loss', loss)
```

```
                return loss

        def validation_step(self, batch, batch_idx):
            x, y = batch
            x = x.type(torch.FloatTensor)
            y = y.type(torch.FloatTensor)
            y_pred = self(x)
            loss = F.cross_entropy(y_pred, y)
            self.log('val_loss', loss)
            return loss

        def test_step(self, batch, batch_idx):
            x, y = batch
            x = x.type(torch.FloatTensor)
            y = y.type(torch.FloatTensor)
            y_pred = self(x)
            loss = F.cross_entropy(y_pred, y)
            acc = Accuracy(task='multiclass', num_classes=4)
            acc_score = acc(y_pred, y)
            self.log('acc_score', acc_score)
            self.log('test_loss', loss)

        def configure_optimizers(self):
            return torch.optim.Adam(self.parameters(), lr=0.01)
```

Note that we transform the predictions and the actual values into a `torch.FloatTensor` structure for computing the `loss()` function. We set cross-entropy as the `loss()` function, which is typically used in classification. In the testing stage, we also evaluate the accuracy of the model.

3. Finally, here's the workflow for training and testing the model based on PyTorch Lightning's `Trainer`:

```
model = TSCResNet(output_dim=4)
datamodule = TSCDataModule(train_df=train, test_df=test,
    batch_size=8)
early_stop_callback = EarlyStopping(monitor="val_loss",
    min_delta=1e-4,
    patience=20,
    verbose=False,
    mode="min")

trainer = pl.Trainer(
```

```
        max_epochs=100,
        accelerator='cpu',
        log_every_n_steps=2,
        enable_model_summary=True,
        callbacks=[early_stop_callback],
    )


trainer.fit(model, datamodule)
trainer.test(model, datamodule)
```

Essentially, after defining the model, the training and testing process with PyTorch Lightning's `Trainer` is similar to that shown in the previous recipe.

How it works...

ResNets have shown promising performance in TSC problems. The idea is to learn the difference (residual) between the original input and a transformed output obtained from a convolutional layer. In the preceding code, we create a neural network that takes as input three parameters:

- `in_channels`: The number of input channels, which is equal to 1 because our time series are univariate

- `out_channels`: The number of output channels from each residual block

- `num_classes`: The number of classes in the dataset

The layers of the neural network are composed of three residual blocks named `ResNNBlock`. Residual blocks are the cornerstone of ResNets and are designed to solve the vanishing gradient problem. You can check the implementation of the residual blocks named `ResNNBlock` at the following URL: `https://github.com/PacktPublishing/Deep-Learning-for-Time-Series-Data-Cookbook`. The output from the residual blocks is passed on to a linear layer.

The following figure shows the confusion matrix for the ResNet:

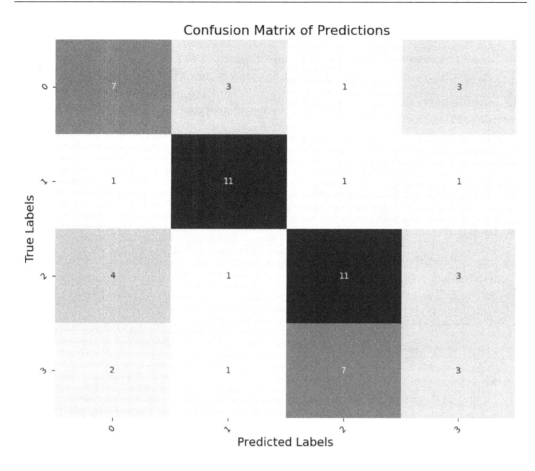

Figure 8.4: Confusion matrix for the ResNet

Like in the previous recipe, we wrap the implementation of the ResNet with the PyTorch Lightning framework. In the testing stage of this recipe, we also include the accuracy metric, which tells us the percentage of cases the model gets right. This metric is commonly used in TSC problems, though it might not be very informative for datasets with an imbalanced target distribution.

Tackling TSC problems with sktime

In this recipe, we explore an alternative approach to PyTorch for TSC problems, which is sktime. sktime is a Python library devoted to time series modeling, which includes several neural network models for TSC.

Getting ready

You can install `sktime` using `pip`. You'll also need the `keras-self-attention` library, which includes self-attention methods necessary for running some of the methods in `sktime`:

```
pip install 'sktime[dl]'
pip install keras-self-attention
```

The trailing `dl` tag in squared brackets when installing `sktime` means you want to include the optional deep learning models available in the library.

In this recipe, we'll use an example dataset available in `sktime`. We'll load it in the next section.

How to do it...

As the name implies, the `sktime` library follows a design pattern similar to scikit-learn. So, our approach to building a deep learning model using `sktime` will be similar to the workflow described in the *Tackling TSC with K-nearest neighbors* recipe.

Let's start by loading the dataset:

```
from sktime.datasets import load_italy_power_demand

X_train, y_train = \
    load_italy_power_demand(split="train", return_type="numpy3D")

X_test, y_test = load_italy_power_demand(split="test",
    return_type="numpy3D")
```

In the preceding code, we load a dataset concerning energy demand in Italy. You can check the following link for more information about this dataset: https://www.timeseriesclassification.com/description.php?Dataset=ItalyPowerDemand.

The data was originally used in the following work:

Keogh, Eamonn, et al. *Intelligent icons: Integrating lite-weight data mining and visualization into GUI operating systems.* Sixth **International Conference on Data** Mining (**ICDM**'06). IEEE, 2006.

We use `load_italy_power_demand` to load the train and test sets as numpy data structures.

Now, let's see how to build different types of neural networks using this dataset.

Fully connected neural network

We start by training a fully connected neural network. The configuration of this network, including `loss()` and `activation()` functions, is passed as arguments to the `FCNClassifier` instance:

```
from sktime.classification.deep_learning.fcn import FCNClassifier

fcn = FCNClassifier(n_epochs=200,
    loss='categorical_crossentropy',
    activation='sigmoid',
    batch_size=4)

fcn.fit(X_train, y_train)
fcn_pred = fcn.predict(X_test)
```

The training and inference steps are done using the `fit()` and `predict()` methods, respectively. If you're used to scikit-learn methods, this approach should be familiar to you.

Convolutional neural network

As we learned in the *Convolutional neural networks for TSC* recipe, convolutional models can be an effective approach to classifying time series. Here's the implementation available on `sktime` with `CNNClassifier`:

```
from sktime.classification.deep_learning.cnn import CNNClassifier

cnn = CNNClassifier(n_epochs=200,
    loss='categorical_crossentropy',
    activation='sigmoid',
    kernel_size=7,
    batch_size=4)

cnn.fit(X_train, y_train)
cnn_pred = cnn.predict(X_test)
```

You can also set other parameters concerning convolutions, such as `avg_pool_size` or `n_conv_layers`. Check the documentation for a complete list of parameters at the following link: https://www.sktime.net/en/stable/api_reference/auto_generated/sktime.classification.deep_learning.CNNClassifier.html.

LSTM-FCN neural network

Recurrent neural networks can also be useful for this problem. Here's a combination of an LSTM with a fully connected layer that is available in `LSTMFCNClassifier`:

```
from sktime.classification.deep_learning.lstmfcn import(
    LSTMFCNClassifier)

lstmfcn = LSTMFCNClassifier(n_epochs=200,
                            attention=True,
                            batch_size=4)

lstmfcn.fit(X_train, y_train)
lstmfcn_pred = lstmfcn.predict(X_test)
```

This method also includes an attention mechanism that improves classification accuracy significantly.

TapNet model

The **TapNet** (short for **time series attentional prototype network**) is a deep neural network designed for TSC. It was originally created to handle multivariate time series, but it's also applicable to univariate ones. Here's how you train this model using `sktime`:

```
from sktime.classification.deep_learning.tapnet import(
    TapNetClassifier)

tapnet = TapNetClassifier(n_epochs=200,
                          loss='categorical_crossentropy',
                          batch_size=4)

tapnet.fit(X_train, y_train)
tapnet_pred = tapnet.predict(X_test)
```

This model can manage a low-dimensional space (small number of features), and work well under a semi-supervised setting – that is, when there's a large number of unlabeled observations available.

InceptionTime model

`InceptionTime` is a state-of-the-art deep learning method for TSC problems. In practice, `InceptionTime` is an ensemble of deep convolutional neural networks that is inspired by the inception architecture created for computer vision tasks:

```
from sktime.classification.deep_learning import(
    InceptionTimeClassifier)
```

```
inception = InceptionTimeClassifier(n_epochs=200,
        loss='categorical_crossentropy',
        use_residual=True,
        batch_size=4)

inception.fit(X_train, y_train)
inception_pred = inception.predict(X_test)
```

The model also includes optional residual connections, which, in the preceding code, we use by setting the use_residual parameter to True.

Evaluation

We can use standard classification metrics to evaluate the performance of TSC models. Here's how to compute the accuracy of the models we trained in this recipe:

```
from sklearn.metrics import accuracy_score

perf = {
    'FCN': accuracy_score(y_test, fcn_pred),
    'CNN': accuracy_score(y_test, cnn_pred),
    'InceptionTime': accuracy_score(y_test, inception_pred),
    'TapNet': accuracy_score(y_test, tapnet_pred),
    'LSTMFCN': accuracy_score(y_test, lstmfcn_pred),
}
```

The results are shown in the following figure:

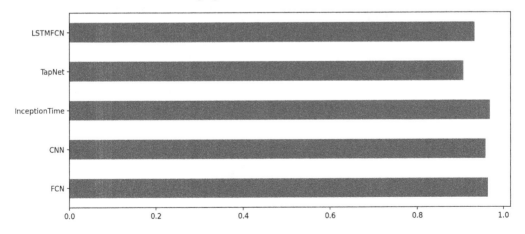

Figure 8.5: Accuracy of the models

Overall, `InceptionTime` appears to be the best approach for this particular problem.

How it works...

In this recipe, we use the `sktime` Python library to build deep-learning models for TSC. While you can use PyTorch as we've shown in the other recipes of this chapter, `sktime` provides an extensive toolkit for tackling TSC tasks. Since `sktime` follows the philosophy of scikit-learn, most of the work is done using the `fit()` and `predict()` methods of the respective class.

There's more...

You can check the documentation of `sktime` for other models, including some that are not based on deep learning. Here's the link: `https://www.sktime.net/en/stable/users.html`.

In most of the models we used in this recipe, we set the parameters to their default values. But, you can create a validation set and optimize the configuration of the models for better performance.

9

Deep Learning for Time Series Anomaly Detection

In this chapter, we'll delve into anomaly detection problems using time series data. This task involves detecting rare observations that are significantly different from most samples in a dataset. We'll explore different approaches to tackle this problem, such as prediction-based methods or reconstruction-based methods. This includes using powerful methods such as **autoencoders (AEs)**, **variational AEs (VAEs)**, or **generative adversarial networks (GANs)**.

By the end of this chapter, you'll be able to define time series anomaly detection problems using different approaches with Python.

The chapter covers the following recipes:

- Time series anomaly detection with **Autoregressive Integrated Moving Average** (**ARIMA**)
- Prediction-based anomaly detection using **deep learning** (**DL**)
- Anomaly detection using a **long short-term memory** (**LSTM**) AE
- Building an AE using PyOD
- Creating a VAE for time series anomaly detection
- Using GANs for time series anomaly detection

Technical requirements

The models developed in this chapter are based on different frameworks. First, we show how to develop prediction-based methods using the `statsforecast` and `neuralforecast` libraries. Other methods, such as an LSTM AE, will be explored using the PyTorch Lightning ecosystem. Finally, we'll also use the PyOD library to create anomaly detection models based on approaches such as GANs or VAEs. Of course, we also rely on typical data manipulation libraries such as `pandas` or `NumPy`. The following list contains all the required libraries for this chapter:

- `scikit-learn` (1.3.2)
- `pandas` (2.1.3)
- NumPy (1.26.2)
- `statsforecast` (1.6.0)
- `datasetsforecast` (0.08)
- `0neuralforecast` (1.6.4)
- `torch` (2.1.1)
- PyTorch Lightning (2.1.2)
- PyTorch Forecasting (1.0.0)
- PyOD (1.1.2)

The code and datasets used in this chapter can be found at the following GitHub URL: `https://github.com/PacktPublishing/Deep-Learning-for-Time-Series-Data-Cookbook`.

Time series anomaly detection with ARIMA

Time series anomaly detection is an important task in application domains such as healthcare or manufacturing, among many others. Anomaly detection methods aim to identify observations that do not conform to the typical behavior of a dataset. In practice, anomalies can represent phenomena such as faults in machinery or fraudulent activity. Anomaly detection is a common task in **machine learning** (**ML**), and it has a few dedicated methods when it involves time series data. This type of dataset and the patterns therein can evolve over time, which complicates the modeling process and the effectiveness of the detectors. Statistical learning methods for time series anomaly detection problems usually follow a prediction-based approach or a reconstruction-based approach. In this recipe, we describe how to use an ARIMA method to create a prediction-based anomaly detection system for univariate time series.

Getting ready

We'll focus on a univariate time series from the M3 dataset, which is available in the `datasetsforecast` library. Here's how to get this data:

```
from datasetsforecast.m3 import M3
dataset, *_ = M3.load('./data', 'Quarterly')


q1 = dataset.query('unique_id=="Q1"')
```

In the preceding code, we start by loading the M3 dataset using the `load()` method. Then, we use the `query()` method to get the univariate time series with an identifier (`unique_id` column) equal to Q1. Now, let's see how to detect anomalies in this dataset.

How to do it...

We'll build a forecasting model and use the corresponding prediction intervals to detect anomalies.

1. We start by creating a forecasting model. While any model would work, in this recipe, we focus on ARIMA. Here's how to define this model using the `statsforecast` library:

    ```
    from statsforecast import StatsForecast
    from statsforecast.models import AutoARIMA

    models = [AutoARIMA(season_length=4)]

    sf = StatsForecast(
        df=q1,
        models=models,
        freq='Q',
        n_jobs=1,
    )
    ```

2. Now, we are ready to fit the model and get the forecasts:

    ```
    forecasts = sf.forecast(h=8, level=[99],
        fitted=True).reset_index()
    insample_forecasts = sf.forecast_fitted_values().reset_index()
    ```

    First, we use the `forecast()` method to get the predictions. In this example, we set the forecasting horizon to 8 (h=8). We also pass two additional parameters: `level=[99]`, which means that we also want the model to predict the intervals with a 99% confidence level; `fitted=True`, which tells the model to compute the training forecasts. We use the `forecast_fitted_values()` method to get the forecasts from the training set.

3. Then, we identify anomalies based on whether the point forecasts are within the prediction intervals made by the model. This is done as follows:

```
anomalies = insample_forecasts.loc[
    (
        insample_forecasts['y'] >=
        insample_forecasts['AutoARIMA-hi-99']
    ) | (
        insample_forecasts['y'] <=
        insample_forecasts['AutoARIMA-lo-99'])]
```

The preceding code checks whether the training predictions (`insample_forecasts['y']` object) are within the 99% prediction intervals. Any observation that does not pass this check is considered an anomaly.

4. Finally, we use the `plot()` method from the `StatsForecast` class to plot the anomalies:

```
StatsForecast.plot(insample_forecasts, unique_ids=['Q1'],
    plot_anomalies=True)
```

Here's what the plot looks like:

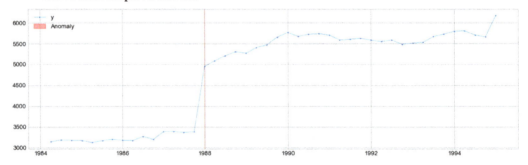

Figure 9.1: Example of an anomaly identified by ARIMA

How it works...

We used the `AutoARIMA` implementation available in the `statsforecast` library to create the ARIMA model. This approach automatically selects the best parameters for the model. We set the seasonal length to 4 since the frequency of the data is quarterly. The fitting process is carried out by a `StatsForecast` class instance.

Prediction-based methods work by comparing the forecasts of a given model with the actual values of the series. In this case, we use an ARIMA model, but other methods can also be used. Moreover, we consider an approach based on prediction intervals. Specifically, an observation is considered an anomaly if its value is outside of the predicted interval. In the code shown in the previous section, we considered a prediction interval with a 99% level, but you can test a different value for your problem.

There's more...

In this recipe, we focus on ARIMA to get prediction intervals, but you can use any other model with such capabilities.

You can check the following URL for more details about how to use the statsforecast library for prediction-based anomaly detection: https://nixtla.github.io/statsforecast/docs/tutorials/anomalydetection.html.

Prediction-based anomaly detection using DL

We continue to explore prediction-based methods in this recipe. This time, we'll create a forecasting model based on DL. Besides, we'll use the point forecasts' error as a reference for detecting anomalies.

Getting ready

We'll use a time series dataset about the number of taxi trips in New York City. This dataset is considered a benchmark problem for time series anomaly detection tasks. You can check the source at the following link: https://databank.illinois.edu/datasets/IDB-9610843.

Let's start by loading the time series using pandas:

```
from datetime import datetime
import pandas as pd

dataset = pd.read_csv('assets/datasets/taxi/taxi_data.csv')
labels = pd.read_csv('assets/datasets/taxi/taxi_labels.csv')
dataset['ds'] = pd.Series([datetime.fromtimestamp(x)
    for x in dataset['timestamp']])
dataset = dataset.drop('timestamp', axis=1)
dataset['unique_id'] = 'NYT'
dataset = dataset.rename(columns={'value': 'y'})

is_anomaly = []
for i, r in labels.iterrows():
    dt_start = datetime.fromtimestamp(r.start)
    dt_end = datetime.fromtimestamp(r.end)
    anomaly_in_period = [dt_start <= x <= dt_end
        for x in dataset['ds']]

    is_anomaly.append(anomaly_in_period)

dataset['is_anomaly']=pd.DataFrame(is_anomaly).any(axis=0).astype(int)
dataset['ds'] = pd.to_datetime(dataset['ds'])
```

The preceding code involves several steps:

1. Loading the dataset and corresponding labels using the `pd.read_csv()` function.

2. Processing this dataset into a tabular format with three main pieces of information: the time series identifier (`unique_id`), the timestamp (`ds`), and the value of the observation (`y`).

3. Processing the labels into a new Boolean column called `is_anomaly` that denotes whether the corresponding observation is an anomaly.

Here's what the series looks like:

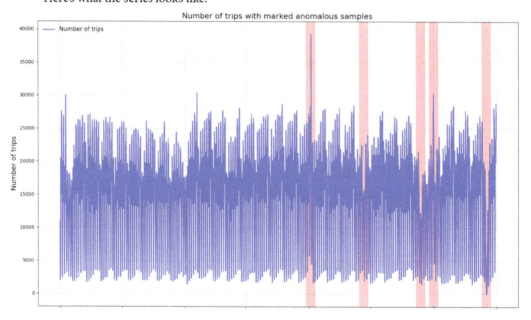

Figure 9.2: New York City dataset with marked anomalies

How to do it...

Now, we use the taxi trips dataset to train a forecasting model. In this recipe, we'll resort to the `neuralforecast` library, which contains implementation for several DL algorithm:

1. Let's start by defining the model as follows:

```
from neuralforecast import NeuralForecast
from neuralforecast.models import NHITS

horizon = 1
n_lags = 144
```

```
models = [NHITS(h=horizon,
    input_size=n_lags,
    max_steps=30,
    n_freq_downsample=[2, 1, 1],
    mlp_units=3 * [[128, 128]],
    accelerator='cpu')]

nf = NeuralForecast(models=models, freq='30T')
```

We use an input size (`n_lags`) of 144, which corresponds to 3 days of data as the time series is collected every 30 minutes (`freq='30T'`).

2. After defining the model, we can train it using the `fit()` method:

```
nf.fit(df=dataset.drop('is_anomaly', axis=1), val_size=n_lags)
```

Before the fitting process, we drop the `is_anomaly` variable that contains anomaly information. Now, the idea is to use the model to forecast the values of the time series. Any significant deviation from the actual value is considered an anomaly. Let's look at the training predictions.

3. We can get the training (or insample) predictions by calling the `predict_insample()` method, like so:

```
insample = nf.predict_insample()
insample = insample.tail(-n_lags)

abs_error = (insample['NHITS'] - insample['y']).abs()
```

In the preceding code, we get the training sample and remove the initial n_lag observations to align the predictions with the actual data. Then, we measure the absolute error of the model by taking the absolute difference between the predictions and actual values.

4. Visualize the absolute error in the training data along with the marked anomalies:

```
preds = pd.DataFrame(
    {
        "Error": abs_error.values,
        "ds": dataset["ds"].tail(-n_lags),
        "is_anomaly": dataset["is_anomaly"].tail(-n_lags),
    }
)

preds = preds.set_index("ds")

predicted_anomaly_periods = find_anomaly_periods(
    preds["is_anomaly"])
```

```
setup_plot(preds.rename(columns={"Error": "y"}),
    predicted_anomaly_periods, "Error")
```

In the interest of conciseness, the plotting functions are not shown. You can check them out in the GitHub repository. The plot is shown in the following figure:

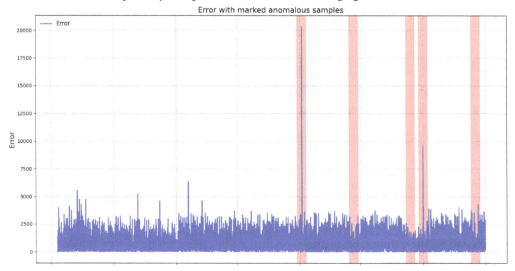

Figure 9.3: Absolute error by the Neural Hierarchical Implementation
for Time Series (NHITS) model and marked anomalies

Large errors occur during two of the anomalies, though the model also misses some anomalies.

How it works...

As seen in the previous recipe, we use a forecasting model to identify anomalies in a time series. In this case, instead of using prediction intervals, we rely on the absolute error of the model. A large error indicates a potential anomaly in the time series.

We use the neuralforecast framework to build a DL forecasting model based on the NHITS method. NHITS is a model that extends **Neural Basis Expansion Analysis (NBEATS)** and is based on a **multilayer perceptron (MLP)** type of architecture.

This involves transforming the data into an appropriate format and training the model using auto-regression.

There's more...

In this recipe, we focus on a univariate time series dataset and a particular forecasting method (NHITS). Yet, it's important to note that the prediction-based approach for anomaly detection can be applied to different settings (such as multivariate time series) and with other forecasting methods.

During the training phase, we need to define an error threshold above which we flag an observation as an anomaly. We will explore several implementations with this feature in subsequent recipes.

Anomaly detection using an LSTM AE

In this recipe, we'll build an AE to detect anomalies in time series. An AE is a type of **neural network (NN)** that tries to reconstruct the input data. The motivation to use this kind of model for anomaly detection is that the reconstruction process of anomalous data is more difficult than that of typical observations.

Getting ready

We'll continue with the New York City taxi time series in this recipe. In terms of framework, we'll show how to build an AE using PyTorch Lightning. This means that we'll build a data module to handle the data preprocessing and another module for handling the training and inference of the NN.

How to do it...

This recipe is split into three parts. First, we build the data module based on PyTorch. Then, we create an AE module. Finally, we combine the two parts to build an anomaly detection system:

1. Let's start by building the data module. We create a class called `TaxiDataModule` that extends `pl.LightningDataModule`. Here's the constructor of the class:

```
Import numpy as np
import pandas as pd
import lightning.pytorch as pl
from pytorch_forecasting import TimeSeriesDataSet
from sklearn.model_selection import train_test_split

class TaxiDataModule(pl.LightningDataModule):
    def __init__(self,
                 data: pd.DataFrame,
                 n_lags: int,
                 batch_size: int):
        super().__init__()

        self.data = data
```

```
        self.batch_size = batch_size
        self.n_lags = n_lags

        self.train_df = None
        self.test_df = None
        self.training = None
        self.validation = None
        self.predict_set = None
```

The `TaxiDataModule` class takes two inputs besides the dataset: the number of lags (context length) and the batch size.

2. Next, we code the `setup()` method, where the data is prepared for training and testing the model:

```
    def setup(self, stage=None):
        self.data['timestep'] = np.arange(self.data.shape[0])
        unique_times = \
            self.data['timestep'].sort_values().unique()

        tr_ind, ts_ind = \
            train_test_split(unique_times, test_size=0.4,
                shuffle=False)

        tr_ind, vl_ind = \
            train_test_split(tr_ind, test_size=0.1,
                shuffle=False)

        self.train_df = \
            self.data.loc[self.data['timestep'].isin(tr_ind), :]
        self.test_df = \
            self.data.loc[self.data['timestep'].isin(ts_ind), :]
        validation_df = \
            self.data.loc[self.data['timestep'].isin(vl_ind), :]

        self.training = TimeSeriesDataSet(
            data=self.train_df,
            time_idx="timestep",
            target="y",
            group_ids=['unique_id'],
            max_encoder_length=self.n_lags,
            max_prediction_length=1,
            time_varying_unknown_reals=['y'],
        )
```

```
        self.validation = \
            TimeSeriesDataSet.from_dataset(
                self.training, validation_df)
        self.test = \
            TimeSeriesDataSet.from_dataset(
                self.training, self.test_df)
        self.predict_set = \
            TimeSeriesDataSet.from_dataset(
                self.training, self.data, predict=True)
```

In the preceding code, we start by splitting the data into training, validation, and testing sets. Each of these is transformed into a `TimeSeriesDataSet` class instance.

3. The data loaders are implemented as follows:

```
def train_dataloader(self):
    return self.training.to_dataloader(
        batch_size=self.batch_size, shuffle=False)

def val_dataloader(self):
    return self.validation.to_dataloader(
        batch_size=self.batch_size, shuffle=False)

def predict_dataloader(self):
    return self.predict_set.to_dataloader(
        batch_size=1, shuffle=False)
```

Essentially, the data loading process is similar to what we did before in the forecasting tasks. You can check, for example, the *Multi-step and multi-output forecasting with multivariate time series* recipe in *Chapter 5*.

4. Now, we focus on the AE model, which is split into two parts: an encoder and a decoder. Here's an implementation of the encoder in a class called `Encoder`:

```
from torch import nn
import torch

class Encoder(nn.Module):
    def __init__(self, context_len, n_variables,
        embedding_dim=2):
        super(Encoder, self).__init__()
        self.context_len, self.n_variables = \
            context_len, n_variables
        self.embedding_dim, self.hidden_dim = \
            embedding_dim, 2 * embedding_dim
        self.lstm1 = nn.LSTM(
```

```
            input_size=self.n_variables,
            hidden_size=self.hidden_dim,
            num_layers=1,
            batch_first=True
        )
        self.lstm2 = nn.LSTM(
            input_size=self.hidden_dim,
            hidden_size=embedding_dim,
            num_layers=1,
            batch_first=True
        )

    def forward(self, x):
        batch_size = x.shape[0]
        x, (_, _) = self.lstm1(x)
        x, (hidden_n, _) = self.lstm2(x)
        return hidden_n.reshape((batch_size,
            self.embedding_dim))
```

5. The decoder is implemented in a class called `Decoder` that also extends `nn.Module`:

```
class Decoder(nn.Module):
    def __init__(self, context_len, n_variables=1, input_dim=2):
        super(Decoder, self).__init__()
        self.context_len, self.input_dim = \
            context_len, input_dim
        self.hidden_dim, self.n_variables = \
            2 * input_dim, n_variables
        self.lstm1 = nn.LSTM(
            input_size=input_dim,
            hidden_size=input_dim,
            num_layers=1,
            batch_first=True
        )
        self.lstm2 = nn.LSTM(
            input_size=input_dim,
            hidden_size=self.hidden_dim,
            num_layers=1,
            batch_first=True
        )
        self.output_layer = nn.Linear(self.hidden_dim,
            self.n_variables)

    def forward(self, x):
```

```
batch_size = x.shape[0]
x = x.repeat(self.context_len, self.n_variables)
x = x.reshape((batch_size, self.context_len,
    self.input_dim))
x, (hidden_n, cell_n) = self.lstm1(x)
x, (hidden_n, cell_n) = self.lstm2(x)
x = x.reshape((batch_size, self.context_len,
    self.hidden_dim))

return self.output_layer(x)
```

6. The two parts are combined in an `AutoencoderLSTM` class that extends `pl.LightningModule`:

```
import torch

class AutoencoderLSTM(pl.LightningModule):
    def __init__(self, context_len, n_variables, embedding_dim):
        super().__init__()
        self.encoder = Encoder(context_len, n_variables,
            embedding_dim)
        self.decoder = Decoder(context_len, n_variables,
            embedding_dim)

    def forward(self, x):
        xh = self.encoder(x)
        rec_x = self.decoder(xh)
        return rec_x

    def configure_optimizers(self):
        return torch.optim.Adam(self.parameters(), lr=0.001)
```

In the `forward()` method, the encoder part takes the original input (`self.encoder(x)`) and transforms it into a reduced dimension (`xh` object). Then, the decoder reconstructs the original input data based on `xh`.

7. Then, we implement the training, validation, and prediction steps:

```
import torch.nn.functional as F

def training_step(self, batch, batch_idx):
    x, y = batch
    y_pred = self(x['encoder_cont'])
    loss = F.mse_loss(y_pred, x['encoder_cont'])
    self.log('train_loss', loss)
```

```
        return loss

    def validation_step(self, batch, batch_idx):
        x, y = batch
        y_pred = self(x['encoder_cont'])
        loss = F.mse_loss(y_pred, x['encoder_cont'])
        self.log('val_loss', loss)
        return loss

    def predict_step(self, batch, batch_idx):
        x, y = batch
        y_pred = self(x['encoder_cont'])
        loss = F.mse_loss(y_pred, x['encoder_cont'])
        return loss
```

8. We train the NN using the `Trainer` class from PyTorch Lightning. We use 144 lags, which amounts to 3 days of data. We also apply early stopping to guide the training process:

```
N_LAGS = 144
N_VARIABLES = 1
from lightning.pytorch.callbacks import EarlyStopping

datamodule = \
    TaxiDataModule(
        data=dataset.drop('is_anomaly', axis=1),
        n_lags=N_LAGS,
        batch_size=32)

model = AutoencoderLSTM(n_variables=1,
        context_len=N_LAGS,
        embedding_dim=4)

early_stop_callback = EarlyStopping(monitor="val_loss",
    min_delta=1e-4,
    patience=5,
    verbose=False,
    mode="min")

trainer = pl.Trainer(max_epochs=20,
    accelerator='cpu',
    callbacks=[early_stop_callback])
trainer.fit(model, datamodule)
```

9. After training, we can apply the model to the test data as follows:

```
dl = datamodule.test.to_dataloader(batch_size=1, shuffle=False)
preds = trainer.predict(model, dataloaders=dl)
preds = pd.Series(np.array([x.numpy() for x in preds]))
```

In the preceding code, we transform the `test` object from the data module into a data loader. We use a batch size of 1 without shuffling to process each instance sequentially. Then, we use the `trainer` object to get the predictions. The following figure shows the reconstructed error in the test set:

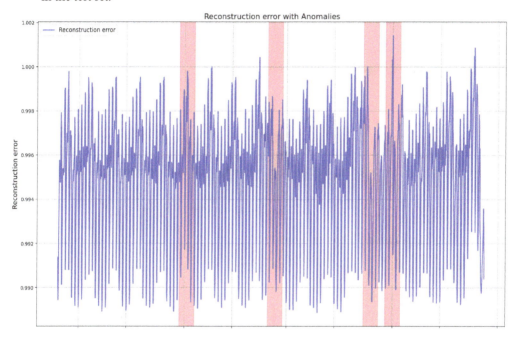

Figure 9.4: Reconstruction error by the AE and marked anomalies

In most cases, the peaks in reconstruction error coincide with the anomalies.

How it works...

The workflow in the data module may be familiar because it follows the same ideas behind the forecasting models we've built in other chapters; for example, in the *Multi-step and multi-output forecasting with multivariate time series* recipe in *Chapter 5*. But, in this case, we're not interested in predicting the future values of the series. Instead, at each time step, both the input and the output of the model are recent lags of the series.

An AE is composed of two main parts: an encoder and a decoder. The encoder aims to compress the input data into a small dimension, which is referred to as the bottleneck. Turning the input data into a small dimension is important to make the NN focus on the most important patterns in the data, disregarding noise. Then, the decoder takes the data encoded in the reduced dimension and tries to reconstruct the original input data. Both the encoder and the decoder of the NN are based on a stacked LSTM AE. Yet, you can use different architectures for these components.

The `Encoder` class extends the `nn.Module` class from `torch`. This particular encoder consists of two LSTM layers. These layers stack on top of each other as detailed in the `forward()` method. The `Decoder` class also contains two stacked LSTM layers that are followed by a densely connected layer.

In the training step of the AE, we pass a batch of the lagged time series (`x['encoder_cont']`) to the model. It produces an object called `y_pred`, which is the reconstructed input. Then, we compute the **mean squared error** (MSE) (`F.mse_loss`), which compares the original input with the reconstructed one.

Building an AE using PyOD

PyOD is a Python library that is devoted to anomaly detection. It contains several reconstruction-based algorithms such as AEs. In this recipe, we'll build an AE using PyOD to detect anomalies in time series.

Getting ready

You can install PyOD using the following command:

```
pip install pyod
```

We'll use the same dataset as in the previous recipe. So, we start with the dataset object created in the *Prediction-based anomaly detection using DL* recipe. Let's see how to transform this data to build an AE with PyOD.

How to do it...

The following steps show how to build an AE and predict the probability of anomalies:

1. We start by transforming the time series using a sliding window with the following code:

    ```
    import pandas as pd
    from sklearn.preprocessing import StandardScaler

    N_LAGS = 144
    series = dataset['y']
    input_data = []
    ```

```
for i in range(N_LAGS, series.shape[0]):
    input_data.append(series.iloc[i - N_LAGS:i].values)

input_data = np.array(input_data)
input_data_n = StandardScaler().fit_transform(input_data)
input_data_n = pd.DataFrame(input_data_n)
```

In the preceding code:

- We get the value column of the time series and store it in the series object.

- Then, we iterate over the dataset using a sliding window similar to an auto-regressive approach. This way, the time series is represented by its past number of lags(N_LAGS) at each time step.

- We standardize the data using `StandardScaler` from `scikit-learn`, which is an important step for training NNs such as AEs.

2. After preprocessing the data, we define the AE based on PyOD and fit it using the dataset:

```
from pyod.models.auto_encoder_torch import AutoEncoder

model = AutoEncoder(
    hidden_neurons=[144, 4, 4, 144],
    hidden_activation="relu",
    epochs=20,
    batch_norm=True,
    learning_rate=0.001,
    batch_size=32,
    dropout_rate=0.2,
)
model.fit(input_data_n)
```

The fitted model contains outlier scores based on the reconstruction process. Anomalies tend to have higher scores. These scores are available in the `decision_scores_` attribute of the model:

```
anomaly_scores = model.decision_scores_
```

Here's the distribution of the scores:

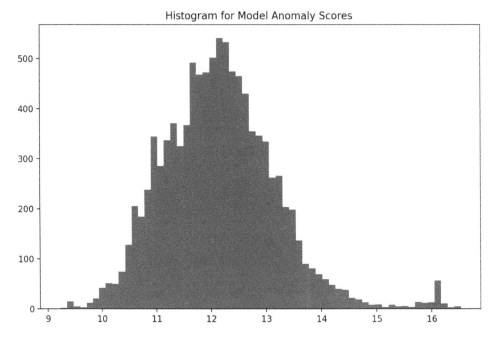

Figure 9.5: Histogram with the anomaly scores produced by the AE

3. Regarding the inference step, we can use the `predict()` and `predict_proba()` methods. The `predict()` method works as follows:

    ```
    predictions = model.predict(input_data_n)
    ```

4. The `predict_proba()` method works as follows:

    ```
    probs = model.predict_proba(input_data_n)[:, 1]
    probabilities = pd.Series(probs, \
        index=series.tail(len(probs)).index)
    ```

5. The probabilities represent the probability of each observation being an anomaly. You can plot the probabilities using the following code:

    ```
    ds = dataset.tail(-144)
    ds['Predicted Probability'] = probabilities
    ds = ds.set_index('ds')

    anomaly_periods = find_anomaly_periods(ds['is_anomaly'])
    setup_plot(ds, anomaly_periods)
    ```

Here's what the probabilities look like along the training set:

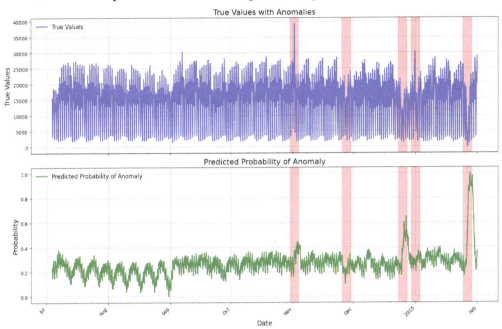

Figure 9.6: Anomaly probability scores produced by the AE

Again, the anomaly probability score peaks coincide with some anomalies.

How it works...

The PyOD library follows a design pattern similar to `scikit-learn`. So, each method, such as `AutoEncoder`, is trained using the `fit()` method and produces predictions based on a `predict` or `predict_proba()` method.

We use the `AutoEncoder` class instance from the `auto_encoder_torch` module. The library also contains the equivalent method but with a TensorFlow backend. We create an instance of the model and set up a few parameters:

- `hidden_neurons=[144, 2, 2, 144]`: These parameters detail the number of hidden units per layer. The input and output layers have a number of units equal to the input size, which is the number of lags. The hidden layers of the AE typically have a low number of units to compress the input data before reconstruction.

- `hidden_activation`: The activation function, which is set to the rectified linear function.

- `batch_norm`: A Boolean input that represents whether batch normalization should be applied. You can learn more about this at the following link: `https://pytorch.org/docs/stable/generated/torch.nn.BatchNorm1d.html`.

- `learning_rate`: The learning rate, which is set to `0.001`.

- `batch_size`: The batch size, which is set to `64`.

- `dropout_rate`: A dropout rate between the layers for regularization, which is set to `0.3`.

In this recipe, we created another AE for anomaly detection. This involves transforming the time series using a sliding window, similar to what we did for building forecasting models for auto-regression. The model predicts whether each observation is an anomaly based on the outlier scores. The threshold is set automatically by the model, though you can pick your own as well.

There's more...

Deciding whether an observation is an anomaly involves analyzing the anomaly scores of the model. You can use different approaches, such as percentiles or standard deviations. For example, consider an observation an anomaly if the reconstruction error is above some percentile (such as 95) or if the reconstruction error is above two standard deviations.

> **Note**
> We used the prediction from the training data for illustration purposes. Working with a test follows a similar approach.

Creating a VAE for time series anomaly detection

Building on the foundation laid in the previous recipe, we now turn our attention to VAEs, a more sophisticated and probabilistic approach to anomaly detection in time series data. Unlike traditional AEs, VAEs introduce a probabilistic interpretation, making them more adept at handling inherent uncertainties in real-world data.

Getting ready

This code in this recipe is based on PyOD. We also use the same dataset as in the previous recipe:

```
N_LAGS = 144
series = dataset['y']
```

Now, let's see how to create a VAE for time series anomaly detection.

How to do it...

We begin by preparing our dataset, as in the previous recipe:

1. The dataset is first transformed using a sliding window, a technique that helps the model understand temporal dependencies within the time series:

```python
import pandas as pd
from sklearn.preprocessing import StandardScaler
import numpy as np

input_data = []
for i in range(N_LAGS, series.shape[0]):
    input_data.append(series.iloc[i - N_LAGS:i].values)

    input_data = np.array(input_data)
    input_data_n = StandardScaler().fit_transform(input_data)
    input_data_n = pd.DataFrame(input_data_n)
```

2. After transforming the dataset, we define and fit the VAE model using PyOD's VAE class. The configuration of the VAE class includes specifying the architecture of the encoder and decoder networks and various training parameters:

```python
from pyod.models.vae import VAE
from tensorflow.keras.losses import mean_squared_error

model = VAE(encoder_neurons=[144, 4],
        decoder_neurons=[4, 144],
        latent_dim=2,
        hidden_activation='relu',
        output_activation='sigmoid',
        loss=mean_squared_error,
        optimizer='adam',
        epochs=20,
        batch_size=32,
        dropout_rate=0.2,
        l2_regularizer=0.1,
        validation_size=0.1,
        preprocessing=True,
        verbose=1)

model.fit(input_data_n)
```

3.   The fitted VAE model is then used to generate anomaly scores. These scores reflect how well each data point conforms to the pattern learned by the model. Points with higher scores are more likely to be anomalies:

```
anomaly_scores = model.decision_scores_
```

How it works...

A VAE is a NN model that stands out for its ability to handle data's latent or hidden aspects. Unlike traditional AEs, which map inputs to a fixed point in a latent space, VAEs transform inputs into a probability distribution, usually a normal distribution, characterized by mean and variance. This way, every input is associated with a region in the latent space rather than a single point, introducing an element of randomness and variability.

The decoder network then samples points from these estimated distributions and attempts to reconstruct the original input data. The training process involves two key objectives:

- Minimizing the reconstruction error ensures that the decoder can accurately recreate the input data from latent representations.

- Regularizing latent space distributions to be close to a standard normal distribution. This is typically achieved by minimizing the Kullback-Leibler divergence. The regularization process prevents overfitting and ensures a well-structured and continuous latent space.

Once trained, the VAE can be employed for anomaly detection. The VAE should be able to reconstruct normal data (similar to what it was trained on) with relatively low error. Conversely, data points significantly different from the training set (potential anomalies) will likely be reconstructed with higher error. Therefore, the reconstruction error serves as an anomaly score.

A high reconstruction error suggests that the data point does not conform well to the learned data distribution, flagging it as an anomaly:

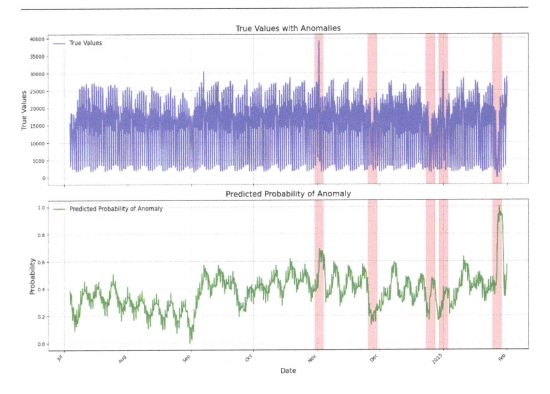

Figure 9.7: True values, true anomalies, and the probability of anomalies predicted by the VAE

This comparison helps us evaluate the performance of our VAE in real-world scenarios.

There's more...

One of the most interesting aspects of VAEs is their ability to generate new data points. By sampling from learned distributions in the latent space, we can generate new instances that are similar to the training data. This property can be particularly useful in scenarios where data augmentation is required.

Moreover, the probabilistic nature of VAEs offers a natural way to quantify uncertainty. This can be particularly beneficial in settings where it's relevant to assess the confidence of the model's predictions.

Using GANs for time series anomaly detection

GANs have gained significant popularity in various fields of ML, particularly in image generation and modification. However, their application in time series data, especially for anomaly detection, is an emerging area of research and practice. In this recipe, we focus on utilizing GANs, specifically **Anomaly Detection with Generative Adversarial Networks (AnoGAN)**, to detect time series data anomalies.

Getting ready...

Before diving into the implementation, ensure that you have the PyOD library installed. We will continue using the taxi trip dataset for this recipe, which provides a real-world context for time series anomaly detection.

How to do it...

The implementation involves several steps: data preprocessing, defining and training the AnoGAN model, and finally, performing anomaly detection:

1. We start by loading the dataset and preparing it for the AnoGAN model. The dataset is transformed in the same way as before using a sliding window approach:

```
import pandas as pd
from sklearn.preprocessing import StandardScaler
import numpy as np

N_LAGS = 144
series = dataset['y']
input_data = []
for i in range(N_LAGS, series.shape[0]):
    input_data.append(series.iloc[i - N_LAGS:i].values)
    input_data = np.array(input_data)
    input_data_n = StandardScaler().fit_transform(input_data)
    input_data_n = pd.DataFrame(input_data_n)
```

2. AnoGAN is then defined with specific hyperparameters and trained on the preprocessed data:

```
from pyod.models.anogan import AnoGAN

model = AnoGAN(activation_hidden='tanh',
    dropout_rate=0.2,
    latent_dim_G=2,
    G_layers=[20, 10, 3, 10, 20],
    verbose=1,
    D_layers=[20, 10, 5],
    index_D_layer_for_recon_error=1,
    epochs=20,
    preprocessing=False,
    learning_rate=0.001,
    learning_rate_query=0.01,
    epochs_query=1,
    batch_size=32,
    output_activation=None,
```

```
    contamination=0.1)

  model.fit(input_data_n)
```

3. Once the model is trained, we use it to predict anomalies in the data:

```
  anomaly_scores = model.decision_scores_
  predictions = model.predict(input_data_n)
```

4. Finally, we visualize the results to compare the model's predictions with actual anomalies:

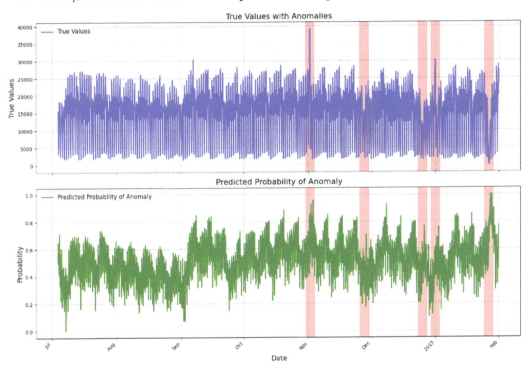

Figure 9.8: True values, true anomalies, and the probability of anomalies predicted by a GAN

How it works...

AnoGAN is a model that employs the principles of GANs for the specific task of anomaly detection in time series data. The core idea behind AnoGAN is the interaction between two key components: the generator and the discriminator.

The Generator is tasked with creating synthetic data that resembles the true time series data it has been trained on. It learns to capture the underlying patterns and distributions of the input data, trying to generate outputs that are indistinguishable from the real data.

The Discriminator, on the other hand, acts as a critic. Its role is to discern whether the data it reviews are genuine (actual data points from the dataset) or fabricated (outputs generated by the Generator). During training, these two components engage in a continuous game: the Generator improves its ability to produce realistic data, while the Discriminator becomes better at detecting fakes.

The reconstruction error is once again used to identify anomalies. The Generator, being trained only on normal data, will struggle to reproduce outliers or anomalous instances. Thus, when the reconstructed version of a data point diverges significantly from the original, we find a potential anomaly.

In practice, the reconstruction error can be calculated using various methods, such as MSE or other distance metrics, depending on the nature of the data and the specific requirements of the task at hand.

There's more...

While AnoGAN provides a novel approach to time series anomaly detection, it is worth exploring variations and improvements. For instance, one might consider tuning the model's architecture or experimenting with different types of GANs, such as **conditional GANs (CGANs)** or **Wasserstein GANs (WGANs)**.

Index

packtpub.com

Subscribe to our online digital library for full access to over 7,000 books and videos, as well as industry leading tools to help you plan your personal development and advance your career. For more information, please visit our website.

Why subscribe?

- Spend less time learning and more time coding with practical eBooks and Videos from over 4,000 industry professionals

- Improve your learning with Skill Plans built especially for you

- Get a free eBook or video every month

- Fully searchable for easy access to vital information

- Copy and paste, print, and bookmark content

Did you know that Packt offers eBook versions of every book published, with PDF and ePub files available? You can upgrade to the eBook version at packtpub.com and as a print book customer, you are entitled to a discount on the eBook copy. Get in touch with us at customercare@packtpub.com for more details.

At www.packtpub.com, you can also read a collection of free technical articles, sign up for a range of free newsletters, and receive exclusive discounts and offers on Packt books and eBooks.

Other Books You May Enjoy

If you enjoyed this book, you may be interested in these other books by Packt:

Time Series Analysis with Python Cookbook

Tarek A. Atwan

ISBN: 978-1-80107-554-1

- Understand what makes time series data different from other data
- Apply various imputation and interpolation strategies for missing data
- Implement different models for univariate and multivariate time series
- Use different deep learning libraries such as TensorFlow, Keras, and PyTorch
- Plot interactive time series visualizations using hvPlot
- Explore state-space models and the unobserved components model (UCM)
- Detect anomalies using statistical and machine learning methods
- Forecast complex time series with multiple seasonal patterns

Modern Time Series Forecasting with Python

Manu Joseph

ISBN: 978-1-80324-680-2

- Find out how to manipulate and visualize time series data like a pro
- Set strong baselines with popular models such as ARIMA
- Discover how time series forecasting can be cast as regression
- Engineer features for machine learning models for forecasting
- Explore the exciting world of ensembling and stacking models
- Get to grips with the global forecasting paradigm
- Understand and apply state-of-the-art DL models such as N-BEATS and Autoformer
- Explore multi-step forecasting and cross-validation strategies

Packt is searching for authors like you

If you're interested in becoming an author for Packt, please visit `authors.packtpub.com` and apply today. We have worked with thousands of developers and tech professionals, just like you, to help them share their insight with the global tech community. You can make a general application, apply for a specific hot topic that we are recruiting an author for, or submit your own idea.

Share Your Thoughts

Now you've finished *Deep Learning for Time Series Cookbook*, we'd love to hear your thoughts! Scan the QR code below to go straight to the Amazon review page for this book and share your feedback or leave a review on the site that you purchased it from.

`https://packt.link/r/1-805-12923-6`

Your review is important to us and the tech community and will help us make sure we're delivering excellent quality content.

Download a free PDF copy of this book

Thanks for purchasing this book!

Do you like to read on the go but are unable to carry your print books everywhere?

Is your eBook purchase not compatible with the device of your choice?

Don't worry, now with every Packt book you get a DRM-free PDF version of that book at no cost.

Read anywhere, any place, on any device. Search, copy, and paste code from your favorite technical books directly into your application.

The perks don't stop there, you can get exclusive access to discounts, newsletters, and great free content in your inbox daily

Follow these simple steps to get the benefits:

1. Scan the QR code or visit the link below

https://packt.link/free-ebook/978-1-80512-923-3

2. Submit your proof of purchase
3. That's it! We'll send your free PDF and other benefits to your email directly

www.ingramcontent.com/pod-product-compliance
Lightning Source LLC
Chambersburg PA
CBHW080632060326

40690CB00021B/4907